Church Planting Road Map

JAMES R. NIKKEL

church
planting
r o a d   m a p

Church Planting Road Map

Copyright © 2004, Dr. James Nikkel

All Scripture quotations, unless otherwise specified, are from *The Holy Bible, New International Version.* Copyright © 1973, 1978, 1984 International Bible Society. Used by permission of Zondervan Publishing House. All rights reserved.

ISBN: 1-55306-734-7

**For more information or
to order additional copies, please contact:**

Dr. James Nikkel
2892 Crossley Drive
Abbotsford BC Canada, V2T 5H2
E-mail: james@nikkel.com

Guardian Books is an imprint of *Essence Publishing,* a Christian Book Publisher dedicated to furthering the work of Christ through the written word. For more information, contact:
20 Hanna Court, Belleville, Ontario, Canada K8P 5J2.
Phone: 1-800-238-6376 • Fax: (613) 962-3055.
E-mail: publishing@essencegroup.com
Internet: www.essencegroup.com

Printed in Canada
by
Guardian
B O O K S

Dear Church Planters,

This book is dedicated to the many Canadian church planters who are faithfully serving Christ, in the interest of living out the great commandment of love, and working at the global disciple-making mandate.

Table of Contents

Acknowledgements

First I want to gratefully acknowledge the fact that God has been faithful according to His promise of being present and giving His empowerment. I thank Him for the privilege of serving Him in the area of evangelism and church planting for many years, and for now nudging me to write and publish this book.

It has been my great privilege to serve Christ together with my faithful and supportive wife, Elfrieda. She has been my constant encourager, partner and intercessor. I especially thank her for giving so much of her time, wisdom and counsel during the preparation of the manuscript of this book. Thank you, Elfrieda, for the many hours that you put into word processing, and formatting the manuscript.

I take great joy also in acknowledging the support and encouragement that my four sons, Bruce, Kevin, Dale, and Chris have been in prodding me to write and publish this church planting book. They have been part of so many of the church planting experiences that have provided the backdrop for this book. Thank you for your vision and faith for this book to be written.

It has been my privilege to have many great ministry mentors and leaders from across Canada and beyond, who have been a great influence and an example of vision to me. I gratefully acknowledge both the leaders from my denomination, the Mennonite Brethren, and the many great friends from the broader Canadian Christian community, who have challenged me to faithfulness, and sometimes risk-taking ministry ventures.

Finally, I thank God for the many church planters from various Canadian provinces and culture groups with whom I have been able to serve. Many of the principles of this book have come from the front lines of church planting experiences with them. Meeting and working with church planters has always been an energizing and invigorating time. Thank you to all of you.

It is by the grace and faithfulness of God that this book promoting church planting has been written. May the work of the harvest be expanded as a result.

Introduction

This book has a history and a life of its own. It has been in the making for many years, involving practical life experiences, and ministry in the trenches of both the local church and the wider Christian body.

Some of the original concepts of this book were carved out in the academic rigours of the Doctor of Ministry program at the Fuller Theological Seminary, on the subject of church planting. It was here that many of the basic principles of church planting and outreach became a passion for the writer.

Some other parts of this book were born out of the centennial celebrations of the Mennonite Brethren Church of Canada in 1988 on the occasion when church planting was championed under the banner of the Antioch Plan. This historic occasion resulted in the writing and development of a manual known as Antioch Blue Prints, a manual designed to encourage rigorous church planting, as did the model Antioch Church. Churches were encouraged to become more like the Antioch church.

The Antioch Centennial plan had a two-fold vision for

the future: 1) each person to be committed to the Antioch model of: daily witness, spiritual worship, generous giving, and Holy Spirit guidance; 2) each church to be committed to the Antioch pattern of evangelism growth, community rapport, church planting and conference action. For the writer, this centennial was a watershed occasion of a commitment to more aggressive and intentional church planting. The Antioch church is still a constant source of challenge and motivation to the writer. In many ways this book is calling Christians to the Antioch mission model of aggressive church planting.

The most significant contributions to this book have come from the many church planters with whom I have worked over the years. Many of the church outreach principles have been learned in the church planting field environment.

It has been a privilege to work together with some twelve different cultural groups involving more than fifty churches within five Canadian provinces. It is the spiritual fruit of these church plants that makes it all worth while. Many people have become followers of Christ and meaningfully involved in the church. The church is the hope of the world, because it is being built by Christ, the church founder.

Another piece in the development of this book came from the classroom. In the past decade there have been numerous opportunities to teach church planting modules and courses in several Bible Colleges and Seminaries. This gave the occasion to further merge the writer's practical church planting experiences with theological reflection in the context of classroom interaction. This resulted in the compilation of the manual *Antioch Blue Prints for Church Planters,* which also became the textbook for some of the courses.

The Church Planting Road Map is taking the above-mentioned experiences, manuals, and some classroom materials, and merging these into a church planting document to be used for encouraging church planters and for training prospective church planters.

The contents of the book begin with a description of the Canadian church planting landscape. The text then devotes a significant chapter to providing theology and motivations for church planting.

Another emphasis of the book is on the practical steps and stages of a church plant under different conditions. The writer seeks to maintain a practical bent throughout the book. Besides describing the church beginnings, the book gives significant space to the description of a church planter. The actions of a church planter need to be specific, intentional and missional.

The other main section is about witness and outreach. Church planting is about evangelism, both personally and corporately. The goal of every church plant is to bring people into the Kingdom. Our experience shows that under the right church planting conditions, about one third of the new attenders will be new to the faith, one third will be people returning to the faith, and one third will be stable Christians who are ready for leadership involvement.

The purpose of this book is twofold: first, to build a strong biblical rationale for aggressive church planting, and secondly, to describe how church planting can be done in the 21st century. It incorporates the various contemporary churhc planting movements to assure relevance for all generations.

The readers of this book will likely be those who have interest in seeing the great commission accomplished. They could be church leaders, prospective leaders, college students and teachers, and specifically church planters and church outreach leaders.

ONE

Contextual Challenges

The building of Canada was not the result of a week-end excursion. It rose out of the efforts of explorers, missionaries, builders, and teachers. It would be an overstatement to say Canada was a Christian nation, but this country was developed by many who had a vision that this new land would be a place where God would be honoured, and whose people would serve Jesus Christ. Over hundreds of years immigrants came with a determination to make something for themselves, shaped by an understanding of God's care and leading. Canadians today are inheritors of this enormous investment.

Brian Stiller, *Don't Let Canada Die by Neglect.*

Church planting under any circumstances is a huge challenge. In a post-Christian or post-modern society the challenge is multiplied. This book is written from thirty years of church planting experiences in the growing secular Canadian environment. This chapter describes the past century of religious turmoil and spiritual challenges in

Canada. Furthermore, it describes the personal challenges of Canadian people in the midst of a post-modern reality. The various expressions of pluralism have left Canada a spiritual mosaic ready for serious church planting.

A. Captured By An Urgent Vision

The world today needs people that are captured by a dream that consumes their every thought and action. When people are consumed by a vision it preoccupies them like a fire burning in their soul. It is like a romance, about which you dream by night and daydream while awake.

Daily, people enjoy the benefits of men and women who are remembered for their visions and courageous actions that have resulted in a changed world. Edison's dream of electricity, Wright's dream of air transportation, Ford's dream of an automobile, or Pasteur's vision for health care are examples of breakthrough dreams and visions that have changed the world. Major accomplishments usually have their beginnings with a seemingly impossible dream and a strong desire to achieve a clearly-defined set of goals. In more recent times, the computer and other technologies have changed the world of communications and relationships. It all starts with a dream and a vision.

In more recent times there has been an emergence of heroes who have acted upon a vision with great determination. The heroic cross-Canada run by Terry Fox against the great odds of running with only one leg, set in motion a new confidence in youth. The *Man in Motion* world tour of wheelchaired Rick Hansen also demonstrated forcefully that people of vision can accomplish great things. Other examples of people who are captured by a vision that has consumed their lives are Mother Teresa, Charles Colson, and Billy Graham, along with many more missionaries around the world.

The heroes of Scripture are those that have been able to combine vision and promise with courageous action. In the Old Testament it was men such as Abraham, Moses, Noah etc., and in the New Testament we have the example of Peter, James and

Paul, and many others whose most noteworthy and remembered qualities are their visionary faith and courageous action.

The supreme example of living out the full purposes of life is Jesus, the Word made flesh. The call is for all to follow in the footsteps of Christ. He had a vision that embraced the world. When Christ emerged from the grave as the resurrected Lord, he was consumed with the vision and call to make disciples of all people. His post-resurrection appearances clearly show his priority and preoccupation to bring salvation to all. Today the Lord still calls out to his followers to go into all the world and make disciples. The Lord is looking for men and women who are consumed and captured by his world-wide vision.

One of the great needs for our day and our times is for people of more faith and greater visions. More people are needed in churches and conference agencies who can combine great thoughts with history-changing action.

Today Christians need to believe that God would like to use the past 100 years of Canadian pilgrimage as a gateway into the next century, expecting greater things from God. Every Christian needs to believe that the power of the Holy Spirit is available for the accomplishment of greater things in our lives, like vigorous church planting.

The challenge of the present day is for leaders of vision to rise up to the work of vigorous church planting. For the church to fulfill its mandate of reaching all nations, a major church planting movement is required.

B. Challenged By A Pressing Reality

While there are many churches in North America that have a good balance of church outreach and nurture, there are also many that are weak on the side of outreach and growth. The result is that the majority of churches in Canada are on a plateau or in decline. The situation differs from church to church.

1. Some churches have become more accustomed to hearing about missions, sending support to missions and talking about

missions, than being the church in mission to their immediate community.

2. Evangelism lay leaders from within our churches have not always found their churches responsive to their witness visions, and have consequently joined forces with evangelism organizations outside of the church, leaving the churches void of evangelism leadership.

3. In some churches the work of evangelism is left primarily to the pastor, while the membership provides encouragement, support and prayer.

4. In some churches the work of evangelism has not been assigned to anyone in particular but to everyone in general, resulting in only sporadic and occasional church witness efforts by a few burdened individuals. In some situations the church has defaulted on evangelism with no one in charge.

5. The work of evangelism has not received the same careful planning and leadership that the worship and education programs of the local church may have received. Consequently, many churches have not developed their outreach leadership, evangelism gifts and witness effectiveness.

6. Many churches have not provided adequate organizational structures or assigned outreach leadership to facilitate an ongoing church evangelism ministry.

7. Many churches live in isolation from the community at large and have little or no community attendance beyond their regular worshippers. Such churches are in danger of misunderstanding or misrepresenting the community's needs, feelings and opportunities.

8. Many churches practice the great commission of making disciples, more in terms of nurturing and educating Christians, rather than reaching and winning new people for Christ, and then teaching the new converts.

9. There are some congregations that are not ready to grow. The thought of changing their church friendship patterns, or of welcoming strange new people, and maybe even changing the

church programs to meet the need of new attendees, is too great a threat for some.

10. There are a few churches that are taking up the challenge of planting a daughter church. Most churches are satisfied with staying together, keeping their people, and enjoying the fellowship of their friends and family.

C. Personal Faith Ineffectiveness Factors

Many Christians today are finding themselves on a slippery slope regarding their personal faith. For many, the church has become an optional practice. There are many steps and stages in the loss of personal peace and Christian joy. Some of the reasons for the faith slide are:

1. Knowledge without Commitment

In many situations today, people have knowledge without commitment and obedience. This has produced a powerless structure of faith without works.

2. Worship without Obedience

Whenever people define their obedience to God in terms of worship only, they have short-changed the discipleship track. Worship cannot be a substitute for witness and service.

3. Devotions without Scripture

The flood of popular people's theology and devotional booklets has created a generalized, rather than specific, awareness of the Word of God. The Scriptures need to have a priority place in the Christian's devotional life.

4. Principles without the Person

As it is in many situations, so it is with salvation; it is not what is known but who is known. One's fellowship and commitment is to Christ the Saviour, which goes beyond a support of Christian principles. The Christian's life is in Christ the Saviour.

5. Witness without a Door

Today, sharing has become for many a generalized dialogue about God the Creator. Witness is sharing what Christ has done to make possible the forgiveness of sin. The witness dialogue has become God-centred conversation without focusing in on Christ the Way, the Truth, the Life.

6. Traditions Rather than Cults

Today it is not popular to talk about false cults or false teachers. It is more popular to talk about other religious traditions alongside the Christian faith. There is an exclusiveness that must be proclaimed which knows only one Mediator/Saviour.

7. Conversion Without Transformation

Salvation is clearly more than an educational process. The theology of conversion must be based on God's love and forgiveness in Christ. It involves a miracle of grace and transformation by the Spirit of God, as people open themselves in repentance and faith.

8. Temporal rather than Eternal

Many efforts of mission today are more social in nature than spiritual. The priority mission of Christ, as culminated in His death for people's sins, must always remain the central focus of the gospel.

9. Presence without Priority

Many Christians are in the world without an intentional purpose. They are insulated and isolated from those whom they are to win. These people are preoccupied with their Christian connections and have no time left for bringing others into the faith.

10. Faith without Holiness

The radical nature of discipleship is all but forgotten by many. A new emphasis on the holiness of God and the devastation of sin is needed. To be in the family of God includes godly living.

D. Canadians In Religious Turmoil

A Century Of Struggles

The Church in Canada has gone through a century of radical change and religious indifference. Canada was born in the context of religious convictions. The founding fathers sought to create a nation that would reflect and respect the Judeo-Christian principles and values. It has taken Canada only a little more than one century after Confederation to change itself from a nation with Christian values to a nation of secular pluralism.

At the time of Confederation in 1867, several centuries of active church and missionary life had already characterized Canada. The religious faiths that were brought to Canada in the eighteenth and nineteenth centuries very much molded the religious fabric of Canada. Many of the early immigration and pioneer arrivals to Canada were motivated by a missionary spirit. This explains the rapid growth of the Roman Catholic and the Anglican churches across Canada, and the Baptist Church and others in the Atlantic provinces. Those who immigrated to Canada out of motives of ethnic survival, political and religious freedom, and economic gain did not come with a missionary zeal and national concern, and so did not see their church mushroom across the nation, as was the case with the earlier missionary explorers.

1. Evangelical Uncertainty—1900–1945

The first half of the twentieth century still very much reflected the faith of the nation's founding fathers. As the immigrants kept pouring into Canada, they gave priority to the expression of their faith. The first three decades after confederation are described by John Grant as decades of religious controversy, denominational collisions, and missionary contests over who would dominate the religious scene.[1]

With the turn of the century came a rapid influx of immigrants who represented religious minorities, or people with convictions that were often indifferent to the values cultivated by the earlier pioneers. Rural values became threatened as the cities began to emerge. The notion of establishing the Church as one of the first concerns in the settlement of an area began to be threatened. The governments began to pass protective legislation such as the Lord's Day Act in 1906, and to provide religion in schools. Other organizations, in the interest of temperance, prohibition, and moral reform, pushed for legislation to outlaw liquor traffic, etc.[2] Their social and moral concerns were soon dubbed as a social gospel movement, and became a red flag movement for the evangelical churches. These social concern groups consolidated their interests by moving into unification talks that led to the formation of the United Church in 1925.

The First World War years did not help the theological controversy that was developing between the social gospel groups, and the emergence of conservative fundamentalism. Several evangelical movements emerged amidst the process of church union and the social gospel emphasis, namely, Prairie Bible Institute (1922), the Pentecostal Church (1919), the Nazarene Church of Canada (1908), and growth of the Alliance Church, which was started in 1890. These new evangelical groups became the opposition to the more liberal church trends. The Depression of the thirties greatly affected the Church. Church budgets needed to be cut by thirty to forty percent. Pastors' wages fell by forty percent or more. Churches began to respond with "restoration funds" and "keeping faith" campaigns and social "self-help" agencies. The need for social reform gave rise to new social political movements like the CCF and Social Credit parties. The depression helped the churches to rethink their priorities. The evangelical church, particularly the fundamentalist churches, felt the gospel was being compromised by the social concerns agenda of the church.

The shock of another war in 1939 brought to a head the anti-war debate among the churches, and the serious consideration of taking a pacifist stand. Despite the freedom of conscience consensus, most churches, except for the Anabaptist, joined in support of the nation's call for soldiers.[3] The war brought about a serious debate on the theology of life, social justice and church purpose. The more conservative evangelical churches found themselves withdrawing from the ecumenical discussions for fear of liberalism. By the end of the war the mainline churches were more ready for church growth than were the evangelical groups. The war had, however, brought about a cynicism about church life that clearly surfaced in the sixties.

2. Post-War Religion Boom—1945–1960

The return of the war veterans generated a new enthusiasm for Christian values and church life, which resulted in a mid-century growth spurt for the churches generally. The returning soldiers were ready to give the Church their support and to make the Church the door through which they could re-enter family and society life. During this period the United Church built 1,500 churches and some 600 manses.[4] The Lutherans also launched an effective program of church extension through their "mission developers." Most of the church growth during these years was in suburban areas. Some of the growth was formed by small group Bible studies, inspirational conferences, lay church service clubs and camps. Lay involvement and laity witness became prominent, resulting in an anti-clerical mood.

The post-war climate was conducive to the emergence of new parachurch organizations and groups like the Mormons and the Jehovah Witnesses. While the mainline churches were rallying their people to deal with social issues, the evangelical groups were following a more conservative and formal expression of the gospel. The evangelicals were, for the most part, bypassed by this religious surge mainly because "the evangelical denominations represented a protest against the typical mind-set of post war religion."[5]

Reginald Bibby suggests that this Golden Era of church boom is somewhat deceptive against the backdrop of population growth. In actual fact, he says, Canada's dominant religious groups saw their membership proportion shrink when compared to the growth of the Canadian population.[6] This was also the time when the Quebec Canadians were undergoing a quiet revolution, where institutions previously controlled by the church were taken over by the government, a transfer which basically meant shifting the power from the Catholic hierarchy to the Catholic laity.

3. Church Exodus—1960–1980

The decade of the 60s brought to the surface the simmering discontentment of many dissatisfied church people. A rebellious mood against institutional forms and traditional systems emerged as part of the decade's character. The Church was seen as being one of the strongholds of something that was no longer very satisfying, and so the church exodus erupted. Three interesting patterns began to emerge. The Protestant Church attendance dropped sharply from a high of 60% in 1945 to 45% by the mid-fifties, and to less than 30% by the mid-sixties and then stabilized at about 25% in the mid-eighties and near 20% in the nineties. The Catholic Church decline started a little later, from a post World War II high of 80%, to 60% by the mid-seventies, to about 40% by the mid-eighties.[7]

The evangelicals on the other hand, began to see signs of growth during this period, whereas during the postwar boom when the mainstream churches were in a growth mode, the evangelicals seemed to be preoccupied with themselves and missed getting a piece of the ready harvest.

The Church in the 60s and 70s was under severe attack. Pierre Burton led the way with his scathing criticism of the Church in his book *The Comfortable Pew*. Many people joining in the church exodus felt as Pierre Burton, who said "There is a growing skepticism about the Church, a feeling not only that it is all talk and no action, but also that it is all double-talk based on double-think."[8] The Vatican II efforts of renewal were in part a response to the growing feeling that church modernization needed to be on the agenda, and that the Church needed to adjust to the contemporary world.[9]

The Christian Church of the eighties and nineties continued to lose ground in Canada. The Charter of Rights of the early eighties brought about a more formalized process to the demise of Canada as a so-called Christian nation. The courts were clogged with cases that sought to remove all reference to the Christian faith upon which our nation was built, to assure the equal rights of individuals. The Vancouver writer in the *Canada at a Glance* column, speaking to the Canadian Radio-television and Telecommunications Commission on behalf of the Canadian Christians concerned about media, has aptly said, "There are blatant examples of anti-Christian bias nationally and especially locally."[10] The nation's lawmakers in Canada who started the century with passing laws to assure the continuance of the nation's respect for the Judeo-Christian values, are concluding the century in an attempt to purge the nation's laws of those things that would reflect a Judeo-Christian value preference.

4. The Current Canadian Situation—Late 80s and 90s

The church exodus of the past number of decades has produced a large population that has a vague knowledge of church life and Christian faith and has a fragmented practice. Canada now consists of a population that has taken on a secularized pluralism. It is now a nation that has moved from having convictions about the Christian faith, to merely showing courtesies to all faiths. David Roberts, one of the religious editors in the *Faith* column, describes the essence of Canadian pluralism. He says,

> We are a pluralistic bunch. Many Canadians believe in God, but not exclusively a Christian God. Indeed, those who criticize government policy on religious grounds, must recognize the Bible as an important but not exclusive source of ethical insight... our society draws from various sources for moral direction.[11]

The same kind of thinking was applied by Jimmy Williams, a former manager of the Toronto Blue Jays, at the time when he curtailed the team's traditional clubhouse chapel sessions, and prohibited team members from appearing in video promotions of Christian organizations, at least not in Blue Jay uniform, because "it might be unfair to other religious groups." The reason given for the recent ruling by the Ontario Public School Board to ban exclusive use of the Lord's prayer in favour of a variety of readings and prayers or drop them altogether, is because "no one religion should be allowed to dominate." The motion to terminate the distribution of Gideon Bibles by the Vancouver School Board in the fall of 1989 follows the same logic. The spokesman for the Vancouver School Board, describing the new School Act says, "School must be conducted in a strictly secular and non-sectarian manner and the board interprets the distribution of scripture to go against the Charter of Rights." These examples indicate to what extent Canada has become pluralistic and secular in its thinking. The current debate on gay marriages and the homophobia accusations further show the lack of Christian tolerance today.

In the *Understanding Our Times* seminar, Brian Stiller, then executive director of the Evangelical Fellowship of Canada, describes the secularization process in Canada as the ungluing of the social contract between the evangelicals and the mainstream, mainline church. His analysis is very helpful. For the first half of the twentieth century, the country was ruled basically by mainstream church politicians who had an unwritten contract of trust with the non-political religious population that the country lawmakers "assumed the existence of God and agreed on the value of biblical morality for Canada." Stiller contends that the basis of government began to shift in the 50s and 60s away from the Judeo-Christian value system, to a system of pluralism which considers all religious world views and value systems as valid choices.[12]

In a sense, this century of Canadian history resembles a checkerboard, according to Stiller, where the first half of the century the Canadian "game board" itself was assumed to be framed in Christian principles, with the other religions being the squares, and players permitted to play on what was essentially considered to be a Christian board. The second half of the century the checkerboard became secular and the Christian ideology became one of the squares or players on the board, alongside many other faith players who were making their strategic moves to influence and control the game of values. For the Christian position to be heard on the game board requires deliberate presence and action on the part of the Christian public. The Christian value system is no longer automatically advanced or followed within the Canadian system as it was assumed to be fifty years ago.

5. A Changed Society of Secularism (Post-modernity)

There is hope for a society in change if the Church will learn to understand it. The last fifty years have rendered Canada a new face.

Canada has moved as a nation from what was loosely described as a Christian nation to a nation of pluralism. The focus of Canada has shifted from a concern of doing what is right before God to the concept of having one's personal wishes and individual rights fulfilled.

Lesslie Newbigin is helpful in providing a base of understanding to the western culture of urbanization and pluralism, by describing secular decision-making in two spheres: the private and the public. He says,

> The public world is a world of facts that are the same for everyone, whatever the values might be; the private world is a world of values where all are free to choose their own values and to pursue such courses of action as will correspond with them.

He suggests that the present western secularized post-enlightenment world view of the public and private worlds is fast becoming the basis of the emerging world culture. The Bible, Church or any other faith experiences have been relegated to the private world of personal values and choices.

> This religious paradigm shift helps us to understand why our secularized society is preoccupied with removing religious practice from the public arena of life because it is seen as belonging to the private world. Newbigin, however, strongly argues that the Bible also belongs to the public world of factual knowledge and so should be given its place in the field of academic investigation. Furthermore, he suggests that every person is a unity where the most private prayers and the most public acts are integrated as one being.[13]

The post-modern Canadian environment is a growing challenge for the church.

E. Characteristics Of The Canadian Religious Landscape

There are many evidences that the Canadian social context is being affected by the changing post-modern environment. In a limited and general way, the following observations represent the Canadian population's profile and expressed values.

1. Socialization Shift

The rapidly changing environment has resulted in the erosion of loyalties. This in turn has resulted in changing relationships, instability, and mobility. This has created a shift of the family's socialization centre. Local community centres are feeling the lack of loyalty and involvement, since much of the socialization has shifted to the workplace, employment centres, or urban commercial centres. The commercialization of leisure has also affected the neighbourhood. The malls have increasingly become entertainment centres, leaving the local playgrounds empty.

2. Individualism

There appears to be a shift away from the emphasis of the common good of society to individual rights and preferences. The Canadian Charter of Rights has facilitated minority considerations over the majority preferences. Personal freedoms and pleasures are high on the scale of Canadian values. Self-sufficiency, materialism, and hedonism are frequent by-products of individualism. Individualism often postures itself in an anti-institutional way.

3. Tolerance

Canadians have a high commitment to diversity. Don Posterski identifies tolerance as the new golden rule which expresses itself as "I'll do my thing and you do your thing."[14] One-way thinking belongs to another age, in a world of pluralism. In this climate of tolerance, the idea of censorship, restrictions, or judgments and persuasions of viewpoints like evangelism, is unacceptable.

4. Morality

In a post-Christian world, morality is a matter of personal choice. Traditional morals are seen as Victorian or archaic. Morality is situational and personal. In such an open society alternative values are often pushed, and traditional values are seen as dangerous and intolerant. In this environment Christians are seen as narrow, out-of-date, and almost untrustworthy. Issues of faith are not deemed suitable or appropriate for public life.

5. Biblical Truth

The notion of absolutes and biblical authority has no place in the post-modern environment. All beliefs and behaviours are seen as equally valid. There is little room for objective universal truth. Propositional truth is gone and has little or no public relevance. When biblical truth is reduced to little more than private feelings and personal experiences, it is a challenge to share the exclusive claims of Christ's salvation.

6. Spirituality

The traditional Christian Church is under serious evaluation. For many it has lost its meaning. The rise of spiritual experimentation and syncretic universalism has left the Church struggling with a declining attendance. Alan Roxburgh has summarized the position of the Church well by saying, "Christians are waking up to the fact that this is no longer our world. Once the main highway of culture, we have become a gravelled back road along which fewer people are choosing to travel."[15] While Canadians are attending church less, they are nevertheless registering high levels of spirituality and a belief in basic orthodox tenants of faith. Spirituality is expressed and experienced in a wide range of ways in this environment.

7. Disconnectedness

The church-going population in Canada is experiencing a disconnection. They feel silenced and disenfranchised. The rapid secularization, with the majority accepting a new culture that is being stripped of its Christian value, has left the Christians alienated and silenced in the marketplace and public area. The church has been marginalized. Many Christians have opted for a closet Christianity with or without the Church.

8. Consumerism

As a response to the reality of a declining church attendance, many churches have stepped up their advertising and adopted a church marketing campaign that promises a satisfied church experience. The result is that churchgoers are demanding for church to be their way. This ha's in turn created some churches that resemble a carnival because people want to be entertained; others resemble a smorgasbord where people can pick and choose what they want; others are more like fast food outlets that provide a quick spiritual fix; and still other churches are selling themselves as warm fuzzies where attendance will make them feel better. This consumer-like church fad has left a divided church landscape, with some retreating back to the basics, and others assuring themselves that the Church must become more attractive to the unchurched. There is a sense that the emerging generation is more interested in going back to church basics.[16]

9. Canadian Church Statistics

Church attendance in Canada has declined in the past century from 60% of the population in attendance in the mid forties, to near 20% by the year 2000. Canada's youth church attendance is around 15%. The young people seem to mirror the beliefs and practices of the adults in their interest in the ultimate questions of life and death. It is important to note that by the late 90s, the mainline church attendance continued to drop to 15% or less, while the evangelical church attendance rebounded to near 50%. Even though Canadian church attendance is sporadic, a high percentage of Canadians still plan to use the church or synagogue for their life cycle events: 75% for child dedications and baptisms, 82% for weddings, and 85% will use the church for funerals. At present, 80% of the 15–25-year-olds identify with a religious organization.

Canadians have separated belief from belonging. While church attendance is 20% or less, their belief percentages are significantly higher.

• 85% of adults and 84% of youth believe in the existence of God
• 79% of adults and 81% of youth believe in the divinity of Jesus
• 65% of both groups believe in life after death

Canadians practice their faith in a fragmented way, and use the church only as needed and wanted. Reginald Bibby has provided the Canadian church a huge service with his nine national surveys since 1974 regarding Canadian church patterns. The statistics in this section need to be credited to his research.[17]

10. *Positive Future*

There are some positive values emerging among many Canadians. There is a growing emphasis on "Green Values," which look for natural, nutritious, healthy, and chemical-free foods. Along with this comes an emphasis on recycling waste to protect the environment. There is an emphasis on making the world a better and more peaceful place. Most Canadians have a passion for justice and equal opportunity. The Canadian emphasis on education, health care, job opportunities, safety, and a high standard of living, have made Canada one of the top-ranking nations of the world.

11. *Church Recovery*

The Church is the hope of the world. There are recovery signs on the horizon. Many young people are pursuing a new spirituality. Churches are being transformed, and the worship is being renewed. Many churches have become more missional in their focus. Donald Posterski sees hope in Christian engagement and dialogue on the issues of diversity. He challenges the Church to accept, appreciate, and influence its society through praying, caring, and communicating.[18]

There is much reason for Canadian Christians to be optimistic. Christians are spiritually empowered beings who emit light, provide salt, and have an aroma that attracts because of their Christ-like-ness. There appears to be a religious renaissance underway all over the globe which has also given Christianity a new lease on life. Sociologist Peter Berger concludes that the assumption that we live in a secular world is false. In fact, he says that "the world today with some exceptions is as furiously religious as it ever was."[19]

F. Canadian Expressions Of Pluralism

1. There are the faithful mainline church worship regulars who are often more sure of their denominational identity than they are of the personal application of their faith.

2. There are the evangelical conservative Protestant churches who are at times overly sure and definitive of their personal faith. For

the most part, this group has a strong commitment to evangelism.

3. There are the churches who come from a strong tradition of institutional faith and liturgical worship style. Many young people are looking for a more formal practice of faith.

4. There are the new Canadian minority language groups who have brought with them the worship of their ancestors. Many of these are unacquainted with the gospel of Jesus.

5. There are the exclusive "other gospel"-type churches that tend to follow a "Bible plus" gospel which is often considered to be cultic or truncated.

6. There are the church dropouts or the neo-secularized non-church attendees who have a tradition and memory of belief that has been abandoned for lack of practicality or necessity.

7. There are the occasional church shoppers or consumers who use the church as a special service agency depending on the cycle of life they are in or on the time of year.

8. There are the second-generation unchurched who are "secular neo-pagans" with little or no knowledge or concern of Christ and church life.

9. There are the "Generation Xers" who often see themselves alienated from the mainstream of society and for the most part from the church.

10. There are the unchurched Christians or TV Christians who practice their faith in isolation of any church or denomination. They "home school" their faith life.

11. There are the first Canadians or Aboriginals for whom life and worship flow as an integrated stream within the context of their natural environment.

G. Implications Of Secularism For Christians

1. The world has stopped coming to church for the most part, which means the Christians will need to find a way other than the Church to dialogue with the unchurched population.

2. The world has also stopped using the Bible as its basic reference point of right and wrong. This means that Christians will need to learn to stand against the popular tide of secular ethical norms. Society is not the moral authority on ethical matters for the Christian. True Christians are committed to biblical faithfulness, and so will need to reject cultural assimilation regarding lifestyles.

3. The secular trends that fuel the spirit of this world today provide an opportunity for the body of Christ to be a distinct alternative to the spirit of worldliness by being a united force within a non-Christian culture. The Church must resist being assimilated into the patterns and priorities of the world.

4. The Christians will need to learn how to distinguish and discern that which is from above and that which is from this world. Sometimes non-Christians know better what is appropriate behaviour for Christians than do the Christians themselves.

5. The new goal for the Christians will need to be one of influence, acceptance, and cultural engagement. The Christian cannot shrink back and be intimidated by pluralism or cultural diversity, says Posterski.

6. The Christians in Canada are suffering from the "cultural blender effect" in which there seems to be little difference between a Christian and a non-Christian. If the differences are only marginal, why should the unbeliever bother with a Christian commitment which seems to be more words than action?[20]

7. The pressure is for the church today to demonstrate spiritual reality and Christian integrity. Only a radical demonstration of love and concern will gain the attention of a world that is fatigued by the publicity of church leadership failures and scandals. The rumours in the world today of what Christianity is do not ring with good news. A new image of integrity, humility, and love needs to be seen by the world.

8. Christians in a pluralistic or secular society face the pressure from society that frowns on aggressive recruitment of people

outside of their group. Twelve percent of Canadians believe strongly in sharing their faith, while 45% of Canadians strongly disagree about Christian faith sharing.[21]

9. Christians need to concentrate their efforts on those who have some affinity toward Christians either by their background, belief, or by friendship. Those who are participating in religion in a fragmented "here and there" fashion may well be ready for a new commitment that involves them fully. Bibby refers to these people as "Affiliates" who could be won. (1995)

10. Witness with any effect in a pluralistic society needs to flow from a non-judgmental, accepting and caring committed person. There is a need to enter into the Christian dialogue with people; a ping-pong-like dialogue with someone who does not yet play too well. The game goal with a new player is to keep the volley going, not to score a quick lead.

11. The Christian Church needs to realize that it has inherited a two-dimensional faith structure: Christianity and Christendom. Christianity is the God-given Good News of the gospel, and Christendom is the human vehicle or structure that has cradled, constituted, and delivered the gospel over the centuries. It is the Christendom part that is being challenged today, not the true gospel. The church needs to hear the call for change on how the gospel is celebrated today.

12. Most of the inter-church disunity and denominational segregations have occurred more as a result of differing views on Christendom rather than Christian gospel understanding. This is not the time for the Christian Church to divide its energies over how to do church. It is time for the Christians to align and unite themselves against the common enemy of their soul, the devil, rather than looking for differences and reasons for further evangelical church divisions. The diversity of church expressions needs to be affirmed rather than fought, particularly in this consumer-oriented society. People want a choice regarding church style and faith.

NOTES——

[1] John Webster Grant, *The Church in the Canadian Era* (Burlington, Ontario: Welch Publishing Company, 1988) p. 82.

[2] Grant, p. 100.

[3] Grant, p. 150.

[4] Grant, p, 161.

[5] Grant, p. 179.

[6] Reginald W. Bibby, *Fragmented Gods* (Toronto: Irwin Publishing, 1987) p.14.

[7] Bibby, p. 17.

[8] Pierre Berton, *The Comfortable Pew* (Toronto, Ontario: McClelland & Stewart, 1965) p. 129.

[9] Bibby, p.19.

[10] Winnipeg Free Press, Jan. 20, 1990

[11] Winnipeg Free Press, November, 1988.

[12] Brian Stiller, *Understanding Our Times* Lecture Series (Willowdale, Ontario: Evangelical Fellowship of Canada).

[13] Lesslie Newbigin, *Foolishness to the Greeks* (Grand Rapids, Michigan: Eerdmans Publishing Company, 1986) p. 135.

[14] Don Posterski, *Reinventing Evangelism* (Downers Grove, Illinois: InterVarsity Press, 1989). p. 66.

[15] Alan Roxburgh, *Reaching the Next Generation* (Vancouver, British Columbia: Regent College Publishing, 1993) p. 45.

[16] James Packer, *Hot Tub Religion* (Wheaton, Illinois: Living Books, 1987).

[17] Bibby, *Fragmented Gods*, General Statistics Source.

[18] Donald Posterski, *Reinventing Evangelism*, p. 32.

[19] Peter Berger in Reginald Bibby, *Restless Gods* (Don Mills, Ontario: Stoddart, 2002) p. 2.

[20] Donald Posterski, *Faith Today*, March/April, 1990.

[21] Angus Reid Survey, 1996.

• Two

Biblical Foundations

The primary mission of the Church and therefore of the churches is to proclaim the gospel of Christ and to gather believers into local churches where they can be built up in the faith and made effective in service, thereby planting new congregations throughout the world.

David Hesselgrave, *Planting Churches Cross-Culturally.*

The Foundations section of this book is an attempt to establish what Christ had in mind when He said He would build His church. It is a theological reflection on the nature and essence of a church and how it gets to be established. This chapter is about making sure a church planter understands what the church that is being planted should look like.

There is an urgency about establishing the church. It is for this redemptive cause that God the Father sent His Son, and it is for this cause that Christ died and rose again, and it is for the same cause that the Holy Spirit was released into the world. This divine cause of establishing churches or redemption centres is the same cause for which the followers of Christ are called. This task of making disciples is the primary task of the church. There is an urgency about this mandate which Christ has given to believers. The following urgencies provide powerful motivations for rigorous biblical church planting.

1. People are Redeemable

God loves the world and wants all people to have eternal life and to live a life empowered by His purpose and presence. People can be set free and given a life of joy and peace (John 3:16; 2 Cor. 5:17).

2. Provision has been Made

There is no salvation outside of Jesus Christ. Jesus is the only way to the father. The Christians are called to proclaim Christ. People need the Lord for salvation (John 14:6; Acts 16:31).

3. People are Lost

People are lost and condemned in their sins without salvation in Christ. The good news is that Jesus has died for our sins and offers forgiveness as a free gift to all who believe (Rom. 3:23; 5:1).

4. The Command has been Issued

To make disciples is a command of Christ. The will of God is for the world to hear and believe. The primary task for the believing world is to make Christ known among all the nations. The mission of Jesus has become the mission priority of every church (Matt. 28:18-20).

5. The Lord is Coming

The day of the Lord is coming, and only those who have accepted Christ will receive the reward of heaven and so escape the condemnation of God. There is an urgency of time in preparing to meet our God (1 Cor. 15:50-58).

The command to make disciples of all nations is the primary task of the church. Every member has the responsibility to be a witness to Christ through the power of the Holy Spirit and to call men and women to be reconciled to God. The gospel is the power of God for salvation and is able to meet the total needs of every person. The gospel of God's kingdom and his reign is experienced through Christ the King.

A. God's Design For The Church

1. The Church as the Promised Blessing

The Church in this world needs to be seen as part of the history of God. God is working out a plan which He conceived before the world and will consummate in future history. The Church is part of God's spiritual lineage. God's promised blessing to Abraham overflows to include all nations and all families of the earth. In this divine historical process Jesus Christ as the seed of Abraham links all of Christ's followers to be Abraham's descendants. The promised blessing to Israel is now also extended to the Church.[1]

2. The Church as Signs of God's Kingdom

The Church is clearly subject to the Kingdom of God and reign of God. It has been described as the continued activity and rule of God in history and beyond. The Kingdom is to be preached (Mark 1:15), to be sought (Matt. 6:33), to be received (Mark 10:15), to be entered (Mark 9:45); it can be possessed, expressed and manifested (Rom. 14:17; 1 Cor. 4:20), and it can be forfeited or taken away (Matt. 21:43; 1 Cor. 6:9-10). The Kingdom of God is a reality from which all sin and works of darkness are excluded.[2] A new church makes the Kingdom of God a visible and practical reality. Christ warns that his followers will find themselves in the midst of clashing kingdoms. It is a cosmic war against the prince of this world, but the Kingdom of light is overcoming the kingdom of darkness. It is a battle for the allegiance of human hearts. In church planting the message of the Kingdom of God brings hope, joy, and freedom.

3. The Church as the Incarnation of Christ

The church is the continuation of Christ's incarnation in this world. The followers of Christ are His hands, feet, voice, and his continued activity. The church is the body of Christ, of which he is the head and cornerstone. The body of Christ is the incarnate mission and message. The church expresses words and deeds of God incarnately in the world. The responsibility of representing God to the people of this world is immense. The church needs to be constantly concerned about the fact that it must be an accurate incarnation of the good news and a consistent follower of Christ.[3]

4. The Church as the Cultural Steward

The cultural mandate of the church stands as a balance parallel to the evangelistic mandate. The cultural mandate has its roots in Gen. 1:26: "They will have power over the fish, birds and all animals, domestic and wild, large and small." Verse 26 suggests that God is putting Adam and Eve in charge over God's earthly creation, which is known as the cultural mandate of God. In the New Testament this mandate is expanded to include loving your neighbour (Matt. 22:37-39). C. Peter Wagner claims that this delegated cultural mandate includes "the distribution of wealth, the balance of nature, marriage and the family, human government, keeping the peace, cultural integrity, and liberation of the oppressed" and that we need to include feeding the hungry and assuring justice for all.[4] God's people are agents for doing good. Every Christian and every church needs to in some way participate in the fulfillment of the cultural mandate. The cultural and evangelistic mandates are like the two wings of a bird.

5. The Church as a Redemptive Agent

The church has been called to be the voice for heavenly concerns here on earth. It has an evangelism mandate and priority. God's purpose for the Church is to be a messenger of the gospel. Every Christian has the responsibility to be a witness to Christ through the power of the Holy Spirit. It was the design of God that the Church would take on the responsibility of sharing the good news worldwide as redemptive co-workers with God. The Church, both individually and corporately, is the vehicle or basic agent for God's vision of global redemption. As such, its people are called ambassadors, peace makers and witnesses. God had in mind a missional church and sent it into the world as an instrument for his mission. Church mission is rooted in God's redemptive purposes to restore and reconcile the world to himself.[5]

6. The Church as a Divine Legacy

The church is the fulfillment and realization of what God intended through Christ's sacrifice. God was creating for himself a covenant people who by faith would embrace the gift of God. The Church, like Israel, is to be a distinct people, a people of God, over whom God is God and the people know they are his people (Exodus 6:7). The Israel of the Old Testament and the believers' church of the New Testament are a continuation of God's design for His creation.[6] When we establish a new church, we are collaborating with God in the realization of His redemptive purposes. By planting churches, we are creating centres and outposts for God's redemptive activity to take place. Church planting is a God-driven exercise through human hands.

B. Building On Scriptural Church Images

Much is learned about Christ's intent for the church from the biblical images used in describing the Church. The very nature of the Church can be seen through this rich Biblical church imagery. Church planting should reflect the dynamics suggested in these picturesque concepts of the believers' community.

1. The Kingdom of God—The Church in Kingly Relationships

This term used some hundred times in the gospels, suggests elements of submission, power, rule, and of sovereign extension, Lordship and authority. God's people are to be seen as being part of the present and future Kingdom of God. It suggests a sense of majesty, loyalty, and commitment. People of God's Kingdom carry the titles of sons and heirs of God (Matt. 3:2; Matt. 4:23; Matt. 6:33; Matt. 13:38).

2. The Church of God—The Church in Divine Perspective

One is reminded of the believers assembled together in worship, prayer, and communion by the word *church*. The meeting together of believers, or the "called-out ones" usually required buildings, and so are called churches, or the believers' meeting place. *Ecclesia,* or church, means congregation, continuing community, the gathering, called together, pilgrims together. The term *church* stands in stark contrast to individualism (Matt. 16:18; Romans 16:16).

3. The People of God—The Church in Family Terms

This phrase emphasizes the church's dignity, value, privileges, and ownership. In an age of isolation and loneliness, it is good news to know that believers are the chosen people of God. The challenge is to live up to this calling by sharing God's love and life. To be a people of God also implies that Christ's followers are not a people of this world but a community of faith with heavenly concerns. God's people are to Him a royal priesthood, a holy nation and a consecrated people (1 Pet. 2:5,9; Rev. 1:6).

4. The Body of Christ—The Church in Medical Terms

The Church as a body is the New Testament's most common metaphor, and focuses on the relationship and unity of the members. The focus here is on the unity and identity that the body has with Christ as its head. This Church is seen as identifying with the sufferings and victories of Christ. This integral relationship emphasizes our dependency, unity and growth in Christ. It also shows a functional relationship between members and the use of their spiritual gifts under Christ's authority (Eph. 5:23-32; 1 Cor. 12:14; Col. 1:18).

5. God's Building—The Church in Contractor's Language

Christ says that he will build his Church. Paul tells the Corinthians they are God's building. Peter talks about stones being built into a spiritual house. The building analogy is particularly suitable in that it has foundation, dimensions, function, and ownership. The imagery of doors, windows and rooms all have dwelling overtones of spiritual form and function (Matt. 16:18; Eph. 2:20-22; 1 Cor. 3:9; 1 Pet. 2:5).

6. The Temple of God—The Church in Clergy Language

The Church as God's temple communicates the ideas of being part of God's sacred field or holy dwelling place. Closely related to this idea is that of being earthen vessels or tents hallowed for His use. It suggests a people of holiness, and of temple worship activity such as prayer, forgiveness, reconciliation, and sacrifice. In this temple image the foundation of Christ has great prominence and the believers as living stones are perfectly fitted (1 Cor. 3:16-17; 1 Tim. 3:15; Eph. 2:20-22; 1 Cor. 6:19).

7. The Bride of Christ—The Church in Romantic Language

The Church as the bride of Christ is one of the most picturesque images. It brings to mind the Church's honorable position and suggests a relationship of love, purity, and intimate devotion. It also suggests a future hope of inheritance and present life of companionship and fullness. His people are a special treasure to Him and a covenant people of faithfulness. The bride, in her beauty, is to attract lovers to herself (Matt. 25:6; 2 Cor. 11:2; Eph. 5:22-32; Rev. 20).

8. The Army of God—The Church in Military Terms

The Church with its triumphant Saviour stands victorious within the battle ground. However, the church must fight on in view of the enemies' lingering activity. The church is called to put on the armour of God to resist the prince and power of the air. Our alignment to Christ and the proper use of our spiritual weapons are marks of God's army. Servanthood, submission and single commitment are central to being a good soldier (Eph. 6:10-20; 2 Tim. 4:7).

9. People of the Way—The Church in Traveller's Perspective

The suggestion in this designation is one of careful lifestyle and directional living. Such people know where they are going and whom they are following. It represents a pilgrim people on the way to the promised land (Acts 9:2; John 14).

10. The Vineyard and Field of God—The Church in Gardeners' Terms

With Christ as the vine and the believers as the branches, the growth is guaranteed. To be part of the garden of God places the focus on fruit, flowers and produce. It is significant to see that

God has an expectation of productivity from his people (John 15; Ps. 1; 1 Cor. 3:9).

11. The Fold of God—The Church in Ranching Language

Christ pictured as the good shepherd and the believers as sheep within his fold, suggests a position of security, safety and well-being. It further depicts the believer as following the shepherd to green pastures and fresh waters (John 10; Ps. 23).

12. A Royal Priesthood—The Church in Functional Language

The church in this term suggests function, purpose and involvement. It suggests a special calling of spiritual activity. It places the believers into a position of intercession and divine positioning (1 Pet. 2:5, 9; Rom. 1:6; 5:10).

Church planting according to these images requires the exercise of divine vision, faith and power. Human wisdom and knowledge is insufficient and incapable in extending the Kingdom of God. Our confidence is in the faith that we are co-labourers with Christ in God's Kingdom. And when Christ says that he will build the church which He loves, and for which He has died, we are assured of Kingdom growth.

C. Planting Kingdom Communities

God's plan for his followers is repeatedly described in Scripture in corporate kingdom terms. God is creating for Himself a people where He will be their God and they will be His people. This God and people relationship makes for a passionate community that cares about following and serving Christ, as well as caring and loving one another. Shenk and Stutzman in *Creating Communities of the Kingdom*, which inspired this chapter heading, refer to Kingdom communities where various divergent language groups worship together in a community of joy and love as an unprecedented miracle of grace.[7]

Each church that is planted needs to reflect the Kingdom characteristics of God's people. The family of God is an intentional community that represents and champions the cause of Christ in this world. Every new church needs to assure that the basic Kingdom blueprints are manifest in the development of the new church.

Every new church that is planted is a sign of God's Kingdom being realized in this world. Every person that accepts the gospel becomes a citizen of God's Kingdom who by faith has moved from the Kingdom of darkness into the Kingdom of light. When the followers of Christ begin to function as the body of Christ it results in various observable Kingdom community characteristics. These constitute the basic parameters and foundational pieces of a new church.

1. Faith Community—The Relationship to God

The Church is built on the premise that to believe in Christ is to have personal salvation. In Christ a person receives spiritual, eternal life. The Church is a spiritual community where spiritual life is experienced and shared. When the spiritual life is shared and nurtured it results in a community fellowship and discipleship. The ultimate privilege of the faith community is to be a worshipping community. In worship the body of Christ celebrates its relationship with God. Worship is a communal celebration of praise, of breaking bread together, of hearing and responding to the word of God.

2. Caring Community—Relating to One Another

Loving and caring for one another are basic to the Kingdom life. This includes bearing one another's burdens and sharing in times of need. It is a community of trust and forgiveness. In God's family there needs to be an accountability to one another regarding biblical faithfulness and appropriate Kingdom behaviours. Loving one another also includes admonishing one another and encouraging each other in good deeds. One of the defining marks of a caring community is the value and expression of unity in the body.

3. Pilgrim Community—Relating with the Future in Mind

The believers' Church does not belong to the world. It is a journey of eternal life. The Christian belongs to the Kingdom of heaven. In this heavenly journey the community of faith often experiences suffering, rejection and humiliation. It is a journey of non-conformity to the world, where the kingdom of this world and the Kingdom of God clash, due to conflicting values and purposes. Our treasures belong to another Kingdom. The believers have the hope of eternal life, the prepared place for those who accept Christ as the way, the truth, and the life.

4. Witnessing Community—Relating to the World at Large

The church is a community of witness, both individually and corporately. Both in life and in Word, it represents the redemptive cause of Christ in the world. The church invites people to participate in the grace of Christ. The witnessing posture of the believing community is symbolized by the basin and towel. The church should be known for its grace giving and generous qualities. It is to be a sweet savour and light-emitting presence in the world. The fruit of God's spirit in the believer's life will be the primary attraction to the unbelieving. Personal harmony, peace of heart, and deeds of love become major connecting points when Christ is lifted up as the Saviour of all who believe. The church has a message of good news which it is privileged and mandated to freely share. The church is the hope of the world.[8]

D. Footprints From The Galilean Hills

The four gospels provide the foundational principles for the Church which was to be born on the day of Pentecost. From the Galilean hills we observe Christ painting the picture of the Church He is building. The gospels give us a preview of the emerging Church. The church-planting lessons found in the gospels are both instructive and encouraging.

1. Christ Provides the Church Foundation

Christ is clearly the Church builder for He says, "I will build my Church" (Matt.16:18). He is also the church's foundation on which the church is to be carefully built. Christ is also described as the head of the Church (1 Cor. 3:10-13; Eph.5:23); He loves the church and cares for it (Eph.5:25-27). Christ is God's sacrificial gift to humanity, making Him the way, the truth and the life (John 14:6). The Marshal McLuhan adage of the medium being the message is clearly true of Christ. On the Galilean hills the proclaimer becomes the proclaimed, where the messenger becomes the message.

2. Christ Provides the Church Vision

Christ had a Church vision that would provide personal transformation. He came to set the captives free, to restore, enrich and fulfill the lives of people (Luke 4:18-19). Christ had a vision to enlist people to become his followers, co-labourers, and worshippers. As we follow Christ through the Galilean Hills we see a vision of rigorous Kingdom activity involving sowing, reaping, seeking, knocking, restoring, teaching etc. Christ had a sacrificial vision that involved sacrifice, servanthood and suffering. He set a high standard for those who would be His followers.

Christ had a twofold vision involving both faith sharing and deeds of kindness. When the world observes the faith community, following Christ's vision of "loving your neighbor" by protecting the vulnerable, defending the powerless, and helping the poor and hurting, then they have truly validated their faith and reflected the nature and image of God. In the present word-weary western society the Church will need to build many bridges of love and goodwill in order to fulfill the vision of making disciples of all nations.

3. Christ Provides the Church Ministry Model

There are many examples of ministry activity in the gospels which become lessons for church ministry today. When Christ called his disciples to follow Him (Mark 2:17) He indicated that they would become fishers of men. This soon became a reality, when He sent them out in twos with witnessing instructions (Matt. 10). He was modelling faith-sharing and he demonstrated it at the well with the Samaritan woman. Christ is a model in lifestyle witness and ministry which demonstrates in the market place, the villages, cities, roadsides, hillsides, waterfronts, private homes, and in religious places. In these different places we find Christ relating to people while eating, resting, walking, lodging, boating, teaching, debating, healing, and forgiving sin. He included a broad spectrum of people in His daily activities. We find Him in ministry among the curiosity seeking masses, as well as the hidden and fearful seekers, the despised and rejected, the hurting and broken-hearted, the sick and weary. But we also find Him among the arrogant opposers of the truth, the high-profile scribes and Pharisees, and among the professionals of His day. The Galilean Hills are rife with models for church planting leaders. A closer look also displays a variety of ministry methods by Christ as popularized by Robert Coleman. He observes that Christ was incarnate, selective, confrontational, inspirational and instructive.[9]

4. Christ Provides the Church Planting Essentials

a) The Good News

Christ has provided the salvation sacrifice. He has made available the gift of eternal life. We have the good news of grace and forgiveness. The power of the Word of God has been given to the believers. It is like a two-edged sword that breaks open the hearts of people. The gospel is the seed that is sown by faithful witnesses and is the power unto salvation to all who believe (Rom.1:16).

b) The Holy Spirit

The presence of Christ's spirit empowers the believers for witness and equips them for service. He guides the people into outreach opportunities and provides prayer assistance and scriptural understanding. The Holy Spirit is the presence of Christ which makes it possible to live a fruitful Christian life.

In the life of a prospective believer the Holy Spirit brings conviction of sin. He opens the mind of a seeker to understand the gospel. It is the Holy Spirit that brings eternal life and forgiveness to those who respond to the gospel in faith.

In the life of the Church the Holy Spirit inspires the exercise of worship and unites the body of Christ in the spirit of fellowship. The Spirit also exposes error and protects the body from the enemy. The body is built up and strengthened by the Spirit of Christ. The Spirit generates the fruit of the Spirit in the life of faithful followers of Christ.

c) The Avenue of Prayer

The invitation to the believer to bring his/her concerns to God is one of the greatest resources available. In prayer and confession one finds forgiveness and peace. The believer's friendship with God is nurtured in prayer. Prayer connects the Christ followers to the missional agenda of God. Prayer releases the power of God for protection over the influences of Satan. The battles of life and death are won in prayer. Prayer opens the doors of opportunity and guides the pathways of the believers.

d) The Harvest Labourers

Christ promises to provide harvest labourers as we ask Him. He opens the human eyes to the harvest opportunities. The Lord reminded the disciples that the harvest is plentiful, meaning that there are many people who are open to the gospel. He also suggests that before the rejoicing of the sower and the reaper can happen, the hard work of many others, which results in the harvest, needs to be done (John 4:38).

e) The Motivation

Christ says that those who serve Him are on the honour role of God (John 12:26). It is a great privilege to be called by Christ to be coworkers with Him in the harvest (1 Cor.3:9). The motivation for serving Christ is in the fruit and the result of the work. The motivation furthermore comes from the presence of Christ's spirit, which produces joy and peace in the harvest. The reward of heaven at the end of life is the ultimate prize for those who finish the race.

5. Christ Provides the Profile of a Biblical Disciple

In order to implement the disciple-making assignment, a clear profile of a disciple is needed. The gospels provide us with a picture of what a disciple should look like. Not all who claim the name Christian have the understanding that Christ has for His followers. A true disciple demonstrates the following behaviours:

a) Believes in Jesus for Personal Salvation

A follower of Jesus accepts the death of Christ to be substitution for one's sins and gives evidence of possessing spiritual life (2 Cor. 5:17).

b) Follows the Teaching of Jesus

A disciple begins to take the Bible seriously as the basis for right and wrong. He or she is a learner and teachable. A follower takes baptism, sacrifice and stewardship seriously (Matt. 10:39).

c) Takes a Position Against Sin and Evil

Followers of Jesus commit themselves to a holy life and take on a resistant attitude toward sin (Luke 9:23).

d) Lives by Faith Awaiting Christ's Return

A believer lives out life in dependence on God the Father and awaits a future with Christ (1 Thess. 1:10; Matt. 24).

e) Continues in the Word/Abides in the vine

Bible study, scripture memory and meditation are regular activities in the believer's life (Heb. 11:6; John 15).

f) Promotes Love, Unity and Peace

Christians are to be known for their love for one another and for their spiritual fruit (Gal. 5:22).

g) Communicates with God in Prayer

In prayer the true Christian learns to share daily concerns with the Lord and to take strength from our Father in heaven who keeps us from entering into temptation (Luke 22:40).

h) Attends the Worship Services Regularly

A true follower wants to be in the company of other believers. The public worship and praise of God inspires commitment and faithfulness in word and deed (Heb. 10:25). A disciple also takes joy in worshipping with tithes and offerings.

i) Demonstrates his Faith Through Baptism

A serious follower seeks to obey Christ in all of His teachings, including baptism and church faithfulness, usually called membership (Mark 16:16).

j) Gives open testimony and witness to Christ

A true believer has a desire in his/her heart to share the good news of forgiveness with others (Acts 1:8).

k) Demonstrates a Servanthood Life in Love

Serving Christ and others are basic essentials to the Christian life. What one does to others in humble service, one has done unto the Lord (Matt. 10:40).

The problem today is that people do not want to submit to God's portrait of discipleship. They want to do their own thing. This has resulted in a type of "cheap grace" that looks for God's mercy without the Christian disciplines. Bibby calls this a consumer "pick and choose" type of religion of fragmentation where the user is the boss.[10]

6. Christ Provides the Church-Planting Mandate

The Church has received its outreach and disciple-making mandate of word and deed from Christ. The effectiveness of fulfilling the great commission of making disciples of all nations will be dependent on how well God's people live out and obey the great commandment of love. The body of Christ authenticates its faith through deeds of love.

Christ gave the great commission command (Matt. 28:18-20) as a victory statement that flowed from His lips just after He had overcome the world of sin and death through his sacrificial death and miraculous resurrection. It is now possible for the entire world to be reconciled to God; hence the command, "Go therefore and make disciples of all nations." This great commission statement has been hailed as the great missionary charter and the church's mission statement since the first century. Wherever this mandate has been implemented, new churches have been established. This great commission mandate is best implemented through Church multiplication.

The details of Matt. 28:18-20 provide the church-planting parameters and church mission understanding. The seed thoughts of the great commission were already evident in Christ's prayer for the believers in the world (John 17). The calling and sending out of his twelve disciples and later the seventy-two with witnessing instruction in Matt. 10 again provided much information and experience on what later became the great commission. At the end of each of the gospels a statement of outreach expectations is given. The clearest statement for the global church-planting task comes from Matt. 28:19-20. The great commission provides:

a) Clear Authorization—all authority has been given for this world-wide assignment involving both heaven and earth.

b) Clear Objectives—it evolves going out to make disciples or calling people to follow Christ.

c) Clear Fundamentals—there is a clear expectation of witnessing, teaching, preaching, baptizing, and observing Christ's teaching.

d) Clear Parameters—this mandate is global in scope. It is to involve all nations, tribes, and clans.

e) Clear Promise—the presence of Christ will be with his followers in the implementation of this global assignment.

The great commission starts with Christ's authority and concludes with Christ's continuous presence. This non-negotiable assignment is to be carried out worldwide by all those who belong to Christ. It is clearly focussed in its purpose of making disciples or diligent followers of Christ. The primary motive for this evangelism/mission assignment is not so much the plight of the unconverted or the eternal blessing of the believer, albeit both are powerful motives, but it is foremost the church's duty to obey the express order and command of Christ "to make disciples of all nations."

E. Blueprints From The First Churches

A case study of the New Testament churches would provide the church planter with many practical lessons on the nature and function of the early churches. The fact that churches were emerging wherever the gospel was preached indicates that the great commission, when obeyed, is really a church-planting commission. The first two churches known as the Jerusalem Church and the Antioch Church provide significant insight on the emergence and development of churches.

The Jerusalem Church as the Church Birth Occasion

The Jerusalem church needs to be seen as the church in its birth or realization. On the Galilean hills the church was present in precept, prelude or in principle, and on the day of Pentecost the church principles of the four gospels were converted into the actual church launch or birth. The arrival of the first church was accompanied with an array of sound effects and natural display of the miraculous, much the same as was present when God provided the ten commandments and when God sent his Son to be born in Bethlehem. It seems that whenever God breaks into space and time with a new presence, revelation, or creation, it is done with a miraculous display of power. The second coming of Christ will happen under similar miraculous conditions.

When the church was launched on the day of Pentecost, it came with power and high visibility. It was the Church on its maiden voyage in God's chosen Jerusalem city. From this church launch the church planter can draw many transferable lessons (Acts 1-2).

1. They were united in prayer and worship.

2. They were introduced to the Spirit filled life.

3. The message was understood in their native tongue.

4. The message was boldly proclaimed.

5. The preaching was about Christ's death and resurrection.

6. The message concluded with a call for repentance for salvation.

7. Those who accepted the message were baptized and added to the Church.

8. They devoted themselves to the apostles' teaching, to fellowship, to the breaking of bread and to prayer.

9. The apostles did many wonders and miraculous signs, leaving everyone in awe.

10. The believers were together and had all this in common; they

sold their possessions and gave to anyone as he had need.

11. Every day they continued to meet together in the temple courts.

12..They broke bread together in their homes and ate together with glad and sincere hearts, praising God and enjoying the favour of all the people.

13. The Lord added daily to the number who excepted the gospel.

14. As the church grew, they chose deacons for food distribution and ministers for prayer and preaching.[11]

The coming of God's Holy Spirit and the birth of the first church were simultaneous events. Jesus had predicted that upon his ascension the Holy Spirit would be sent to replace his physical presence. With the coming of the Holy Spirit and the launch of the Church in Jerusalem, the stage was set for the great commission to be launched through the Antioch Church.

THE ANTIOCH CHURCH AS THE GATEWAY CHURCH

The Antioch Church can be described as the watershed church since it was the doorway church for the great commission. In the Antioch Church the gospel moves from Jewish soil to Gentile territory. By the working of God's spirit the Antioch Church becomes a model church for missions and church planting. This second church has all the necessary characteristics needed in a church-planting situation (Acts 11-14).

1. Focus in Hardship

They kept their focus on Christ in the midst of persecution and scattering (11:19).

2. Cross-cultural Witness

They were telling the good news to the Jews, Greeks, and people from Cyprus and Cyrene (11:20).

3. Spiritual Empowerment

The hand of the Lord was with them, making them effective and purposeful (11:23).

4. Ministry Fruitfulness

They saw a great number of people believe and turn to the Lord (11:23).

5. Leadership Spirituality

The church accepted the leadership of Paul and Barnabas who were good men full of faith and the Holy Spirit (11:24).

6. Congregational Integrity

They showed evidence of the grace of God which gave them the name "Christian" (11:23).

7. Foundational Teaching

The leaders provided concentrated Bible teaching to great numbers of people (11:26).

8. Prophetic Influence

They responded to the prophetic voice of the prophets regarding church needs abroad (11:27).

9. Social Generosity

They shared in the needs of others by giving according to their ability (11:29).

10. Dynamic Worship

They worshipped and responded to God with prayer and fasting (13:2).

11. Holy Spirit Impact

They responded to the leading of the Holy Spirit to send out missional leaders (13:2).

12. Church Reproduction

They sent out Paul and Barnabas for aggressive church planting (13:2).

13. Harvest Celebration

The church gathered to celebrate what God had done and how he opened doors for them (14:26-29).

F. Lessons From The Church-Planting Journeys of Paul

The Antioch Church set in motion the three missionary or church-planting journeys with Paul and Barnabas. Again these apostolic exploits are rife with church-planting lessons. The goal of this section is to follow Paul with church-planter eyes, and note the transferable principles.

1. Launching Dynamics from the Antioch Church (Acts 13:1-3)

- The church was prepared through prayer, fasting and listening
- The local church sent them out.
- They sent out a church-planting team.
- The Holy Spirit directed the church.
- The people in persecution started churches.
- Their strongest leaders were sent out.
- The mother church was planting churches.
- The Holy Spirit prompted their journey.

2. Strategic Implementation Principles (Acts 13:4-11)

- They started near Barnabas's birth place in Cyprus.
- They concentrated on entire cities and regions.
- The synagogue was a major target area.
- The bold proclamation of the Word was primary.
- They concentrated on responsive individuals and the God-fearing (Acts 13:7).
- They used homes for meetings (Jason—Acts 17:5, Justin—Acts 18:7).
- They discussed the Scriptures on neutral ground like the courtyard (Acts 28:17).
- They evangelized while being in prison (Acts 16:25).
- They gave personal testimony of their conversions (Acts 8; 26)
- They experienced miracles for the glory of God (Acts 19:11)
- They engaged in intellectual debates on Mars Hill.
- They stood up against evil (Acts 17:16).
- They responded to invitations like Macedonia (Acts 19:9).
- They conducted extended Bible seminars.

3. Leadership Lessons from the Church Plants

- They were financially self-supported (Acts 20:33-35).
- They appointed elders from the indigenous areas (Acts 14:23).
- They called elders together for instructions (Acts 20:17).
- They recruited team leaders from the field (Acts 16:1-2).
- They worked according to gifts; some planted, some watered, some harvested (1 Cor. 3:6-7).
- They consulted with the apostles on critical issues (Acts 15).
- They regrouped and realigned to solve conflicts (Acts 15:39).
- They reported their results to the sending church (Acts 14:27).
- They made changes in their plans as the Spirit closed or opened doors (Acts 16:6).
- They adapted their message to their audiences whether Greek or Jew (1 Cor. 9:20).

4. Church Plant Follow-up in Acts

- They back-tracked for pastoral care (Acts 14:21-22).
- They wrote letters of encouragement, instruction, apologetics, and doctrine (Acts 15:30-31).
- They conducted short-term Bible schools (Acts 11:26).
- They addressed social needs (Acts 11:28-29).
- They gave exhortations and warnings (Acts 20:1,28).
- They prayed for the new believers night and day (1 Thess. 3:9-10).[12]

It is important to note that the front-line church-planting leaders in Acts were known for their courage and boldness. Opposition and persecution did not stop them from obeying the vision of Christ. They were leaders filled with the spirit and given to prayer and fasting. They followed the priority of preaching the Word and the gospel of Christ with boldness. They knew the transforming power of Christ, and obeyed the calling that they had received from the Lord.

5. Church Planting Supervisory Leadership of Paul

The Apostle Paul provides many practical and positive lessons on how to give oversight leadership. It is important for each new church to have an accountability group or a person who will from time to time provide some valuable insights and guidance. Church planters have a high need to share their experiences and frustrations with someone who understands and cares for their situation. They need to hear words of encouragement and support from their oversight leaders. The apostle Paul provided a good oversight model.

a) He provided church-planting oversight with a thankful spirit (1 Cor. 2; Romans 1:8). He came in simple faith and not with elegant words. He came with words of affirmation and appreciation and found great satisfaction and joy in their accomplishments.

b) He provided church-planting oversight that was personal and relational (1 Thess. 2:8). He gave leadership that was self-giving and sacrificial. He kept them in his heart, through his prayers, repeated visits, and personal letters.

c) He provided church-planting oversight that was practical and instructive (Acts 20:16-24). He was practical in combining his field trips with teaching and admonition. In his travels he always sought to take someone with him for practical reasons and for training purposes.

d) He provided church-planting oversight that was progressive and strategic (Acts 13-17). His leadership patterns reflect a strategy that moved progressively from region to region and city to city. Paul was always thinking in expansion terms and of doing more.

e) He provided church-planting oversight to meet the church planter's personal needs. Paul was willing to lend a sympathetic ear and to hear their stories. He frequently sent personal greetings and messages to them which indicates a deep affection and caring model of supervision.

f) He provided church-planting oversight that produced leadership (Acts 14:23). In new areas he assigned elders to take charge, and in some areas he decided to stay for a time to give leadership himself.

G. Church Planter Theological Non-negotiables

For a new emerging church to reflect the Biblical blueprint and designs of God, it will need to have a church-planting leader who is committed to establishing a church that follows the church patterns of the Bible. A church development is different and distinct from other organizations. The foundation of a church is a divine project where Christ is building his Church (Matt.16) through human partnership. As co-labourers with Christ, the church planters need to be deeply committed to the purposes and values of Christ.

The following church planter's statement of faith can serve as an orientation or self-examination for church-planting theological readiness.

1. Theological Harmony

The planter must believe that God the Father, God the Son, and God the Spirit work together in a redemptive harmony and priority to bring about the salvation of all people.

2. Great Commission

The planter must believe that the great commission assignment as given by the resurrected Lord is a mandate and charter for church planting.

3. Great Commandment

The planter must believe that the great commandment of love and compassion is an indispensable partner to the effective implementation of the great commission.

4. Harvest Orientation

The planter must believe that the seeds of the gospel, when planted into responsive soil, will produce a harvest of fruit.

5. Co-labouring

The planter must believe that the calling to be in partnership with God, as his witnesses and ambassadors of heaven, bring salt, light and life, in Christ's behalf. Christ builds his church through believers that have the keys to the Kingdom and have been empowered with spiritual gifts.

6. Spiritual Dependence

The Planter must believe that prayer is the doorway to effective ministry, spiritual power, and harvest. It is the daily guidance of the Holy Spirit that keeps the leader on track.

7. Unbelief

The planter must believe that the sin of unbelief carries the eternal punishment of condemnation and judgment; that non-Christians are victimized and enslaved by Satan until they respond to Christ in faith.

8. Conversion

The planter must believe that people are redeemable and need to be born again in the spirit by faith and repentance; that in Christ people are transformed, forgiven and adopted into the Family of God.

9. Church

The planter must believe in the local body of Christ for all believers. The goal is to bring people to new life in Christ and into meaningful fellowship and ministry of the local church.

10. Expansion

The planter must believe that we have been called to represent Christ within a given church planting area, that the ministry is that of evangelism beyond the walls of the church.

H. Basic Biblical Orientation For Church Planting

1. Church planting is God's program for this world; it is his predetermined method of propagating and nurturing the faith worldwide.
2. Evangelism and church formation go hand in hand. Wherever evangelism is happening, there a church needs to emerge.

3. Everyone who is brought to an experience of salvation in Christ needs to have a place for worship, fellowship, and maturing. This the church provides.

4. The personal sharing of Christ with others, together with the evangelistic efforts of the church, have a common purpose of bringing new people to Christ and into the fellowship and ministry of the local church.

5. God is depending on the "believers' Church" to spread the gospel of salvation and "body life" to all people. There is no contingency plan. Personal salvation and the embodiment into a church is God's design for all.

6. Church planting is a normal expectation and function of every church. Each contains the seed for more churches. Church planting is not really an option or an exception.

7. Church planting best fulfills the great commission. It holistically and systematically implements the mandate to preach, teach, evangelize, and baptize.

8. Church planting is the biblically-preferred method of doing evangelism. Paul clearly models the priority of establishing churches from place to place.

9. A new church is God's corporate gift to a community. Through the faithfulness of the Church, God is making his personal presence and ministry available to the people of the community.

NOTES——

[1] Ralph D. Winter, *Perspectives on the World Christian Movement*: "The Living God, a Missionary God," by John R.W. Stott, p. 17.

[2] George W. Peters, *A Theology of Church Growth* (Grand Rapids, Michigan: Zondervan, 1981) p.42. Another valuable source regarding the reign of God is: Darrell Guder, *Missional Church* (Grand Rapids, Michigan: Eerdmans. 1998) pp. 93-109.

[3] Stuart Murray, *Church Planting* (Waterloo, Ontario: Herald Press, 2001) p. 43.

[4] C. Peter Wagner, *Church Growth and the Whole Gospel* (Cambridge: Harper and Row, 1981) p. 31.

[5] Elmer Martens, *God's Design* (Baker Book House: Grand Rapids Michigan, 1981) p.252.

[6] Eddie Gibbs, *Church Next* (Downers Grove, Illinois: InterVarsity Press, 2000) p. 51.

[7] David Shenk & Erwin Stutzman, *Creating Communities of the Kingdom* (Scottdale, Pennsylvania: Harold Press, 1988) p. 213.

[8] Walfred Fahres, *Building on the Rock* (Scottdale, Pennsylvania: Herald Press, 1995).

[9] Robert Coleman, *Master Plan of Evangelism* (Revell, NJ: n.p., 1963).

[10] Reginald Bibby, *Fragmented Gods* (Toronto, Ontario: Irvin Publishing, 1987) p. 80.

[11] Shenk & Stutzman aptly describe the Jerusalem apostolic church as having nine characteristics. pp. 93-95.

[12] David Hesselgrave in *Planting Churches Cross-Culturally* (Grand Rapids, Michigan: Baker Book House, 1980) appropriately describes Paul's church-planting cycle or methodology in ten strategic and logical steps, p. 58.

THREE

Divine Calling

> When the pulpit is on the decline, the church is on the decline. When the preaching is in crisis, the church is in crisis. And both crises stem from a failure to understand the nature of the divine Word. In the sermon it is God talking to humans, and not merely humans talking about God.[1]
>
> James Daane, *Preaching With Confidence.*

Many believe the call of God applies mostly to missionaries and maybe pastors, and the rest of the people do not have to worry about God's call. There are certain times when people hope they understand God's will, namely when choosing a spouse or a career. This chapter examines the call of God common to all and the call of God specifically to apostolic ministries. It seeks to clarify the meaning as well as the misconceptions regarding God's will. Important to this section are the guidelines for discerning the will of God. It is crucial for the church planters to know that they are planting because they have been called to do so. Unless the planters have a clear conviction and call from the Lord to plant, they will not be able to withstand the headwinds of challenge which come with this ministry.

A. Understanding The Biblical Ministry Calling

It is true that in some sense all work has elements of ministry in it; however, the call to full-time ministry is different from an 8:30 to 4:30 labour job. It has to do with assuming spiritual responsibility for the destiny of people's lives. A church planter will not survive the headwinds of frontier ministry unless there is a divine calling as a sustaining anchor point.

1. The Ministry Call is Divinely Given

The following scriptures provide the basic understanding for the divine call to ministry.

"You did not choose me, but I chose you and appointed you" (John 15:16).

"I thank Christ Jesus our Lord, who has given me strength, that he considered faithful, appointing me to his service" (1 Tim.1:12).

"See to it that you complete the work you have received in the Lord" (Col. 4:17).

"I have become its (church) servant by the commission God gave me to present to you the Word of God in its fullness" (Col. 1:25).

"...if only I may finish the race and complete the task the Lord Jesus has given me, the task of testifying to the gospel of God's grace" (Acts 20-24).

"Having been called by God...through the gospel" (2 Thess. 2:14).

"Therefore, since through God's mercy we have this ministry, we do not lose heart" (2 Cor. 4:11).

"He has committed to us the ministry of reconciliation" (2 Cor. 5:19).

2. God's Call in the Old Testament

The most common ways of God revealing his will in the Old Testament was through the Word, the commandments, the prophets (1 Samuel 9:9), sacred lot (Joshua 18:6), dreams (Daniel), signs (Judges 6), voice (Genesis 12:1-3) and other miraculous encounters involving animals and natural demonstrations. The call for people to serve also came through chosen leaders.

3. God's Call in the New Testament

With the coming of the Holy Spirit into the world and into people's lives, the revelation of God's will changed from the Old Testament revelation patterns. The New Testament revelation was more through the Scripture and the Holy Spirit. The Scriptures are there for our instruction, guidance, rebuke and correction (2 Tim. 3:14-17). In the New Testament there is an increasing role of the community of believers consulting together to determine the will of God (Acts 15:22). The Holy Spirit through the Word is the primary communication of God's will in our lives. The Lord in fact warns his disciples against looking for signs.

B. Key Elements Of The Ministry Call

1. The Ministry Calling is to Speak for Christ

"He who hears you hears Me, and he who rejects you rejects Me, and he who rejects Me rejects Him that sent Me" (Luke 10:16).

"We are therefore Christ's ambassadors as though God were making his appeal through us. We implore you on Christ's behalf, be reconciled to God (1 Cor. 4:20).

"In Christ we speak before God with sincerity, like men sent from God" (1 Cor. 2:17).

"For it is not you who speak, but the spirit of your Father speaking through you" (Matt. 10:19).

"The proclamation of the word is, not as the word of men

but as what it really is, the word of God" (1 Thess. 2:13).

The prophets saw themselves as the mouthpiece of God.

"Thus saith the Lord" (Hos. 6:5).

"Thus says the Lord" (Jer. 15:19).

2. The Ministry Call is to Proclaim the Word

"Devote yourself to the public reading of scripture, to preaching and teaching" (1 Tim. 4:13).

"So faith comes from what is heard, and what is heard comes by the preaching of Christ" (Rom. 10:17).

"Give our attention to prayer and ministry of the word" (Acts 6:4).

"Is not my word like fire, says the Lord, and like a hammer which breaks the rock in pieces" (Jer. 23:29).

"The word of God is living and active" (Heb. 4:12).

"I am not ashamed of the gospel because it is the power of God, for the salvation of everyone who believes" (Rom. 1:16).

3. The Ministry Call is for Evangelism

"We are Christ's ambassadors as though God were making His appeal through us. We implore you on Christ's behalf: be reconciled to God" (2 Cor. 5:20).

"But you keep your head in all situations, endure hardships, do the work of an evangelist, discharge all the duties of your ministry" (2 Tim. 4:5).

"Therefore go make disciples of all nations" (Matt. 28:19).

"The harvest is plentiful but the workers are few, ask the Lord therefore to send out workers into his harvest field" (Matt. 9:37-38).

"I make myself a slave to everyone to win as many as possible" (1 Cor. 9:19).

"For we are the aroma of Christ... the fragrance of life" (2 Cor. 2:14-15).

> The word of God is powerful enough to work its own way through the resistance of the human heart to achieve its saving purpose. Every attempt to empower the Word by human strategies and techniques is no less than gimmicky which dishonours the Word.
>
> James Daane, *Preaching With Confidence.*

C. Biblical Lessons On God's Call To Ministry

1. *The Ministry Call to Individuals*

There are many examples in both the Old and New Testament where God called people individually to achieve specifically assigned tasks for God.

OLD TESTAMENT EXAMPLES

Abraham—was called to be the father of God's covenant people and to be the channel of blessing to the people of the earth (Genesis 12).

Moses—was called to lead God's people from slavery to freedom.

Nehemiah—was called to rebuild the ruined walls of Jerusalem.

Jonah—was called to preach repentance to the people of Nineveh.

Daniel—was called to be a godly presence and a spokesman for God within a corrupt society.

Isaiah—was called to prophesy of the coming birth of Christ the Emmanuel.

NEW TESTAMENT EXAMPLES

John—was called to announce the coming King as a voice in the wilderness.

Paul—was called to be an apostle to the Gentiles.

Mary—was called to be the child bearer of Christ the Saviour.

Barnabas—was called to be a leader of encouragement to the Antioch Christians.

Timothy—was called to do the work of an evangelist.

71

2. The Ministry Call to Specific Groups

The Gideon army—God specifically chose a small army to achieve a huge task under Gideon's leadership (Judg. 8:36-40).

The twelve disciples—Christ chose the twelve apostles to take charge of the disciple-making command of Christ (Mark 3:13-19).

The church elders—Paul carefully selected and placed elders to be in charge of the newly-formed churches (Acts 14:23).

The deacons—the Jerusalem church chose seven deacons who were known for their wisdom, faith and spirituality (Acts 6:3-6).

The missionaries—Paul and Barnabas were specifically called and sent out to plant churches (Acts 6:3-6).

Each of these specifically called-out groups had carefully-defined qualifications described for them (1 Timothy 3; Titus 1).

3. The Ministry Call to all Believers

God's people are all called to be servants of Christ and all have been given spiritual gifts and talents to do so. Some of the things Christians are called to be:

Co-labourers with Christ (1 Cor. 3:9).
Servants of Christ (John 12:26).
Fruitful abiders (John 15:4).
Faithful worshippers (Heb. 10:22-25).
Witnesses for Christ (Acts 1:8).
Salt and light (Matt. 6:13).
Temples of God (1 Cor. 6:19-20).
Doers of good deeds (James 2:14; Eph. 2:10).
Chosen people (1 Peter 2:9-18).
God pleasers (Romans 12:1-2; 2 Cor. 5:9).
Separated from worldliness (John 17).

4. The Specific Ministry Call of Church Planters

The Scriptures reveal that God has a special spiritual calling for specially-assigned ministry tasks. Examples of divine calling of individuals include: Noah, Moses, Abraham, the prophets, John the Baptist, Paul the apostle, etc.

The church-planting task too, is a special calling that involves apostolic spirit and action. Each church planter should be able to point to a divine call to the church-planting ministry.

> The church planter's ministry calling needs to be clear and specific. It is a call to a specific task which goes beyond the general call to all believers.

D. Understanding And Doing The Will Of God

It is essential for those in ministry to have an understanding of what God wants. Church planting is about fulfilling the will of God. Within the broader redemptive will of God for the world there are different aspects of God's will mentioned in the Scriptures.

BASIC ASSUMPTIONS REGARDING THE WILL OF GOD

1. We can assume that God delights in revealing his purposes and will to his chosen people.
2. We can assume that God's will for individuals will follow the path of the individual's spiritual gift mix and personality make-up.
3. We can assume that God's will incorporates our prayers and desires when expressed from a pure heart.
4. We can assume that the will of God is revealed in the Word of God. God's will for believers is doing what God wants done redemptively in the world, as revealed in the Scriptures.

BIBLICAL PRIORITIES REGARDING THE WILL OF GOD

1. Salvation Will of God (2 Peter 3:9)

God has made provision for all who accept Christ to have eternal life. He is not willing that anyone perish.

2. Moral Will of God (1 Thess. 4:3)

God expects all Christians to reflect the values of the Kingdom of God including, a holy life, submission to authority, being thankful and joyful, etc.

3. Servanthood Will of God (John 12:26)

God expects his followers to be His servants and to live sacrificially for God and others. God's will is about the daily choices we make to honour and serve God.

4. Witnessing Will of God (Acts 1:8)

It is clear that God has empowered the believers to be witnesses unto him as co-labourers and ambassadors of God.

5. Personal Will of God (Eph. 2:10)

God has created the believer to do good works. He expects each person to use his or her best judgments in making the daily decisions about living out a life of godly deeds.

6. Ministry Will of God (1 Tim.1:12)

The call to full-time ministry is a divine call. The call to church planting is similar to that of an apostle or prophet. It is a specific and special call to serve Christ and so fulfill the purposes of God.

7. Present and Future Will of God (Matt. 6:23)

Seeking first God's kingdom is His will, and the future will unfold. The biblical focus on God's will is more about the present life than the future.

In God's sovereign will he reveals His redemption plan; in His moral will He reveals how He expects us to behave; and in His individual will He reveals how we should serve Him. The church planter needs to understand and do God's will.

> The will of God concerns the present more than the future. It deals with our motives as well as our actions. It focuses on the little decisions every day even more than the big decisions we make about the future. The only time we really have to know and do God's will is the present moment. We are to love God with heart, mind, and strength, and we are to love our neighbours as we love ourselves.[2]
>
> Gerald L. Sittser, *The Will of God as a Way of Life*, 2000.

E. Discerning The Ministry Call Of God

1. Evaluate the desire of your heart and look for spiritual qualities suitable for ministry in your life.

2. Look for patterns of involvements in your past that support leadership traits.

3. Look for affirmations and support for ministry from your peers, family, and church friends.

4. The ministry call needs to be discerned and encouraged by the leaders of the home church.

5. Seek opportunities and ministry involvement without high profile recognition to test your ministry heart and passion.

6. Look for a specific event, spiritual experience or a God moment where you felt a definite nudge or call to the ministry.

7. Prepare yourself for ministry through appropriate training and ministry experience.

8. Your spiritual gift, personality and passion need to line up in support of a ministry calling.

9. Heed the advice from spiritual leaders who know you, and listen to how they see your calling.

10. Look for scriptural affirmation and specific passages that "light your path" and guide your decisions.

11. Let the peace of Christ rule your heart and guide your thoughts, and follow the inner leading of the Holy Spirit concerning the ministry calling.

12. Make the ministry decision by faith based on the principles of a sound mind, a heart for God, a need or opportunity, your abilities, and on the evidences that point to a ministry call.

13. Avoid an emphasis on fleeces, signs or other self-prescribed conditions and deadlines that force God's hand.

14. Rely on the Holy Spirit for a growing conviction and excitement in pursuing God's purposes in response to a specific call.

15. Discern God's will and voice in the stillness of prayer, study, and meditation, with a spirit of submission and obedience to do whatever pleases God. It is in the quiet waiting on God that the Holy Spirit places a conviction and assurance in our heart to know what is the right thing to do.

A Christian cannot make a sound judgment without relying on scripture, a heart purified by God, the wise council of others and the circumstances the Lord sends our way... There are five things to consider when relying upon your own judgment.

1. *Make your decision in light of scripture.*

2. *Make your decision in light of giftedness.*

3. *Make your decision according to your ability.*

4. *Make your decision according to your circumstances.*

5. *Make your decision according to an overall strategy.*

Human reasoning is a good thing and a gift from God. We ought to use it within the parameters of God's plan for guidance. We should never resort to human logic in violation of the Bible. Instead, we use sound judgment in accordance with scripture.[3]

Bruce Walthe, *Finding the Willing of God,* 1995.

NOTES——

[1] James Daane, *Preaching with Confidence* (Grand Rapids, Michigan: Eerdmans, 1980).

[2] Gerald Sittser, *The Will of God as a Way of Life* (Grand Rapids: Zondervan, 2000).

[3] Bruce Walthe, *Finding the Will of God* (Gresham, Oregon: Vision House Publishing, 1995).

- FOUR

Crucial Beginnings

The church has a tone to strike against which all other
instruments of the society must be tuned. It is the "A"
that does not vary with the changing of society or the
passing of civilizations. Joy is the clear, pure note of
the Christian which will still be heard over the mush
and meaninglessness of the Information Age. To sound
that clarion note, however, we need to understand
what Christ meant when he prayed that our "joy
might be full."

David McKenna—*Mega Truth*.

The beginnings of a new church are critical to the
growth and development of a congregation. This chapter
looks at the various reasons why new churches are urgently
needed, and provides a biblical and practical motivational
base for planting churches. Equally important to the success
of the church plant is the circumstance of the church's birth.
A healthy birth usually results in a healthy church. The
health of a new church is facilitated by a number of church-
planting systems that are reproducible. These systems are
designed to enhance the church in its mission effectiveness.

The most important factor in the beginning of a church plant is the realization that Christ is the church builder. For the church planter this is a constant source of encouragement.

A. Motivations For Beginning New Churches

There are many reasons why new churches should be planted. Some are outreach-driven and others are for pragmatic reasons, like church overcrowding. In this section, six motivational categories are presented for the purpose of making a convincing case for why many more churches need to be planted. God's creation is no doubt the greatest lesson for church multiplication. The natural fruit garden produces two products: the tasty consumable product, and then the seeds, which need to be planted for multiplication of the fruit. Churches also have these two functions.

1. Biblical Motivations for Church Planting

- Church planting best fulfills the great commission
- Churches are planted because the harvest is plentiful, diverse and ready
- Church planting extends the kingdom of God
- Church planting is the N.T. model for faith expansion
- Christ promises to build the church
- New churches provide new wineskins
- Church planting accomplishes the worldwide goal of evangelism
- Church planting follows the passion of Christ and the heart of God
- Other gospels and cults are countered through more biblical churches
- It hastens the coming of Christ through increased proclamation
- Church planting brings the incarnation of Christ to more areas
- It moves evangelism from decisions to discipling
- It establishes God's kingdom in a visible way
- New churches find more lost sheep
- Church planting enhances the exercise of prayer and faith
- The most effective strategy in reaching the world for Christ is

church planting

- Church planting is the most biblical strategy for reaching the world for Christ

2. Effectiveness Motivations for Planting New Churches

- Church planting provides for immediate convert follow-up and church incorporation
- New churches provide the dynamic needed for effective evangelism
- New churches give more priority to evangelism
- New churches reach more new people
- New churches can better attract drop-outs and disaffiliates
- More new churches set up another generation of churches
- Church planting reverses church decline and plateaus
- New churches grow better than old churches
- New people are more open to attend new churches
- New churches provide for denominational growth

3. Demographic Church-Planting Motivations

- Church planting takes the gospel to where the people are
- Members moving around need churches for worship
- Population growth requires the multiplication of churches
- Church mergers need church replacements in new communities
- New churches are an advantage to an area and invigorate new communities
- There are not enough churches to meet the diverse needs of people
- The demographic shift of communities require new churches to serve new people groups
- A goal of a church for every 1,000 people will require many more churches[1]

4. People as a Key Motive for Planting Churches

- New generations need new church models to be planted
- New churches provide an involvement for the adventurous visionary leaders

- The unchurched need more church options to meet their needs
- New churches provide new spirit, joys and self-image
- New churches make the gospel available to more language groups
- People have church character preferences and need new church styles
- New churches are needed for new immigrants
- New people are more likely to attend new local churches than older ones
- New churches provide involvement for more people
- Conversion retention is best done in new churches

5. Practical Benefits of New Churches

- All of society benefits when more churches produce more devoted followers of Christ
- New churches can break with unwanted traditions and baggage
- New churches are more open to change than older churches
- Aging and dying churches need to be replaced
- Atrophic effect is halted in a new church
- New churches are more attractive to new people than older churches
- New churches provide renewal and revitalization to mother churches
- Church plants mobilize and produce new leaders
- Church plants help break the mono-ethnic homogeneity of a denomination
- New churches facilitate congregational diversity
- New churches balance the denominational church mix with new DNA churches
- It stimulates and inspires area churches
- No one church can meet all the people's needs, so more churches are needed
- Parenting a church is a primary measure of church health
- New churches are a benefit to society's goodwill

6. Historic Church Motivations

- Church planting assures the chain of church continuity

- Historically Christianity is always expanded through the multiplication of churches
- It halts the long-term theological church drift in some denominations
- It continues the reformation corrective of merging ecclesiology and missiology
- Church planting bridges the cultural gap between modernity and post-modernity
- New churches are needed for new movements of God
- To reach the world, many more churches are needed
- Church planting raises harvest awareness from generation to generation[2]

B. Diversity Of Church Beginnings

As there are many ways to start a new business operation, so it is with church planting. Some businesses are government-sponsored, others are family-initiated, still others are driven by individual visions, and many are business extensions. In church planting there are also various new church initiators and sponsors. This section presents four different categories that describe how churches are started.

1. Modality Church Plants Involving a Mother Church

A modality planting situation involves a mother church that in one way or another is helping to start new church. There are a number of options available to churches that are open to participating in a church plant.

a) Parent/Daughter Model

In this situation the mother church plans and launches a daughter church. The sponsoring church usually supplies the planter and a core group of people as well as the start-up finances. (See Parenting Chapter for more details)

b) Church Within a Church Model

This situation could be similar to starting a second or third week-end service. It could be a Saturday evening church with a different emphasis from the other services, but using the same church building. In some situations an associate staff person is assigned to plant this church with an interested group. This group should seek to attract unchurched people and not merely take a group from within the church. Another version of this model is for the church to start a language-specific church where they share their facilities and office services.

c) Satellite Campus Model

In this model the mother church uses her staff and leaders to develop another church campus. This approach usually applies to a larger church with a strong preaching pastor. The sermon is shared by video satellite with the new church. Each location has its own worship team and fellowship group. The uniqueness of this model is that the sermon is shared by both campuses. The church administration is shared, and a common budget is developed and managed.

d) Multi-Congregational Model

In this model the mother church functions as the dominant host culture church. The mother group welcomes other culture groups, to worship with them while at the same time developing their own fellowship and identity. Such a church develops into a multi-cultural church.

e) Church-to-Mission Planting Model

In this situation the mother church works in conjunction with a mission agency to sponsor the planting of a mission church in a cross-cultural or remote area. The mother church often supplies funding and leadership to this project. It also sends some of its own church people to visit this church and to provide short-term help. The church-to-mission model can take many different forms.

f) Church Replanting Model

This is a situation where the mother church needs revitalization or replanting, so it sells its facility and uses the assets to start a new church. The mother church gives birth to a new church through its own sacrificial death.

2. Sodality Church Plants Involving Mission Agencies

A sodality church planting involves a mission agency, para-church group or a denominational organization. A sodality is usually more focused in its organization mission function than that of a church. Sodality leadership is usually more catalytic and independent than congregational leadership. There are a number of approaches in a sodalic church-planting model.

a) Plants by Denominational Boards

In this well-known model, the church denominations give leadership to church planting. The church assumes that the denomination is responsible to organize new church plants.

b) Cluster Church Planting

In this situation, the denomination chooses a city or an area and plans for a number of church plants to happen simultaneously. Again it is denominationally driven.

c) Denomination and Church Combinations

This is a model where the denomination approaches several churches and invites them to join the denominational church planting board to start a church together in a strategically-chosen area. In this situation the denomination usually provides the planter and oversight, while the church provides the launch team and the core people.

d) Mission Board Church Planting

Usually this involves a pioneer mission situation where missionaries are assigned to plant churches. This is the more traditional mission agency church planting model.

e) Saturation Nation-Wide Church Planting

This describes the "discipling a whole nation" (DAWN) process. In Canada it is called Outreach Canada, or Vision 2000. This is a cross-denominational nation-wide model where the various church groups band together to pursue a common church-planting goal for their country. In Canada the goal is to plant a church for every 1,000 people. There needs to be a church for every person.

e) Inter-denominational Agency Church Planting

These inter-denominational church plants are particularly effective in smaller towns or villages. Such churches do not like to be seen as denominational churches even thought they are usually multi-denominational by virtue of their attendance. Often these are low budget, faith-supported church births.

3. Situational Church Plant Beginnings

In this category of church plants, the church beginnings are birthed within a particular circumstance or unique context. These church initiatives are often the result of intentional strategies for a particular environment which requires a new approach or a special technique such as youth culture churches.

a) Tele-marketing Church Plants

Planting churches through a telephone campaign was popularized in the late eighties and is still used by some church planters. It involves organizing a telephone team and then calling thousands of people. The purpose of the telephone call is to inform the people of a new church being started in their area and invite them to the church launch service. They are also asked if they would be interested in being on the new church mailing list. The response of this technique is based on the usual telemarketing percentages.

b) Evangelism Crusade Church Plants

In this situation a church is organized at the end of an evangelism crusade from the crusade converts. The crusade follow-up results in the formation of a new church. This process is successful in countries and places where there is little or no Christian presence.

c) Inter-faith Church Planting

This model involves a number of denominational bodies working together. The ecumenical church planting situation is best suited to remote or industrial towns where the population is not large enough for each church body to plant a church separately.

d) Colonization Church Planting

In a colonization situation, a group of people move into a new area and take up employment there for the purpose of planting a church. This could be initiated by the interested people or by a church body. This also describes the model used when a group of immigrants settle in a new country.

e) Bi-vocational Church Planting

Bi-vocational church planters often do not have a sponsoring body so they plant on their own. These people usually have a dauntless passion and vision to start a new church. They use their employment for financial support and plant the church as time permits. The energy and entrepreneurial spirit invested often result in an independent church.

f) Radio Broadcast Church Planting

While many religious television or radio broadcasts operate from a church base, many are also agency—or personality—driven. There are some instances where churches have resulted from the follow-up of mass media broadcasting. This church-planting model is successful in cross-cultural situations. The best example of a denomination starting as a result of radio broadcasting is the Armstrong Church of God movement.

g) Church Planting by Adoption

In this situation a church is started through the adoption of a Bible study group or an independent ministry. It could also be an independent church that is looking to affiliate with a church body.

h) Church Planting by Fragmentation or Church Splits

Whenever a new church is started as a result of a church split, it usually is not a healthy or ideal church birth. Many churches have been started from existing churches where there were conflicting visions or internal differences that could not be resolved.

4. Style—or Target—Specific Church Plant Beginnings

a) Youth Culture Church Planting

In this situation a church is planted specifically to meet the needs of young people. The style would be such that it attracts and suits the preferences of the younger generation. These churches are often planted from existing church youth groups that already have youth culture events. In larger churches these youth culture churches may constitute one of the church's week-end services. The starting of these churches needs to be very intentional and style-specific.

b) Language-Specific Church Planting

In a multicultural society like Canada, many churches are started in the mother tongue of the immigrant people. The first generation of immigrants require a language—and culture-specific church. The second generation of immigrants are able to integrate into an English-speaking church while still maintaining their ethnic identity.

c) House and Cell Church Planting

The house church movement is an alternative to the traditional church. In some countries the house or cell churches are multiplying rapidly. Because of the relatively simple format and organizational structure, these smaller group churches can develop and start more spontaneously. The parameters of this book do not permit a fuller explanation of both the cell and the house church movements.

d) Urban Centre Street Church Plants

The churches in the city centres usually require a high level of support. New churches that are targeted for the urban city, poor, homeless, or people with substance abuse problems require sponsorships and outside funding for their survival. It is important that such inner-city churches have leaders from the city centres who can understand the kind of church that is needed. The beginnings of these churches usually involve a high level of social ministry.

e) Theological Bent Church Plants

These style—and theology—specific churches are often started in order to nurture a particular church understanding. The churches often have a fringe characteristic or hobby-horse issues that are crusaded. These alternative churches are usually started by individuals who have not found acceptance in the more traditional church. By biblical standards these churches usually do not represent a balanced church presence.

f) Post-Modern Character Church Plants

These churches attempt to make the church understandable and meaningful to people that have limited church background. It is an attempt to attract people from the secular environment. These churches often have a highly interactive and experiential approach to church. These churches tend to be relational, issue-oriented, environmentally-sensitive, and have a focus to personal relevance.

C. Beginning Churches Through Reproducing Systems

CHURCH PLANTING NETWORKS

Increasingly, denominational leaders are working cross-denominationally in establishing various networks and reproducible church-planting systems for the purpose of more effectively bringing in the harvest and fulfilling the great commission.

The kingdom of God has been greatly enhanced through new church-planting systems and networks. The systems are focused on fruitfulness and effectiveness, and embrace a wide spectrum of denominations. These systems have a very sodalic character and a parachurch-like single-mindedness and focus. Growing in momentum are the following systems or networks:

1. Prayer Network

Church planters are encouraged to recruit intercessors who are committed to pray daily for the church planter. Every church-planting effort must be rooted and grounded in prayer. God is the one who builds His church. Any human effort or project is doomed to fail unless God is in it. Church planters are encouraged to build an army of prayer warriors. The church-planting process is encumbered with many barriers and trials which can be overcome with prayer; hence the new and welcomed focus on prayer teams and prayer networks.

2. Recruitment Network/Pastors Factory

This network focuses on leaders who have a particular interest in church planting. Given that leadership is the single most important part of church planting, it is important to recruit quality candidates. The recruitment network identifies and provides training experiences and area group experiences for a pool of pastoral candidates who are interested in someday planting a church. A second leg of this system is the pastor's factory, which has the express goal of preparing church planters. The pastors in the recruitment network that are committed to pursuing a church planting assignment are assigned to the pastor's factory. In this factory network, they are encouraged to go through a church planter's assessment.

3. Assessment Systems

The high cost of church planting and the special gift mix needed to plant churches has resulted in the formation of at least two assessment instruments for the purpose of better assessing suitable candidates for church planting.

a) The Profile Assessment System

This system follows Dr. Charles Ridley's "How to Select Church Planters" system through the behaviour interview which seeks to identify the 13 church planters' behaviours needed for effective church planting. The assumption here is that past behavior is the best prediction of future performance. A team of two assessors does the interview. They are required to follow a definite system and are approved to be interview assessors after a rigorous process of training. The assessment interview takes about 4 hours, after which an extensive report is written on the prospective church planter's qualifications.

b) The Church Planter Assessment Centre

In this assessment system the prospective church planters are assessed in a group of ten to fifteen couples, who spend some four days together in various leadership experiences and aptitude testing. The assessors monitor and evaluate the church planter-like exercises and experiences over the four days and decide as a group on the couple's suitability for church planting. Interviews, reference checks, and peer and self evaluations are all part of the evaluation system. The centre seeks to maintain a ratio of one assessor per couple being assessed. In this system fourteen critical church-planting factors are being evaluated. At the end of this assessment, each couple receives a report card: being recommended, conditionally recommended, or not recommended for church planting.

4. New Church Incubator (NCI)

The New Church Incubator provides a supportive environment of sharing for church planters and their spouses. This group of people meeting together monthly raises church-planting issues pertaining to prayer partner support, vision building, group mobilization, and any other church start-up issues. Because church planters are "thoroughbred" in spirit, and are intrinsically motivated, they need coaching and dialogue to keep them going in the right direction.

5. The Coaching Paradigm

The coaching paradigm provides for a regular hands-on process of helping a church planter succeed. Coaches are trained in the art of active listening, caring, celebrating, strategizing, and challenging. This regular one-to-one ministry coaching within an environment of trust and partnership is producing a new level of confidence and effectiveness in the church planter. This mentoring system is having an empowering effect on personal development, spiritual vitality, and effective outreach. It is also providing a much-needed accountability relationship within our society of individualism, and is providing a new approach of giving supervision.

6. The Parent Church Network (PCN)

This network works with pastors and lay leaders to cultivate commitment to church planting by their congregation. This network promotes the "churches planting churches" idea. Each church in the PCN makes a commitment to begin a new congregation within 18-24 months. The basic agenda for this network is to train churches in the art of parenting a new church. The three P's of this network are: 1) Preparing for parenthood, 2) Planning for parenthood, 3) Proceeding with parenthood. The leaders meet every six to eight weeks.

7. Focusing Leaders Network

The assumption of this network is that in order to refocus the local church, the leaders need to be renewed and focused. This network clarifies the leaders' biblical call and personal mission, and facilitates character growth. The background idea here is that when the church is refocused on its mission, it will take steps to plant a church. So the process moves from a focused leader, to a refocused congregation, to the parenting of a church.

8. Church-Planter Summit or Boot Camp

This is a strategic week for church-planter training. At this training church planters develop strategies and plans for a location-specific church plant. This summit gives them the occasion to work through the development stages of a church plant.

Other systems that are not so clearly defined include the church-planting fund-raising system. With the decline of denominational money, this system may become more pronounced. It needs to be noted also that there is a need for a network or system to encourage faith sharing. To some extent, the church care groups are providing this emphasis. Other systems and networks building around specific family needs and crises are emerging as part of the networking environment.[3]

D. Beginning Churches With Intentional Mission Factors

ESSENTIAL OUTREACH REQUIREMENTS

For the church of Christ today to be effective in the implementation of the great commission, it needs to align itself with the biblical requirements for effective outreach. The records of scripture provide a number of indispensable realities for fruitful witness and evangelism.

1. Empowerment of the Holy Spirit (Acts 1:8)

It is the Spirit of God that empowers the believer for witness. The Spirit guides, enlightens, reminds, convicts, intercedes, and provides new life. The Spirit also opens witnessing doors and makes us attractive and effective through the fruit of the Spirit and spiritual gifts.

2. Confidence in the Gospel (Romans 1:16; 10:17)

Effective witness is the result of being confident that the gospel is the power of God unto salvation. The gospel of Jesus as the only Saviour that can forgive sins is good news. Faith comes from the hearing of the Word. Therefore, we are not ashamed of the gospel.

3. Unity and Love Among Believers (John 17:23; Eph. 4)

Christ made it clear that love and unity among believers are a powerful incentive for people to come to Christ. A disruptive or disunited church has little to offer to a seeking world. Love and unity have evangelistic drawing power for which Christ prayed.

4. Faithfulness (John 15; Gal. 5)

Christ links fruitfulness to faithfulness. If the Christians remain in the vine and keep connected to the Lord, they will experience joy and answers to their prayers. Christ-likeness by keeping in step with the Spirit brings power to a life of words and deeds. Witness is destroyed through lack of integrity and enhanced through prayer and faith.

5. Loving Your Neighbor (Luke 10:27; Mark 12:31)

The great commandment of loving your neighbour is the key bridge to winning people to Christ. In a word-weary society, expressions of love and deeds of kindness go a long way in making a faithful follower of Jesus. When the church shows concern for the powerless and compassion for the needy, it has entered into the world in a Christ-like spirit. Effective outreach demands positive relationships within the world that needs to be reached.

6. Priority for Evangelism (Matt. 1:21)

The great commission declares the purpose of the church to be making disciples of all nations. As Jesus came to seek and to save the lost, so the church needs to be involved. As the shepherd leaves the ninety-nine in search for the one lost sheep, so the church must give priority to bringing people into the fold. This priority must be expressed both individually and corporately. Individuals need to witness where they can, and as a church, evangelism needs to be the driving force of its activity and joy. The church has no more right to keep the faith to itself than individuals have the right to live self-ishly. At the corporate level, the church takes the responsibility to provide opportunities for the community at large to hear and respond to the message of Christ.

E. Church Beginnings Through The Work Of Christ

CHRIST WILL BUILD HIS CHURCH

The hope of the church lies in the fact that Christ is building his Church and the gates of hell will not overcome it (Matt.16:18). This promise that Christ is building his Church, gives it a divine character with eternal dimensions. The church is not an afterthought, but rather God's designed structure within which the Christian faith is shared and nurtured. Christ is the ongoing builder of the church. He is the church contractor and his followers are the church sub-trades, you might say. How then is He building his Church?

1. Through the Provision of Harvest Leadership

It is often said that ministry rises and falls based on leadership. For church planting this is certainly the case, except for the grace of God. The church planter needs to be a person of vision and faith, someone that has a passionate desire to see Kingdom influences extended. Church planting requires the gift of leadership with the ability to organize people to achieve the church-planting goals. A planting leader needs to be able to relate to both the mission culture and the church culture. Personal integrity, spiritual maturity, and a heart for outreach are primary factors in effective harvest leadership. Christ provides harvest leaders as Christians pray.

2. Through the Exercise of Prayer

Prayer tunes the Christians' hearts to line up with the heart of God. Prayer opens the individual's mind to church planting. A sustaining vision for extending the church comes from God as one waits on Him in prayer. Unless the Lord builds the house, its builders labour in vain (Ps. 127:1). The way to assure that you are doing God's will is to commit every step of the way to the Lord in prayer.

3. Through an Intentional Harvest Strategy

The church plant needs to be positioned in the midst of a ripened harvest. There the planter needs to discern usable and effective fruit-gathering methods. The church-planting tasks then need to be broken into workable units. Next a strategy needs to be established that attracts people, meets their needs, and wins them to Christ. Some have referred to the church planter's strategy as the project road map.[4]

4. Through the Work of the Harvest Cycle

Bringing in the harvest is the result of working the cycle of cultivating, sowing, and reaping. Christ refers to the hard work that people have done in the context of celebrating the harvest (John 4:38). Paul instructed Timothy to do the work of an evangelist (2 Tim.4:15) for He knew from experience that evangelism is hard work. Christ builds His church through his faithful, hardworking ambassadors.

5. Through the Full Mobilization of the Body

The design of Christ for his Church is that everyone be given spiritual gifts for ministry. Paul writes to the Ephesian Church with the perspective that every member is a minister (Eph.4:11-12). The leader's role then becomes one of equipping and mobilizing a very diverse body. Christ uses people to build His Church. Some are called to suffer for Christ, others to look after the disadvantaged, and still others to provide public ministries. All have the calling to witness and to share the gospel.

6. Through the Exercise of Worship and Devotion

The Church of Christ is being built by the Lord through faithful followers. Some have described the believer's devotion to take place in three relationship circles: the cell, the congregation, and the celebration.[5] A fourth one that needs to be added is the prayer closet. Christ builds His Church body through a dynamic personal and corporate relationship with the church. People are drawn to Christ as they lift up Jesus their Saviour.

NOTES——

1 Murray Moerman, *Transforming Out Nation* (Richmond, British Columbia: Church Leadership Library, 1998) p. 59.

2 These motivations have been compiled from the writings of numerous church-planting leaders.

3 Two major sources for describing the church-planting reproducing networks are: Kevin Mannoia, *Church Planting the Next Generation*, (Indianapolis, Indiana: Light and Life Press, 1994).

Robert & Steven Ogne, *Churches Planting Churches* (manual), 1995.

4 Paul Becker and Mark William, *Dynamic Daughter Church Planting Handbook*, Section p. 1.

5 C. Peter Wagner, *Your Church Can Grow* (Glendale California: Regal Books, 1976) p. 97.

FIVE

Impact Variations

Every church contains the seed for other churches. The local church was meant to reproduce itself over and over again. As a healthy plant forms seeds that when planted bring forth other plants, so healthy churches form seeds that produce other churches. There is a price to be paid for the planting of that seed. But there is a far greater price to pay if the seed is not planted.

Keith Bailey.

In a diverse society where relevance is a high value, it is important to plan for variations and multiple options in church planting. This chapter deals with some of the variations of church personality, the impact of different church locations, and the diversity of church styles and theologies. It is important to recognize that the focus and emphasis of church planting changes with decades of time, and with the generational preference. The material of this section is presented in charts, lists or outlines for quick church planter reading and for clarity in making comparisons.

A. Variations Between The Traditional Church And The New Church

OLD WINESKINS	SUBJECT	NEW WINESKINS
Complex, well developed; all the extras possible	*Organization*	Simple, bare minimum structure with no extras
Concentrated with a dominant cultural group and common traditions	*Ethnicity*	Wide variety of people with different backgrounds
Clearly identified and distinguishable from non-members' participation	*Membership*	Less emphasis on membership, membership in terms of belonging and participation
More mixture of nurture and commitment with behavioural change	*Conversion*	More process conversion with gradual behavioural changes
Often more a doctrinal reality with historic definitions	*Holy Spirit*	More a present reality and daily resource and presence
Confession is assumed and accepted without much debate	*Confession of Faith*	Traditional views must be proven biblically relevant
Services predictable, routine and formal	*Worship Patterns*	Services are flexible, creative and contemporary
Assumed loyalty with a priority of doing together what cannot be done alone	*Denominational Loyalty*	Discomfort with the bigger organizational network which is often unknown
Leaders are more traditional often believer-focused	*Leadership*	Leaders are more catalytic and and outreach-oriented
Held together by values and experiences that are shaped by many generations	*Church Glue*	Held together by practical relevant experiences that are currently meaningful

B. Variations Of Church Personality

A church is very much like a family in that it develops a corporate personality or character. These body characteristics will have drawing or attraction power for some and a repelling effect on others. It is important therefore to give careful attention to the kind of personality that a church develops. As people are making their choices about church attendance, they will do so very much on the basis of church character. Some churches are bright and joyous, others are sober and more legalistic. Some have an optimistic spirit, and others are more pessimistic.

The characteristics among most churches are varied and mixed. In most churches you can, however, identify a dominant characteristic and perhaps several secondary traits or interests. The leadership families usually set the pattern of the church personality or DNA.

CHARACTERISTICS THAT NEWCOMERS ARE QUICK TO OBSERVE IN A CHURCH

1. Academic Character

Such a church has a large body of people that are in professional life. This church has a high need level for mental stimulation, a formal environment and quality performance.

2. Ministry Character

Such a church is usually relational and caring. It likes to have close fellowship, with a stress on acceptance, honesty, and body involvement.

3. Worship Character

This church sees its emphases and purpose fulfilled basically in a strong Sunday morning worship service. Such a church has a strong emphasis on Bible preaching and good singing.

4. Leadership Character

Some churches have a strong emphasis on leadership by a select qualified group. The function and development of leaders is a common theme for such a church.

5. Missionary Character

This church has a heart for missions. It maintains good communication and financial support for the denomination's mission programs both at home and abroad.

6. Outreach Character

This church has a strong inspirational and enthusiastic character. Much of its efforts are related to reaching out to its neighbours.

7. Denominational Character

Some churches are known for their particular interest and partnership in the brotherhood. They are known for their loyalties to conference programs.

8. Social Action Character

Such churches have developed a conscience and interest in dialogue around world injustices, inequalities and peace concerns.

9. Youth Character

Churches that are situated near university campuses often develop a body character that has special attraction to young people.

10. Ethnic Character

These churches place a high value on the church's traditions, heritage and mother tongue. Homogeneity is considered one of their strengths.

11. Contemporary Character

These churches use contemporary instrumentation, worship teams, new music, life-related messages. These churches seek to be relevant to church visitors.

Don Bauman, in All Originality Makes a Dull Church characterizes churches into five distinct body personalities: (1) soul winning; (2) classroom, (3) life situation; (4) social action; (5) general practitioner. Peter Wagner adds several others to the list and describes two of them as the "rock generation church" and the "spiritual high congregation."[1] More recently, churches have been described as seeker sensitive or seeker targeted

C. Church Variations Due To Location

Church Context Has An Impact On Church Planting

The nature and character of a church is shaped by its geographic environment. The church planter must assure that the kind of church envisioned is compatible with the kind of people in the area. Both the rate of growth and the composition of a church to a large extent are determined by its location or context.

1. City Core Mission Church

Planting a church in the core city will require much patience and many resources. The social complexity and need levels of the people will make growth slow and work heavy. The ministry of the church often becomes a rehabilitation ministry in the core area.

2. Inner-City First Neighbourhood Church

This struggling neighbourhood just outside of the city core business sector is made up of a highly transient population. Planting a church within such a low-income tenant neighbourhood is always very difficult. The church planter will need to expect a large turnover of church attendance with a high level of social need. Often the church in this part of the city takes on a certain style, such as storefront, with a distinctive theological bent.

3. Transition Stepping-stone Neighbourhood Church

In this area many of the residents are first-time and also short-term owners. They buy for resale, making for a tentative, transient character. Planting a church in this kind of neighbourhood is somewhat easier than that in the more core area rental neighbourhood. A church in this neighbourhood will tend to remain small and may often have an ethnic character.

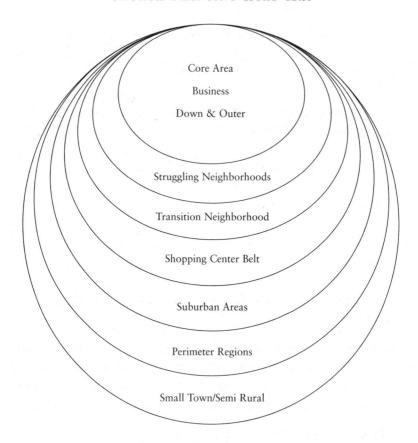

Core Area

Business

Down & Outer

Struggling Neighborhoods

Transition Neighborhood

Shopping Center Belt

Suburban Areas

Perimeter Regions

Small Town/Semi Rural

4. Suburban Neighbourhood Church

When planting a church in a more suburban area, the development of an autonomous, more middle-class church is readily predictable. Since the population is more stable and resourceful, the church in turn reaps similar benefits. Again, the church will take on the character of the people in the area.

5. Small Town/Semi-Rural Church

Church planting in smaller communities is usually more personal. People know each other, and often have for generations. Most have their official historic church ties even though in practice they are not involved. The new church may experience a number of years of struggle until it builds friendship and credibility in the community.

A new church must always adjust itself to its strategic environment. A church in a government centre will operate differently from a church in a trade or manufacturing centre. Similarly, a church in a university city will be different from an emerging church in a military base, farm, or entertainment community.

It should be noted that just as the church location has an impact on the character of the church, so does the church's theology. Church plants vary according to the denomination's philosophy of outreach. The spectrum from mainline churches to evangelical churches parallels a low to a high commitment toward active evangelism. Because church planting is an evangelism program, it follows that evangelical churches are more committed to church planting than churches with a lower commitment to evangelism.

D. Variations Based On Growth Factors/Terminology

Each decade of church leaders seem to generate their own set of church growth factors and terminology. The past three decades have produced spokespersons who represent the values and focus of their decade. Note the changing patterns and the use of terminology to describe the decadal emphasis and the church focus.

1. Church Growth Principles of the Sixties

Donald McGavran[2]
- Church growth expectations
- Mission Imperative/Harvest theology
- Indigenous church planting
- Sociological applications
- Redemption and lift
- People movement conversion
- Growth barrier and readiness
- Indigenous principles

George W. Peters[3]
- Spiritual fullness
- Unity of faith
- Godly leadership
- Functional body
- Discipled members
- Biblical preaching
- Continuous prayer
- Joyful sacrifice and suffering

2. Vital Signs of the Seventies

C. Peter Wagner[4]
- Strong leadership
- Mobilized party

Robert Schuller[5]
- Good accessibility
- Surplus parking

- Suitable sizing
- Celebration worship
- Homogeneity
- Relevant programs
- Clear priorities

- Program inventory
- Satisfied service
- High visibility
- Possibility thinking
- Good cash flows

3. Core Values of the Eighties

Rick Warren[6]

- Vision of fruitfulness
- Purpose-drawn structures
- Life-related messages
- Visitor-friendly strategies
- Ministry through spiritual gift
- Seeker-sensitive focus
- New member assimilation
- Guided spiritual growth
- Clarity of commitment targets
- Positive, upbeat music

Bill Hybels[7]

- Anointed teaching
- People matter to God
- Cultural relevance
- Believer authenticity
- Serving with spiritual gifts
- Loving church relationships
- Functioning small groups
- Excellence for God and people
- Leadership gifts for church leadership
- Every believer a devoted follower

4. Quality Characteristics of the Nineties

Christian Schwartz Research[8]
Universal Characteristics

- Empowering leadership
- Gift-oriented ministry
- Passionate spirituality
- Functional structures
- Inspiring worship
- Holistic small groups
- Need-oriented evangelism
- Loving relationship

George Hunter III[9]
Apostolic Characteristics

- Rooted in Scripture
- Disciplined in prayer
- Understand pre-Christians
- Obey the Great Commission
- Vision of a disciple
- Cultural adaptation/communication
- Believer/seeker small groups
- Involvement by giftedness
- Pastoral care by shepherds
- Variation of outreach

5. Church and City Transformation for 2000 and Beyond

Transformation Expectations[10]

- City Leadership networks
- City prayer worriers and intercessors

- City wide outreach initiatives
- Whole body mobilization
- Reconciliation within and beyond the body
- City-wide gatherings and celebrations
- Transformation of the city
- Saturation church planting
- Redemption of society

SAMPLE CORE VALUES OF GROWING MENNONITE BRETHREN CHURCHES

Northview Community Church Abbotsford, BC	Meeting Place Winnipeg, MB
- God-centered worship	- Biblical functioning community
- People building, nurturing	- People matter to God motivation
- World-focused message	- Culturally relevant communication
- Contemporary communication style	- Devotion to Christ for life change
- Practical teaching of scripture	- Life-transforming worship service
- Entry-level special events	- Small groups for discipling/care
- Small groups, care-giving	- Spiritual growth accountability
- People to people outreach	- Honour God by giving one's best
- Discerned and empowered leaders	- Vision to present the good news
- Authentic biblical lifestyles	- Spiritual direction giving
- Biblical stewardship / management	- Committed to reaching all people
- Cross-cultural mission experiences	- Authentic relationships

Above content based on personal interviews

E. Understanding Urban/Rural Church Variations

Church planting needs to take into consideration the different mind set and values between urban and rural churches. City church planting can be more businesslike, while rural planting needs to be more like a family. The growth rates will also vary greatly from city to rural plants. The variations chart below is helpful in understanding the value system of both groups.

Church Planting Road Map

Subject	City	Semi-Rural
Church Composition	Professionally diverse/complex, a wide spectrum of people represented	There is a dominance of one or two professional groups; more homogenous
People Mobility	People are constantly moving in and out	Core groups remain relatively constant
Spirituality	There is a likelihood of more new Christians, with more spiritual diversity	Majority of church people are 2nd or 3rd generation Christians with spiritual evenness
Family Relationships	Relationships are casual. Little is known of the weekday work patterns of other church people	Church is like an extended family with intimate awareness of one another
Outreach Programs	Public announcements result in anonymous attendance	One-on-one friendships and long-term relationships are the norm
Church Schedules	Church programs are adjusted to suit the business life with breakfast and luncheon meetings	Programs accommodate the farming lifestyle with more seasonal adjustments
Theological Diversity	Church problems reflect the diversity of a city life of secularism	Dialogue reflects a ministry pattern in response to rural life
Opportunity and Challenge	There is involvement in civic functions, ministerials, chaplaincies, counselling, radio, TV	People are involved in their own and nearby towns for their functions and rural celebrations
Values Preferences	People prefer anonymity, mobility, diversity, and change	Rural people prefer familiarity, stability and sameness
Professionalism	Church involvement is often by specialization and professional preference	Church involvement is more by people availability and faithfulness
Information flows	Formal printed materials are used	Information flows informally (grapevine)

Finance	There is a business approach of payment for services given to the church	Services rendered are often gratis with members carrying the cost
Audience	Audience is often more critical and more demanding of competence; there is less lay involvement	People are more tolerant and loving of one another; family style
Personal Ministry	Contact with parishioners is brief and often only in church situations	Visitation is often combined with social visits to the home
Program Visibility	Extensive advertising, using various media gives the program high profile and visibility	Local posters and one-on-one information flow about events lets the people know what is happening; Low profile advertising

F. Impact of Generational Preferences And Differences

New church plants invariably are faced with the challenge of designing a worship service that is relevant for the different age groups within their congregation. The generational variations of the three basic age groups are described in broad strokes below, portraying the different value systems. The list has been compiled from various sources including the writer's own experiences, and provides valuable insights on what will attract and retain the groups in a church plant. This research also indicates how complex it is to have a relevant worship service for all three or more groups in one church service.

Builders	**Boomers**	**Busters**
born before 1946	*born 1947-1964*	*born after 1964*
Influenced by the Depression, WW II world atrocities	Influenced by post-war prosperity, television, rock music, sexual revolution	Influenced by high-tech information, fast foods, double-income parents
program-oriented money to missions	people-oriented money to people	social orientation money to causes

Builders	Boomers	Busters
loyalty to denomination	loyalty to people	loyalty to causes
committed to church	committed to relationships	committed to community
Bible study: content	Bible study: fellowship	Bible study: issues
marriage/retirement	marriage/family	marriage/singles
be formal	be relational	be spontaneous
expository sermons	life-related sermons	issue-oriented sermon
doctrinal hymns	praise songs	new songs
organ/piano	keyboard/guitars	drums/guitar; jazz
low participation	higher participation	lower participation
long-range projects	people-oriented projects	instant-issue projects
campaign evangelism	friendship evangelism	process evangelism
leader/enabler	leader/facilitator	leader collegial
teaching: propositional	teaching: experiential	teaching: incidental
facilities adequate	facility attractive	facility practical
verbal orientation	visual orientation	project orientation
program stability	program variety	program fragmented
be uniform	be unique	be different
guests recognized	guests anonymous	guests hidden
maintain stability	use variety	use spontaneity
ministry for obedience	ministry for satisfaction	ministry for fun
attendance regular	attendance mostly regular	attendance as suitable
dress formal	dress informal	dress casual
drive bigger car	drive van/4x4	drive sports car/truck
sing harmony	sing along	clap along
fixed pulpit	glass pulpit/music stand	no pulpit
natural lighting	bright light	spot lights, strobe etc.

A fourth column of values for the generation X and another for the echo generation could be added to the above values columns. Some research suggests that the younger society has its own cultural values for each three-year segment.

NOTES——

[1] Don Bauman, *All Originality Makes a Dull Church* (Santa Ana, California: Vision House Publishers, 1976).

[2] Donald McGavran, *Understanding Church Growth* (Grand Rapids,

Michigan: Eerdmans Publishing, 1970) p. 335.

[3] George W. Peters, *A Theology of Church Growth* (Grand Rapids, Michigan: Zondervan Publishing, 1981) p. 209.

[4] C. Peter Wagner, *Your Church Can Grow* (Glendale, California: Regal Press, 1976) pp. 32-33.

[5] Robert Schuller, *Your Church Has Real Possibilities* (Glendale, California: Regal Books, 1971) pp. 19-29.

[6] Rick Warren, *The Purpose-Driven Church* (Grand Rapids, Michigan: Zondervan, 1995) p. 85.

[7] Lynne and Bill Hybels, *Rediscovering Church* (Grand Rapids Michigan: Zondervan, 1995) pp. 184-193.

[8] Christian Schwartz, *Paradigm Shift In The Church* (Carol Stream, Illinois: Church Smart Resources, 1999) p. 21.

[9] George Hunter, *Church For The Unchurched* (Nashville, Tennessee: Abingdon Press, 1996) pp. 28-32.

[10] Jack Dennison, *City Reaching*, (Pasadena, California: William Carey Library, 1999) p. 94.

[11] James Nikkel, *Evangelism Canada Digest*, March, 1986, Vol.3, No.1, Urbanization—Rural/city Relationship (Winnipeg, Manitoba: Kindred Press, 1986).

Six

Planting Preparations

Confusion reigns in a society or an institution when issues are not sorted out and acted upon one at a time... the limit of our social energy requires that we deal with one at a time... our system for assimilating information can handle only so many issues. When the system fills us, we close it off against the entry of any new issues.

David McKenna, *Mega Truth*.

This chapter discusses the preparation phases of a church plant. In many ways the preparation phases of a church are similar to that of preparing for the start-up of a restaurant. Many of the same issues need to be decided, such as criteria, name, location, clientele, advertising, and designing the master plan. Choosing the type of restaurant such as family, fast-food, ethnic, or formal dining, is one of the first decisions to be made. Based on that decision, the menu, staffing and hours can be decided. These are some of the same decisions required in the planning of a church.

A. Preparing The Church-Planting Criteria

CHURCH PLANTING COULD BE CONSIDERED IN THE FOLLOWING
SITUATIONS:

1. In a place where a person of peace in the community is opening her/his home as a partner in the church plant (Luke 10:5-8).

2. In such places where conversions have taken place and no church is available for nurture and growth.

3. In those communities where there is no gospel-centred church, or no churches that are aggressively pursuing the fulfillment of the great commission.

4. In places where several families of a particular denomination have a desire to establish a church witness in continuity with their theological traditions.

5. In such places where a group of concerned people have extended a Macedonian call to come and help organize the core group.

6. In places where the population base has several commonalities with the church-planting denomination, and where economic, educational, and/or historical affinities can be identified.

7. Language-specific churches could be considered wherever there is a sizable identifiable ethnic community of 800 or more. New churches are required wherever there are substantial cultural distances or differences between the population segments.

8. In such situations where a denomination is establishing a cluster of churches as a regional development strategy.

9. According to Outreach Canada/Vision Canada, one evangelical church for every 1,000 people could be considered a reasonable criterion.[1]

10. In the larger city, any one denomination might consider planting a church for every 30,000—45,000 people in a given area of the city.

11. As a general principle of involvement, the smaller population

centres should perhaps be serviced by the more interdenominational mission church planters, and the larger population centres should be the target area for the more denominational mission church planters.

12. Church planting should be considered in response to individuals who have a personal sense of divine call or vision to plant a church in a given area.

13. Church planting by adoption should be encouraged in situations where a group has already been established but is looking for a denominational affiliation.

14. In all the above situations, the guidance of the Holy Spirit and the agreement of the denomination in concern must be present for a new church.

PRINCIPLE OF CONSULTATION

Whenever an individual or church is considering a church-planting venture, it should seek the advice and counsel of area or provincial evangelism and church extension agencies in order to assure the best beginnings and suitable timing.

B. Deciding On The Church Paradigm

THE PARADIGM DETERMINES CHURCH ORIENTATION

Subject	Charismatic Power Church	Traditional Evangelical Church	Contemporary Believer's Church	Contemporary Seeker's Church
Value	Experience	Faithfulness	Worship	Relevance
Evangelism	Miracle Evangelism	Friendship Evangelism	Event Evangelism	Attraction Evangelism
Orientation	Holy Spirit Focused	Believer Focus Inter-Generational	Seeker Sensitive Blended	Seeker focus Focus: X's
Preaching	Spontaneous Spirit Led	Exegetical Teaching	Biblical Application	Spiritual Principles

Leadership	Prophetic Voice Personality	Congregational Democratic	Elder Leadership by gifts	Personality Vision Group
Music	Spiritual Songs	Mostly Hymns Harmony	Worship Team Contemporary	Stage Band Clap Along

C. Preparations Through Research And Surveys

Research is a very important part of the church-planting process. The decision to start a church in a given area must be based upon qualifying data along with a deep conviction that God, through his Spirit, is calling the new church into being. The church belongs to Christ the church head.

Research must be relevant. The data gathered must be such that it will help the planners in determining the right location and an appropriate strategy. Good planning and survey was clearly advised by Christ in that he urged his followers to count the cost, look unto the field, and exercise good stewardship.

Good research is valuable for vision building and motivational involvement.

Research can help people see the need.
Research enables people to see the vision.
Research may cause people to want to grow.
Research can be a motivation to people.
Research helps people see an overall strategy.
Research may encourage people to become involved.

Helpful and useful surveys will ask questions concerning the people, the place, and the program.

PEOPLE QUESTIONS:

1. Does the population for the area show a growth or declining trend?

2. Is that area known for people mobility and transiency?

3. Are the people mostly homeowners, renters or apartment dwellers?

4. What are the economic and educational levels of the community?

5. Does the area have a high presence of single-parent families, children or senior citizens?

6. Are there significant numbers of ethnic people in the area?

Program Questions:

1. Are there observable needs that could be met by a new church?

2. How many churches are there presently in the area in question?

3. What percentage of the community is actively involved in church life and what percentage of the community has no church connections?

4. Have there been some recent church starts or stops in the community?

5. Is the great commission evangelism work being accomplished through the existing churches?

6. Are there signs of receptivity, and openness to the gospel in the area in question?

7. Will it be possible to reach and incorporate new people into the church?

8. Are there major barriers or distance factors between the sponsoring denomination and the community (i.e. economic, social, educational, theological, etc.)?

9. What will a new church be able to accomplish in the target area which is not already being done by the existing churches?

10. Are there some families available in the area that are ready to assume church-planting responsibilities?

Place Questions:

1. Are there institutions in the area that will help or hinder a new

church (schools, hospitals, prisons, parks, etc.)

2. Are there some natural boundaries or industrial developments which separate or affect the target area?

3. Is the area subjected to industrial noise or onerous odours?

4. Is the area in question serviced with major traffic arteries and a public transportation system?

5. Does the area have any "wrong side of the track" stigmas or reputations?

6. Does the community have its own communications systems such as newspapers, radio or television stations?

RESEARCH DATA CENTRES:

1. Census Canada
2. Realtor Offices
3. School/District Offices
4. Social Services

5. Chamber of Commerce
6. Municipal Offices
7. Regional Libraries
8. Internet

D. The Community Person Profile

WHO ARE THEY??

From the research, a personal profile of the average person living in the targeted church planting community needs to be developed including:

- What they value
- Are they formal or informal?
- How do they communicate?
- What are their hobbies?
- What are their lifestyles?
- What are their needs?
- Church background
- Level of Biblical awareness
- Personal preferences, etc.[2]

E. Preparing The New Church Preliminary Design

The new church, like any new business or institution, must be developed upon a specific set of principles. The original church vision needs to be spelled out so that the developmental process can proceed around a common understanding or philosophy. A carefully-prepared preliminary design document will help to avoid misunderstanding between the original project pioneers, the first pastor, the new converts or move-ins, and the denomination in concern. This original document summarizes in statement form the intentions and basic understandings of the new congregation. Usually, the original vision-holders and initiators of the new project are the authors of this document.

This preliminary design sets the conceptual parameters and directions upon which the new congregation is launched. This project design should include summary statements on the following:

PRELIMINARY DESIGN OUTLINE

1. Background circumstances and motivations of the new church project

2. Purpose, goal and rationale statements for the new church

3. The target group being ministered to in the church plant

4. Confession of faith and theological orientation

5. Sponsorship and mandate for establishing the new church must be clear. If the church is to be related to the denomination, then the communication, relationship, and accountability lines need to be established.

6. Financial support, both short- and long-term, need to be projected. If conference funding is anticipated, then include the projected along with the anticipated subsidies.

7. Program philosophy and ministry design need to be defined.

8. Leadership roles and organizational principles

9. Membership acceptance and responsibility

10. Mission statement and core values of the church

11. A tentative development time line [3]

F. New Church Master Plan

The church-planting group needs to visualize in their minds of faith what God wants to do. It is important that God's plans be recognized and converted into a flow chart of action. This planning group needs to see the bigger picture of all that is involved in this church plant. The new church master plan is designed to help the church-planting task force to see the project on a time-line from start to finish. Prayer is an essential priority for each of the master plan steps. It is also assumed that the church planter will have coaching and mentoring in the planting process. This master plan converts the visions and dreams for the new church into concrete development steps.

NEW CHURCH MASTER PLAN

1. Affirm the biblical mandate of church planting
2. Determine the church planting area and target group by field surveys
3. Prepare the church-planting preliminary design
4. Determine project sponsor, participating churches/church extension
5. Secure the go-ahead mandate/approval
6. Assign a project facilitator/interim leader/church planter
7. Appoint a task force or launch team
8. Establish a prayer base of intercessors
9. Allocate start-up funds and appoint a treasurer/bank account
10. Develop a start-up program plan, strategy and ministry philosophy
11. Decide on the name of the church
12. Recruit a core group to help launch the program; assign tasks
13. Have a sending and commissioning service
14. Arrange for temporary meeting place
15. Print promotional and invitational literature

16. Arrange for interim donation receipting

17. Purchase worship materials: keyboard, sound system, projectors, offering bags, communion trays, etc.

18. Plan the launch service as an inaugural dedication service

19. Add new ministries to the worship service on a time-line

20. Prepare provisional, operational policies

21. Conduct membership preparation classes

22. Arrange for a baptism service

23. Plan the membership chartering celebration service

24. Launch team resigns, and church elders appointed

25. Apply to government for tax status

26. Church establishes short- and long-term goals

27. Full-time pastor/church planter pastor affirmed by the members

28. Application for denominational church membership is made

29. Blueprinting for permanent facilities

G. Choosing A New Church Name

Attracting the Pre-Christian

The name of a church is very important. It has the power to attract or repel people. The church name is part of the church's welcome mat. The name should be short and be as inclusive as possible in its appeal to the public.

Historically, church names tended to identify the church with a period of history, a theological orientation, certain experiences, a movement or denomination; all of which have meaning and appeal to existing members of a church. The name chosen in a church plant needs to have appeal, or at least be neutral to prospective church attenders. Since the church is called to reach all nations, the name should cater to those that need to be reached.

Church names tend to have specific reference points or orientations. The first seven reference points listed below would have high appeal to church members, and the last three, the human, geographic, and natural reference points, would have more appeal to unchurched people. Most church plants choose their names from the bottom three reference points. The denominational affiliation does not necessarily need to be part of the official name, but should be declared in the church's printed literature.

Church Name—Reference Points or Orientations

1. Historic Reference Point
Lutheran, Reformed, Anglican, Mennonite, Calvinist, Episcopalian

2. Denominational Reference Point
Chilliwack Free Methodist, White Rock Southern Baptist, Clearbrook Mennonite Brethren, Dunbar United, New West Four Square

3. Theological Reference Point
Rose of Sharon, Calvary Church, Eastside Bible Church, Trinity Baptist, Church of God, Maranatha Fellowship, Christ's Church

4. Experiential Reference Point
Fresh Winds, Living Waters, Victory Church, Pentecost Fellowship, Full Gospel, Church of the Redeemed, Sovereign Grace, Revival Fellowship

5. Missional Reference Point
Harvest Fellowship, Missionary Church, Salvation Army, Open Door Church, Gospel Light Church, Glad Tidings

6. Cultural Reference Point
Greek Orthodox, Swedish Baptist, German Lutheran, Indo-Canadian, Chinese Christian Church, Arabic Christian Fellowship, Mennonite

7. Believers' Reference Point
Bread of Life Fellowship, Covenant Church, The Believers Bible Church, Mission Christian Fellowship, Open Bible Church

8. Human Reference Point

People's Church, All Nations Fellowship, The Gathering Place, The Meeting Place, People of Joy Church, People of the Way

9. Geographic Community Reference Point

Westbank Community Church, Willingdon Church, 10th Avenue Alliance, Chilliwack Central Church, Portage Avenue Church, Cedar Park, North Side Community Church, Promontory Community Church

10. Natural Environment Reference Point

Oceanview, Northview, Mountainview, Bakerview, Fraser Heights, Hillside Church, Riverbend, Orchard Park, Silver Hills Church

---

A Name Should Create a Good First and Last Impression

Logan and Rast in Church-Planter's Checklist suggest the name should be:

1. **Catchy**—sound appealing to an unchurched person

2. **Creative**—reflect the creativity of God

3. **Indigenous**—be descriptive of location or primary culture

4. **Related to Purpose**—points toward the purpose of the church

5. **Related to Style**—reflects the church's style of ministry[4]

H. Developing Church Advertising Guidelines

Aggressive advertising within a mass-media culture is an essential part of effective church planting. Care should be taken that new church advertising should not have negative or comparative statements which suggest other churches may be boring or irrelevant.

New church advertising needs to be positive, and present the strength of the new church, based on credible values and purposes in its own right.

1. Aggressive Advertising

a) Church Advertising Values for the Community
- Sends a message that the church is interested in the community
- Raises church visibility and awareness of the new church
- Gives the church planter a public introduction
- Breaks down stereotypes of the church
- Explains what the church is all about
- Creates a positive church image
- Lets the community know when the church plant is happening

b) Advertising Values for the Church
- Creates a public mind set of growth for the church people
- Reinforces the outreach motif
- Combats ingrownness through visitor expectation
- Creates openness and declares more church entry points
- Forces the church to articulate its focus and values
- Provides new rally occasions for the church
- Enhances excellence and pushes the church to be at its best
- Utilizes graphic skills people
- Provides opportunity for market interactions
- Communicates a positive image

2. Saturate the Church's Influence Area with Advertising

a) Clarify Target Areas for Promotion
- Select a geographic area for repeated coverage of 2,500 to 5,000 homes
- Saturate the target area with prayer walks and brochure drop-offs
- Repeat the coverage 6 to 8 times a year in the church "farming area"
- Do door-to-door invitation calls

b) Schedule a Promotional Campaign

- Advertise the initial church-interest meetings with several flyers/newspaper ads. For the launch service distribute monthly flyer for three to four months before the public service
- Advertise for the special calendar days such as Christmas, Valentine's, Easter, Mother's Day etc.
- Have a special brochure for the fall church opener
- Plan and advertise the Thanksgiving and Christmas banquets
- Consider advertising special church anniversaries or seminar series
- A brochure that introduces a new pastor works well

3. Church Advertising Principles

a) Newspaper and Brochure Advertising
- Newspaper advertising tends to attract Christian families
- Door-to-door get the attention of the unchurched
- Seek to get church cover story and pictures into the paper
- If possible, write a column for Easter, Christmas, Thanksgiving etc.
- Write positive letters to the newspaper editors

b) Church Signs and Message Board Advertising
- Place portable sandwich boards at major intersections to the church worship
- Place a visible church entry sign at the main door if location is rented
- Position interior signs to auditorium, nursery and washrooms
- Print signs professionally since they reflect your values
- Assure that sign wording is clear and not crowded to include: welcome, worship time, church name and telephone number

c) Telephone and Internet Advertising
- Advertise in the telephone yellow pages church section
- Advertise in the denominational telephone listings
- Create an attractive web page with good graphics
- Post the church bulletin with sermon titles
- Highlight church mission statement, values and programs
- Give e-mail address, telephone and church location

•Update information regularly

d) Church Office Promotions/Advertising
   •Print co-ordinated business cards, letterhead and envelopes
   •Have a general church information brochure for visitor hand-outs
   •Set up a church information literature table with ministry details and resources
   •Have back issues of church program bulletins available
   •Have friendship and encouragement cards available
   •Publish a monthly/quarterly church family newsletter
   •Have give-aways like calendars, mugs, pens, booklets etc.
   •Keep an idea file of brochures from other churches

Advertising for the Grand Opening

Dr. Ron Bonar recommends six flyers and two phone calls during a six-week period before the Grand Opening of a church. He says it takes a concentrated advertising and telephoning campaign to establish public awareness of the church plant: a "market presence." The flow of repeated advertising unplugs the ears of the unchurched target group so that they can hear the message communicated. People need to see, hear, or read your commercials six times or more before they stick in their minds.[5]

Six-Week Countdown Advertising Schedule

1. Six flyers, one per week before Grand Opening
2. The first telephone call after 3 flyers to ask if they have noticed the flyers in the mail.
3. The second telephone call is made during the week before the Grand Opening, reminding them of the flyers and inviting them to the public Grand Opening service.
4. The final flyer should give clear details about the Grand Opening service, including a map of the church location.

I. The Planter's Countdown Check List

1. Have the appropriate bodies given their approval or authorization for this church planting project?
2. Has the church planter and a leadership team been appointed?
3. Has a preliminary design sheet been written up?
4. Has the church paradigm and name been decided?
5. Has the master plan been developed and time-lined?
6. Has the starting date and location been established?
7. Has the advertising campaign been aligned with the research?
8. Is there clarity on what the start-up worship program will be and what ministries will be placed on hold for later implementation?
9. Has a call been made to the supporting constituency for special prayer regarding this project?
10. Has an adequate church awareness been established in the community through "big day" or "crowd" events?

Benefits of Crowd or Big Day Events [6]

- builds morale and unity
- gets community attention
- expands church vision
- boosts spiritual growth
- mobilizes the congregation
- breaks barriers and records
- creates outreach opportunities
- identifies the committed

---

11. Has an interim treasurer been appointed to handle expenses and to make arrangements for receipting services?
12. Are the basic supplies ready, such as: keyboard, public address system, music, offering bags, communion trays, information table, refreshments, and church bulletins?
13. Are the program people needed for the first three months assigned?

14. Has the church name and letterhead been prepared for correspondence to go out in connection with the start-up programs?

15. Have appropriate advertising materials been printed for distribution in the community and in the newspaper?

16. Has the basic new church program philosophy and ministry goals brochure been printed for handouts to interested persons?

17. Have invitations gone out to the denominational leaders, community officials and mother church to attend the special inaugural launching service?

18. Is there a projected one-year budget to guide the anticipated financial transactions?

NOTES——

1 Murray Morman, *Transforming Our Nation* (Richmond, British Columbia: Church Leadership Library, 1998).

2 Rick Warren, *The Purpose-Driven Church* (Grand Rapids, Michigan: Zondervan Publishing, 1995) p. 170.

3 Esra Earl Jones, *Strategies for New Churches* (New York: Harper and Row, 1976) p. 98.

4 Robert E. Logan and Jeff Rast, *Church Planter Checklist Manual* (Pasadena, California: Fuller Institute, 1987).

5 Ron Bonar, Free Methodist Church Planting Specialist, video series on church planting.

6 Dale Plante, *Church Planting School II Manual* (A Time to Plant Ministries).

SEVEN

Strategic Implementation

If ever the world needs new churches, this is the hour! The time has come to rise up and plant churches across our continent. No one can question our authority, for it is biblical. None can question the method, for it was used by the apostles. No one can question the results, for it is God's way. No one can question its effectiveness, for it reaches every strata of society. It makes no difference; you will find churches in the slums and in the affluent communities.... Let's get on with the job!

Timothy Starr: *Church Planting Always in Season* .

This chapter is about getting the church started in manageable implementation steps. In the start-up steps, the church planter is to the church plant what a contractor is to the house construction. The job is to make sure the blueprint is being followed and that the development is happening in the appropriate sequence. It is vitally important that the sub-trades or launch team are available at the needed times. If this analogy is continued, the goal would be to have an open house, and then the moving in of the permanent dwellers. The end goal is to have a fully-functioning church. The first attenders will be looking for the first service to have programs according to their needs and expectations. It is for this reason that a well-designed first service needs to happen. The big event of this section is the public launch. Everything moves toward the public church birth. The interest meetings, social events and the advertising all are for the purpose of having a major public launching celebration. Once the people are coming, the membership organizing and program development can take place.

A. Start-up Steps And Stages Of A Church Plant

THE IMPLEMENTATION CYCLE

Just as a new house needs to have a master blueprint that determines how and where the construction will take place and how the finished product is going to look, so the implementation steps of the new church need to be time-lined. The church planter needs to be able to answer the questions of what kind of church it is to be, and what the development steps will look like.

Logan and Rast describe the church life cycle as a living organism.[1] As such it closely parallels the life cycle of human beings. Therefore, they use the five major stages of physical growth in the human analogy namely: Conception—the beginnings, Prenatal—the development stage, Birth—the church going public, Growth—maturing process, Reproduction—multiplication.

The development phases need to be distinct steps with measurable activity goals in each phase. Each phase has its priorities, leadership profile, public events and check points. In this book the church planting process is described in terms of a natural sequence of development steps.

The Church Planting Cycle Flow Chart

Church Planting
Steps and Stages

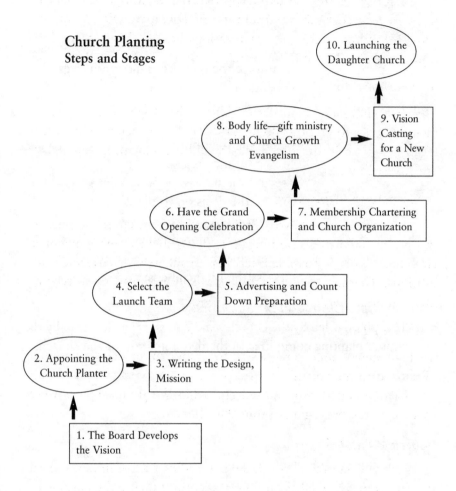

10. Launching the Daughter Church

8. Body life—gift ministry and Church Growth Evangelism

9. Vision Casting for a New Church

6. Have the Grand Opening Celebration

7. Membership Chartering and Church Organization

4. Select the Launch Team

5. Advertising and Count Down Preparation

2. Appointing the Church Planter

3. Writing the Design, Mission

1. The Board Develops the Vision

STEP ONE

VISION CASTING STAGE
Projecting and Discerning

Priorities
- embrace the great commission harvest
- spend time in serious prayer
- discern God's call to proceed
- spin out the vision
- examine the options
- research the area
- secure the necessary permissions
- make the decision to plant
- recruit intercessory teams
- identify the church partners/sponsors
- determine the church type and style
- assess the financial cost and source

Leadership—Church Plant Sponsors
This phase is led by the church plant sponsor which is usually the church planting committee of the denomination or the church.

Public Events
- Parenting congregation meets for approval of the project
- Commissioning and sending service

Check Points:
1. Is this church plant driven by faith and prayer?
2. Is the vision clearly defined?
3. Has adequate research been done?
4. Has the church plant been approved?
5. Is the project launched to reach the unchurched?
6. Do we have faith for the financial resources?

STEP TWO

DESIGN STAGE
Intensive Planning

Priorities
- assess and appoint the church planter
- concentrated prayer for guidance
- decide on location
- develop a profile of the community
- develop the mission statement/values
- project the ministry philosophy
- visualize the development steps
- chart the time-line
- determine the leaders needed for the launch
- describe the organizational principles
- decide on the church name
- open the church bank account
- develop the financial procedures
- plant the seeds of reproduction
- visit the area ministerial
- keep doing evangelism

Leadership—The Planter and Director
This phase is led by the church planter and the director of church extension.

Public Events
- No public events in this phase
- Much prayer time

Check Points:
1. Is the design reasonable for the community?
2. Has the target audience been identified?
3. Is the motivation clear and the plan feasible?
4. Has the nature of the church been clarified?
5. Do the values, mission, and philosophy harmonize?
6. Are the spiritual priorities clear?

STEP THREE

PREPARATION STAGE
Countdown Tasks

Priorities
- prayerfully recruit the launch team
- create a community presence/awareness
- set date for the grand opening
- identify the tasks to be done
- orientate team on values/mission/style
- write up team leaders' job descriptions
- actively recruit new participants
- have several public-interest meetings
- begin home groups
- organize outreach crowd/fishing events
- do some door-to-door surveys/contacts
- get church-plant story into newspaper
- launch aggressive advertising campaign
- print stationary/business cards/envelopes
- set up temporary office and computer
- purchase necessary start-up equipment: key board, sound system, power point, etc.

Leadership Launch Team
This phase is led by the launch team, chaired by the church planter, and coached by the church planting director.

Public Events
- Several interest and information meetings
- Several outreach crowd events to get a critical mass

Check Points:
1. Are all interested people being followed up?
2. Is enough time spent in prayer?
3. Does the launch team understand their job?
4. Are all the members of the launch team involved in outreach?
5. Are the advertising brochures sent out on time?
6. Has the equipment for the launch Sunday been purchased?

STEP FOUR

LAUNCHING STAGE
Grand Opening Service

Priorities
- set goal of 125 people for launch service
- complete the countdown preparations
- arrange for a rehearsal and prayer service
- pray for an effective and fruitful launch
- make Grand Opening a celebration
- include celebrative ribbon-cutting dedication
- include presentation of vision and values
- arrange for a well-run child care
- have photographer take pictures
- have a clear and sensitive gospel presentation
- prepare program bulletin/feedback cards
- have information table with current pamphlets
- arrange refreshments before and after service
- put sandwich board street signs at key corners
- have signs at the entrance with inside directions
- place greeters outside/inside, before/after service
- arrange for more advertising during launch week

Leadership—Launch Team
The launching phase is led by the launch team under the church planter's direction and the coach. After the launch service, the launch team has completed its assignment and a transition team is appointed.

Public Event
- Launch team rehearsal prayer service
- The Grand Opening launch service

Check Points:
1. Is the worship team in tune with the outreach goals?
2. Have the spiritual preparations been looked after?
3. Are the facilities adequate for this major event?
4. Is the location well-marked and easy to find?
5. Are the team participants spiritually ready for the launch?
6. Are the ministry leaders in place for ongoing services?

STEP FIVE

ORGANIZATION STAGE
Membership Chartering

Priorities
- invite attendees to consider membership
- conduct membership orientation classes
- prepare for the first baptism service
- hear testimonies of potential members
- have a membership-chartering service
- present new members with certificates
- set up a suitable record-keeping system
- involve attendees/members in small groups
- register church as a charity with government
- make tithing part of the worship experience
- cultivate ongoing outreach and follow-up
- see that church leaders affirmed by the members
- ensure members take ownership of goals/values

Leadership—Transition Team
After the launch service the launch team is enlarged into a transition team. Some of the launch team members may not continue as transition team members. The transition team serves for one year beyond the membership chartering and they are expected to be members.

Public Events
- Baptism service
- Membership chartering/organizing service
- Regular worship services

Check Points:
1. Is outreach regularly emphasized in the worship?
2. Do newcomers remain the church priority?
3. Does the church organization facilitate church growth?

4. Are membership/baptism classes offered regularly?
5. Are members and attenders mixed together in small groups?
6. Do the planter and leadership team/elders model tithing?

STEP SIX

GROWTH STAGE
Church Development

Priorities
- maintain contemporary worship services
- have newcomer classes and lunches
- ongoing assimilation/integration events
- spiritual gift assessment and involvement
- cultivate ongoing active outreach events
- involve visionary, positive leadership
- keep the multiplication mindset alive
- arrange for permanent facilities
- use special days for outreach
- keep an active advertising program
- train and use new ministry leaders
- develop multiple ministry groups
- opportunity for fellowship and meals
- personal growth of each participant

Leadership—Church Elders
The transition team resigns one year after the membership chartering at which time church elders are appointed as church leaders.

Public Event
- Regular worship
- Special occasion crowd event
- Seasonal banquets, concerts, etc.

Check Points:
1. Are new leaders being recruited, trained and mobilized?
2. Do the ministry leaders have a mindset of excellence?
3. Are the worship services inspiring and challenging?
4. Is the Bible preached and followed for faith and life?
5. Are new people assimilated through small groups?
6. Does evangelism continue to be a church priority?

STEP SEVEN

REPRODUCTION STAGE
Church Multiplication

Priorities
- church planting is defined as a natural part of church life
- multiplication of witnesses, disciplers and small groups
- constantly look for new opportunities to reach people
- cultivate an active church-planting mindset
- appoint an associate for church planting
- develop a new church-parenting strategy
- empower a launch team to start a new church
- develop the new church design
- calendar the new church beginning
- invest much time in prayer
- follow steps and phases of this chapter

Leadership—Launch Team
Assign a church-planting launch team from within the church

Public Events
- New church interest and information meeting
- Fishing-pool, outreach, crowd events

Check List:
1. Is the church healthy enough to reproduce?
2. Do the church core values include church planting?
3. Is the church effectively making disciples?
4. Does the church have a plan to reproduce within two years?
5. Is the senior pastor excited about church parenting?
6. Does the church have finances available for a new church?

B. Public Interest Meeting

Information about the church-planting project must be shared with the community. A suitably-prepared brochure with data on worship location and time, program projections, church affiliation, and an invitation to participate is very important. Community people will not attend something they are not aware of or do not know enough about. It is important to seasonally distribute information about the church in the community. The community must be told over and over again that they are welcome and wanted in the church. The two prime times for launching a new church are in spring around Easter time and fall around mid-September.

Sample Advertisement of Interest Meeting

New Church Option/Information meeting

A new church interest and information meeting for the west area of Abbotsford is taking place as follows:

Date: March 6, 1996—7:30 p.m.
Location: Leisure Center on Talbot and South Fraser Way
Topic: Information on a new church proposal
Sponsor: BC Mennonite Brethren Church Extension

This information meeting is open to anyone interested in exploring the option and feasibility of participation in the beginnings of a new church plant. For more details, contact Extension director James Nikkel.

302—32025 Dahlstrom Ave., Abbotsford, BC V2T 2K7
Phone: (604) 853-6959 / Fax: (604) 853-6990

Information Handouts for the Interest Meetings Should Include the Following:

1. The purpose of the new church

2. Direction and core values

3. Ministries that will be provided

4. Starting detail

5. Some reasons for participating

6. Involvement opportunities

7. Church planter contact information

8. Countdown details[2]

C. Launch Sunday Preparation Priorities

THE GRAND OPENING CELEBRATION

This first public service should be characterized and profiled as a great celebration. It is like a ribbon-cutting ceremony, where the vision and purposes are declared. Special guests and greetings should be part of the event. It should be a specially-prepared event, and should be seen as a pace-setting launching service. Included in this service should be a prayer for the church planter and greetings from the denomination, community leaders or organizations.

1. Attendance Goal

To have 125 people or more present at the launch from within your declared church planting area (critical mass).

2. Program Priorities—Leading up to the Launch Service

- Monthly crowd events (concerts, picnics, etc.)
- Small group house meetings
- Write thank-you notes constantly
- Keep the community flyers going
- Have lots of eating together
- Develop momentum and team spirit

- Hold new convert breakfast meetings
- Have outings together
- Have job descriptions for all jobs
- Track the attendance and keep records
- Have apprentice for most jobs
- Do evangelism

3. Preparation for the First Service

- Three or more flyers announcing the coming event
- Telephone invitations to first service
- Door-to-door surveys and invitations
- Have prayer walks
- Look for people who are not actively attending a church
- Recruit a committed launch team
- Have sandwich board signs on major streets

4. Priorities for the First Service

- Upbeat, accepting atmosphere
- Name tags for launch team
- Dress code: casual/business-like
- Use stage, spot lights if possible
- Well rehearsed: performance level
- Remove all dead spots
- Short drama/lots of music with overhead
- Worship team: keyboard, drums, guitar
- Practical twenty-minute conversational message
- Have child-care option
- State the vision of the church
- Have programs (bulletins)
- Have a low-key offering
- Mention the survey, telephone contacts with gratitude
- Award them with a gift certificate
- Announce your next 4 weeks' sermon titles
- Use quality sound system
- Have coffee, juice and cookies

5. Launch Team Preparation Priorities

- Weekly practice and planning
- Monthly vision-casting meetings
- Prayer times
- Be available to meet and greet worshippers
- Generate enthusiasm
- Guard against negative influences
- Develop literature and pamphlets
- Develop systems for ushers, follow-up, etc.

6. Worship Setting Preparation for the Launch

- Make sure the sandwich board signs are out early at key inter-sections
- Direction signs at front doors and inside
- Entry hosts and exit hosts/greeters
- Welcome table with a host giving out name tags
- Some information about the denominational sponsor
- Refreshment table well-accessible
- Stage props: artificial plants, welcome banner
- Equipment boxes stored away out of sight

D. Trouble-shooting The Beginnings

COMMON SENSE STARTING

1. False Start

Do not start your public service until you are ready. There will be pressure by some to go public before you have all the bases covered. Have a practice service a week before you go public with your worship launch. Make sure the brochure campaign and telephone blitz has been completed.

2. Clarity of Direction

Make sure the type of church you are starting is clearly defined. There will be people coming who will have their own vision and ambitions for this church. Set the direction.

3. Priority Time

Make sure that you give priority time to those who will be helpful in launching the church. Spend time in team-building and in strategy development. Keep the bigger picture in mind and move toward it step by step.

4. Attention People

A new church can easily attract a group of difficult, high-need people. Make sure that the church planter's time is not consumed with people who have constant crises and high attention needs. See them by appointment only and so control and balance your time.

5. Power People

Look out for "wanna-be pastors" or theologically-trained lay people who feel called, but have never been affirmed by the church. Be careful about giving authority and power to unknown individuals. Do not give away assignments on the spur of the moment. Hasty appointments lead to regrets.

6. Delegation of Responsibility

Give assignments to new people on a task-by-task basis. Leadership trust must be earned first. Loyalty to the church planter needs to be assured. Eager leaders may have self-serving agendas such as taking a group out of the church. Define the expectation of each task to be performed.

7. Enemy Attack

Satan will seek to disrupt, destroy and discourage. Be on your guard against impending distractions, disruptions and leadership attacks. Keep a prayer hedge of protection.

8. Keep Evaluating

Have the leadership team evaluate every event and meeting with a view to improving the quality and impact. The church planter will need to be firm in expecting to achieve excellence.

9. Trust God

Church planting is a "God-sized" project, and God is the source of adequate supply. Pray for everything you need and expect God to supply your needs.

10. Keep Momentum

The new church needs to keep things moving and growing, building momentum through new activities, new jobs, new posters, new brochures and new groups. The new church needs to get the reputation of being an action church in town. Make sure you have leaders before you start project diversification.

11. Give Recognition

Give generous acknowledgments to people for their involvement. Write cards, notes and letters. Make phone calls. Surprise people by your thoughtful recognitions. Make individuals your top agenda.

12. Follow Leads

Take people seriously if they hint at being interested in the church. Take the initiative over and over again. Make repeated calls; often people change their minds.

13. Build Profile

Become known in the community by showing up at public meetings and giving volunteer time to other agencies who rely on outside help. (Big Brothers, Kiwanis, chaplaincy, etc.)

14. Newspaper

Use the newspaper for interest stories with pictures. Submit articles, get interviewed, and seek to get publicity wherever possible. Advertise on restaurant place mats or other unexpected places.

15. Establish Permanence

It is important for the church planter to live in the focus area. The church people need to see that you are committed to those in the area.

16. Vision Building

Keep the vision and purpose of the church in the forefront. The people need to hear the vision over and over. New people need to be brought up to speed on what God is calling the church to be and do.

17. Model Evangelism

The church planter needs to spend from 30-40% of the week doing outreach/witness type of work. Church planting is an evangelism project.

NOTES——

[1] Robert E. Logan & Jeff Rast, *Church Planter's Checklist* (Pasadena, California: Fuller Institute, 1987). The manual deals with the different stages of this chapter.

[2] Handouts. It is important to have printed materials for the various church programs.

Eight

Intentional Organization

If you want to build a healthy, strong and growing church you must spend time laying a solid foundation. This is done by clarifying in the minds of everyone involved exactly why the church exists and what it is supposed to do. There is incredible power in having a clearly defined purpose statement.... If you want your church to become purpose-driven, you will have to lead it through four critical phases. First you must define your purposes. Next you must communicate those purposes to everyone in the church on a regular basis. Third, you must organize your church around your purposes. Finally, you must apply your purposes to every part of your church.

Rick Warren, *The Purpose-Driven Church*.

This chapter brings together the various planning pieces of the church. Church goals define the specific things to bring about or carry out the church vision. Goals are a statement of what part of the vision is to be accomplished within a given time frame. The whole idea of setting goals is to plan the church development rather than bumbling along, muddling through and taking it as it comes. Setting goals simply involves writing up the events and activities required to accomplish the vision. In the goals, a declaration is made of what is to be done. It is in response to God's vision. In the philosophy of ministry one brings into being a program plan that is compatible with the vision and goals. In the ministry philosophy one converts the energies and harnesses the resources into program activity in order to accomplish the goals.

After the church has its vision, purpose, and philosophy of ministry in place, it puts together its organizational and leadership structure. The constitution and bylaws assure that the church is stabilized to achieve its purposes. Most important in the new church program are the workers. Unless Christians are ready to be involved and are prepared to sacrifice of their time, God's Kingdom will not be extended. God is calling for labourers and co-workers to work His harvest and to build His temple.

A. Organizing The Church Around A Clear Purpose And Vision

It is very important for a new church, or any church, to organize its ministries around a purpose statement. The philosophy of ministry is basically a written description of what the church expects to do and be. A written mission statement assures that the various ministries of the church are lined up to go in the same direction and serve the stated church purposes.

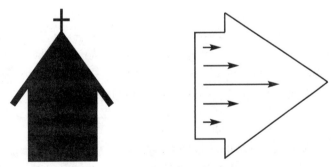

Founding Assumption:
That each new church has clearly stated its vision,
purpose and core values.

In the vision statement, the congregation tries to describe the church from God's perspective. It is a mental picture of what God wants the church to be and do. It is not enough for the church planter to have this vision; the people must share the vision. The entire church needs to build from the same blueprint or vision. The clearer the vision, the more united the implementation process will be. This vision or mental picture of the finished product as given by God must be taken seriously. The basic motivation of all that is to happen in the church comes back to the vision and call that God has placed in the group. The vision, or call, must be written into a basic church purpose statement.

1. Church Vision Statement *(ministry futures)*

The church has a vision to be a congregation that is known to be

- Christ-centred
- Biblically-based
- Culturally relevant
- Believer-affirming
- Family-focused
- Socially winsome
- Community-involved
- Growth-producing
- Outreach-oriented
- Denominationally connected

Rick Warren explains the Saddleback purpose as follows:

> We bring people in, build them up, train them, and send them out. We bring them in as members, we build them up to maturity, we train them for ministry, and we send them out on mission, magnifying the Lord in the process.[1]

2. Church Mission Statement *(ministry purpose)*

The church exists for the purpose of obeying the great commandment of love, and fulfilling the great disciple-making commission of Christ by:

- Expressing faith and allegiance to Christ
- Joining together in exaltation and worship
- Sharing the good news of new life
- Encouraging one another in Christian living
- Expressing care and love to those in need.

3. Church Core Value Statements (ministry guidelines)

a) That the Bible be respected as the basis for faith and life and that the scriptures be taught with a practical life application.

b) That helping people to experience Christ personally and to become meaningfully involved in the life and mission of the church of Christ be a priority.

c) That the worship services be celebrative and uplifting, and carefully orchestrated for contemporary relevance and community involvement.

d) That the ministry of the church be anchored in prayerful planning, small group caring and involvement according to gifts, spiritual maturity, and the empowerment of the Holy Spirit.

e) That the church be led by spiritually-discerned leaders/elders who equip and release others to be involved in ministry.

f) That the church be known for its unity of faith and Christ-likeness in lifestyle and concern for the needs of others.

g) That the church keep connected with the community through special attraction entry-level events, neighbourhood involvement and regular advertising.

h) That the church be a place of grace and trust where restoration of hurts, failures and disappointments are experienced.

i) That the church encourage a life of personal stewardship that helps people practice good time usage, personal self-care, financial discretion, and environmental care.

j) That the church posture itself for an active life of witness, growth, and service within and beyond the denomination.

4. Church Ministry Desired Outcomes

Goals are a set of commitments that are made in faith before God to bring about the vision and mission God has assigned. A carefully developed set of goals keeps the congregation going in a consistent direction. John Haggai, in *Lead On*, says goals must be S-M-A-R-T: Specific, Measurable, Attainable, Realistic and Tangible.[2] Church goals are to the church what a hoop is to a basketball court. The church goals need to be both corporate and personal. The personal outcomes are the same for each individual.

a) Each person to experience salvation in Christ.

b) Each person to become baptized on their faith and become an active member of the church.

c) Each person to grow and mature in Christ.

d) Each person to cultivate a personal devotional life with Christ.

e) Each person to be regularly involved in a corporate worship.

f) Each person to be cared for by the church in a "one-to-one" or group situation.

g) Each person to express their gratitude and love for God through regular financial tithing.

h) Each person to be involved in some form of regular ministry according to their ability and spiritual gift mix.

i) Each person to be sharing the joy of their salvation in witness to others as they have opportunity.

j) Each person to participate in the world-wide mission of Christ.

k) Each person to have a social ministry involved with someone in need.

l) Each person positively supporting the leaders of the church.

m) Each person excited and supportive of the local church.

n) Each person to support the extended ministry of Christ through the conference ministry network.

B. The Bigger Picture Church Philosophy

THREE ORGANIZATIONAL COMPONENTS

The philosophy of ministry describes in program language how the various facets of the church will work together to accomplish the purposes of the church. The philosophy will declare what the church will do and will not do. A philosophy of ministry defines the roles of the various agencies, and assures that they are going in the right direction.

1. Worship Celebration—Front Door Ministry

- the body in unity and oneness
- focus on word, worship, and outreach
- entire worshipping family together
- hearing the Word of God together
- the church together intergenerationally
- common experience in tithes & worship
- seasonal high-visibility events for outreach
- same experience in multiple services (Alternate services are considered a church plant known as a "same place" church plant)

2. Ministry Fellowship Groups—Side Door Ministry

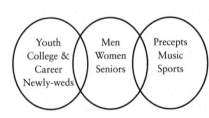

- the body in diversity in varied experiences
- fellowship focused or ministry-directed
- functions in auxiliary to the worship
- group commonality: social and spiritual
- contextual relevance to age, need, content
- friendship fishing pool events
- weekday affinity groups: peer attraction

3. Cell—Care Groups—Home Based Fellowships

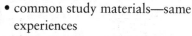

- cell multiplication groups
- focused on personal care-giving
- prayer—fellowship—sharing—growth
- flexible on time and place
- common study materials—same experiences
- open to new people—visitor friendly
- social interaction—spiritual accountability
- spiritual mentoring—apprenticing leaders
- process evangelism

The church can have a clear vision, reasonable goals and a good ministry plan, but if it does not have a united spirit and a harmonious environment, it cannot expect growth from God. Conflict and strife within the body predictably results in church decline, and possible demise or split. The body of Christ must resemble the nature of Christ in its life and work. The fruit of the Spirit must be alive and well in the life of the congregation. Christ made the unity of the believers a high priority.[3]

C. Organizing For Ministry

Doing the work of ministry is the whole point of organizing the congregation. The idea is to free people from being tied up in planning committees as decision makers. The more people that can be channelled into actual ministry, the better. Most church organizations spend more time planning ministry than doing ministry and have more people making ministry decisions than they have people doing the ministry. The organizational structure must guard against an ineffective balance between planning and implementing.

1. Making a Value Choice Between a Decision-Making Priority or a Ministry Priority

a) Many Leaders and Few Workers in Ministry as a Priority

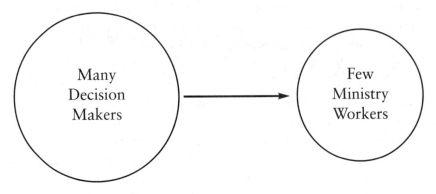

b) Some Leaders and Many Workers in Ministry as a Priority

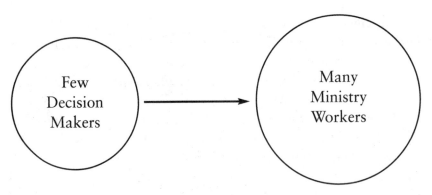

All churches do not need to plan, only those who plan to grow need to do so. Churches that do not need to plan ahead are those that want to stay the same, and keep things to themselves. Churches that plan ahead are those that are interested in new people, and are serious about reaching out to the community. Serious planning is required for those who walk by faith, and for those who follow a vision. New churches need to take much time for evaluation, program adjustment and change. If a ministry is not working out, change must be considered.

2. Developing a Christ-Centred Organization

The new church needs to move forward with an evangelism priority. Church planting is a church evangelism program. The heartbeat of the church is the same as that of the Godhead. The heartbeat of God is about providing a Saviour for the world. The primary purpose of Christ's coming was to seek and to save the lost (humanity). The Holy Spirit has the same redemptive purpose of convicting people of their sin and of empowering people for witness and godly living. The church has the same redemptive priority as that of the Trinity. The church is God's mission committee.

The church needs to organize itself as simply as possible to accomplish its task and fulfill its purposes. The organization needs to be built on the four main pillars of church life with Christ centring each of the four areas.

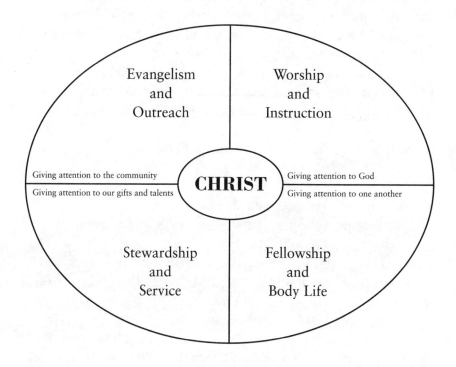

While the church is small each of the above areas may be assigned to the charge of an elder in the church, and as the church grows, a committee or task force may need to be assigned to oversee the four areas of ministry.

PROBLEM

The established churches have become "pro churches" and often expect new churches to operate with the same specialization as the established churches. Leaders must realize that a new church does not come into being as a car loaded with all the extras.

D. The Appointment Of Church Elders

SPIRITUAL PEOPLE WITH LEADERSHIP GIFTS

It is clear from the church-planting records of Paul the apostle that the appointment of elders was a vital part of his church-planting task. The initial church planting leadership came from Paul and Barnabas, after which it was transferred to an elder team from the local church-planting area. The board of elders then took charge of the responsibility of providing spiritual and administrative leadership. In today's setting, the church planter would likely be the chairman of the board of elders for the first year, or until a leader emerges with the spiritual maturity and ministry gifts to take the position.

1. Responsibilities of Elders

a) They are to oversee and shepherd "the flock." That is, they are responsible for the spiritual care and nurture of this church (Acts 20:28-31).
b) They are to instruct, correct, and equip the believers in this church for ministry (Eph. 4:11-13; 1 Tim. 3:2; 2; Tim. 2:24-25).
c) They are to lead in resolving doctrinal and moral issues in an attitude of love and gentleness (Act 15:4,6,23; Gal. 6:1-5).
d) They are to discern and articulate the vision, and goals of the church through prayerful decision-making and meaningful

involvement of the members (Acts 13:1-3; Acts. 6:1-7).

e) They are to formulate and make recommendations on major matters for church approval.

f) They are to coordinate and oversee all the ministries and functions of this church (1 Peter 5:1-10).

g) They are to organize themselves by appointing a vice-chairman, secretary, and overseeing elder for each major department of this church.

h) They are to help believers discover their giftedness and to equip and empower them for ministry.

i) They are accountable first to Jesus Christ, then to each other and the church (Acts 20:28; Heb.13:17; 1 Peter 5:1-5).

2. Elder Duties as Care Group Leaders

In most elder-led congregations, the elders have been discerned and proven by first being leaders of a care group. The elders exercise their primary responsibilities of care-giving and "guarding the flock" by leading a care group. In some churches the elder board consists basically of those who have been spiritually discerned and are prepared to lead a care group along with the pastors who are fellow elders.

3. Initial Appointment of Elders

The first group of elders in a church plant are usually appointed on a temporary basis by the church planter in consultation with the denominational church-planting director. The appointments are temporary because the elders may not be well known and because more qualified leaders could emerge within the first year. The appointment of elders by the church planter follows the model set by Paul.

4. Subsequent Appointments and Discernment Process of Adding Church Elders

a) The elder qualification and duties are taught by the church planter.

b) The number of elders needed is announced to the congregation.

c) A week of congregational prayer for elders is initiated.

d) The members are invited to submit their suggestions to fill the elder vacancies, usually through a bulletin insert.

e) The existing elders discern and short-list the suggested names.

f) The short-listed prospective elders are contacted for availability by the pastor.

g) The list of potential elders for the required vacancies is submitted to the congregation for affirmation.

h) Only as many names are recommended for affirmation as there are vacancies. This is not an election process which creates winners and losers.

i) The primary qualifications for elders are gifts of leadership, wisdom, and discernment along with spiritual maturity.

5. Filling Other Church Ministry Positions According to Spiritual Gifting

The church has the freedom to nominate and elect the other congregational ministry leadership positions. Some churches also fill these positions by appointment to avoid the pain of not being elected.

6. Scriptural Behavioural Guidelines For Elders

a) The elder senses a personal call of God to be an overseer in the church of Jesus Christ (Acts 20:20; 1 Tim. 3:1; Titus 1:5).

b) The elder demonstrates a servanthood attitude towards others in providing leadership willingly according to Scriptures (1 Peter 5:1-3).

c) The elder has a growing marriage relationship with his wife (1 Peter 5:1-3).

d) The elder is able to manage his own family well (1 Tim. 3:4,5).

e) The elder and his wife practice hospitality cheerfully and demonstrate love for others (1 Tim. 3:2; Titus 1:8).

f) The elder and his wife are willing to work together, to the best of their ability, in the work to which God is calling him (1 Cor. 4:1,2).

g) The elder and his wife are not addicted to anything that is controlling their lives (1 Cor. 6:12; 10:23).

h) The elder and his wife are personally committed to Jesus

Christ and his Word (Rom. 12:1,2; 2 Tim. 3:16,17).

i) The elder and his wife have positive and teachable attitudes towards those who are over them in the Lord (Heb.. 13:17).

j) The elder has a respectable Christian reputation in the church and in the community where he lives, works, and relates socially (1 Cor. 4:1-5; 1 Tim. 3:7).

k) The elder desires to do good and pursue personal and practical holiness, seeking to become more and more Christlike (Rom. 8:29; Heb.. 12:14; Titus 1:7-9).

l) The elder has a regular, meaningful personal devotional life (John 15:1-7).

m) The elder does not pursue dishonest gain or the love of money (1 Tim. 3:3).

n) The elder is faithful and able to teach in settings that are formal and informal (Acts 20:20; 1 Tim. 5:17; 2 Tim. 2:2).

o) The elder is able to teach others in sound doctrine, and refute those who oppose sound doctrine (Titus 1:9).

p) The elder is able to exercise self-control over his thoughts, feelings, words, and actions most of the time (Phil. 4:8; 1 Tim. 3:2,3).

q) The elder is not self-willed, overbearing, quarrelsome, quick-tempered, or violent (Titus 1:7).

r) The elder is able to direct the affairs of the church and exercise leadership without lording it over people (1 Tim. 5:17; 1 Peter 5:3).

E. Official Registrations And Record Keeping

START-UP DOCUMENTATION

1. Pastoral License

If the church planters are new to the ministry or to the denomination they will need to apply to the provincial/area denominational office for official licensing and certification procedures. The government requires church pastors to be denominationally approved for ministry certification.

2. Government Charity

Each new church needs to apply to the federal government in order to get a charitable tax number. Official application forms are provided by the charitable organizations branch. Most denominations assist the church in this process.

3. Incorporation

Most churches, upon organization, also apply to the government in order to be officially incorporated as a society. This is not legally required if the church is part of a denomination, since they are covered by its charter.

4. Conference Affiliation

Most conferences have the practice that a new church applies to the provincial/district conference to be recognized as a member church, as soon as possible after their membership-chartering celebrations. The new church is then officially accepted upon recommendation of the denominational agency.

5. Church Documentation

Each new church is requested to submit to the denominational office and to the conference archives a summary story or write-up on how the church was started and what the circumstances were that led to the beginning of this new church.

6. Membership Records

Each new church needs to keep an official set of minutes of all its proceedings as well as an official record of their baptisms, membership, marriages, and funerals. Most conferences have an official membership record book available for this purpose.

7. Government Requirements

The government requires that the church/pastor keep a record of all marriages and funerals, and that appropriate statistical records be kept in a government-provided record book. The church will also need to provide annual financial data to the government.

8. *Essential Resources*

Most church conferences have available for the new pastor's guidance, at a minimum cost, a leadership manual, membership record book, certificates of baptism, certificates of membership, discipleship manual, confession of faith, conference handbook, as well as denominational distinctives and policies.

Sound Health Check

As the human body is subject to good health and poor health, so the corporate body must keep fit and guard against corporate ill health. Some of the more serious afflictions within the body of Christ are an infected tongue, splintered eye, stopped ear, and corrupted mind. The experts of body health refer to the church diseases as ethnikitis, old age, people blindness, hyper cooperation, koinonitis, sociological strangulation, and arrested spirituality. Every church needs to take a health inventory from time to time to assure that it is free from disease.[4]

F. The Organization Of A Church Constitution

In order to determine how the church is to function, it needs to spell out the values that are to be reflected in the church constitution. If the church is to be congregational in government or led by an eldership structure or have any other philosophy of government, the organization principles need to declare the particular system of government that is to be followed. Before the church constitution is written, the church should decide on the values, leadership understanding, and church governance that they want to protect or enshrine in their constitution. Some of the listed principles will need to be placed into the church operational by-laws while some are best fitted into the constitution.

1. Organization Principles

a) The constitution should be crafted in such a way that the goals, values, and mission of the church are effectively accomplished.

b) The constitution should reflect a process which assures that every individual will have an opportunity for guided growth.

c) The constitution should call for a minimum number of persons to be tied up in elected committees and a maximum number involved in church ministry.

d) The constitution should assure that those in ministry leadership positions are church members who in turn are accountable to the church elders/congregation.

e) The constitution structure should make provision for ministers and deacons (leadership team) to emerge and serve from within the congregation based on their gifts, maturity, spiritual calling, and church affirmation.

f) The constitution should allow for generous opportunity for the program leaders/committees to make their own decisions as affecting their ministry.

g) The constitution needs to assure that each program area that is connected to the entire church body has at least one spiritually-approved leader who answers to the church through the church elders. This may vary among denominations.

h) The constitution should assure that key leadership positions are filled on the bases of spiritual maturity, gift discernment, and the availability of suitable people.

i) The constitution should provide for some involvement within the church ministry, in non-elected positions, of those that are not yet members of the church.

j) The constitution should allow for those ministry positions that require a special skill, or a short-term task, to be filled by appointment rather than election.

2. Constituting Service

Some churches have a special constituting celebration service which marks the official organizing of the church. The congregation officially accepts the constitution and the church-planting launch team resigns and the first new church officers are appointed according to the constitution or guidelines. This constituting service is often combined with the membership-chartering service.

3. *Church Constitution/By-laws*

MENNONITE BRETHREN SAMPLE [5]

Date: _____

CHURCH CONSTITUTION

ARTICLE I—CHURCH NAME

This is the formal constitution of the church whose official name is

Name _____

Location _____

ARTICLE II—BIBLICAL CHURCH PURPOSE

The purpose of the church shall be to worship and glorify God by:

a) providing spiritual fellowship and worship for its attenders.
b) providing an evangelism and witness ministry in the community.
c) providing Christian Education and nurture for all participants.
d) promoting mission and services at home and abroad.
e) promoting and following the teachings of the Bible.

ARTICLE III—CONFERENCE AFFILIATION

The church is a member of the provincial/district conference of Mennonite Brethren churches and is thereby also affiliated with the other levels of Mennonite Brethren Conferences. All articles and by-laws of this church shall be in accordance with the above-named Conferences.

ARTICLE IV—CONFESSION OF FAITH

The church accepts the Bible as the supreme and final authority in matters of faith and conduct. The confession of faith of the Conference of Mennonite Brethren Churches shall be the official confession of the church.

ARTICLE V—HISTORIC DISTINCTIVES

The Mennonite Brethren church follows in the Anabaptist traditions of the reformer Menno Simons, who sought to return the church to a practical biblical foundation, personal faith for salvation, and baptism upon the believer's confession. The focus of the reformation included the involvement of all believers in witness, simple worship, and church-affirmed leadership. This radical discipleship included separation from the sins of the world and a commitment to peace and love in family, community, and country.

ARTICLE VI—CHURCH PROPERTY

Real estate and properties acquired by the church shall be officially registered in the name of the Mennonite Brethren Conference and so be protected by the denominational Charter.

ARTICLE VII—FISCAL YEAR/FINANCES

The fiscal year of the church shall end on December 31 of each year. The church treasurer shall be responsible for preparing and presenting to the leadership team and the church the financial statements and the annual budget. The financial records shall be subject to audits as assigned by the church leadership team. The audited financial annual reports/budgets shall be presented to the congregation.

ARTICLE VIII—CONSTITUTION AMENDMENTS

Any church member or committee of the church may with good reason initiate a proposed constitutional change by submitting it in writing to the church moderator or pastor. The leadership team, after review, study, and approval then shall present a notice of motion two weeks prior to presenting the proposed amendment to the membership for consideration. A two-thirds majority vote of the attenders of a duly called meeting are required to carry a motion to amend the constitution.

ARTICLE IX—CHURCH DISSOLUTION

In the event of dissolution or disassociation of this church, all assets remain the property of the denomination. The board of directors of the denomination are the official executors of the church in the event of dissolution or disassociation. The conference executive and the church-planting agency shall be consulted before the church considers dissolution or disassociation.

CHURCH BY-LAWS

ARTICLE I—CHURCH MEMBERSHIP

Section 1: Membership Qualifications

Church membership is open to any person who believes Jesus Christ to be the Son of God and accepts Him as his/her personal Saviour and acknowledges Him as Master and Lord of their life. Anyone who has confessed his sins and repented of them and puts his trust in the love and mercy of God through Christ, and seeks the guidance of the Holy Spirit for a consistent Christian life, and is prepared to publicly witness to this position of faith through the ordinance of baptism or has already done so, is welcome to apply for membership.

Section 2: Reception of Members

It is the responsibility of the church leadership team (elders) to examine the faith of prospective members and to recommend new people to the church for membership. There are four ways that members may be received:

    a) Through baptism by immersion upon a personal faith. (the church practices baptism by immersion because it believes this mode best symbolizes the biblical meaning of baptism and conversion.)

b) Through a certificate of transfer from another church within the same denomination.

c) Through a letter of recommendation, when the applicant is a member of another denomination and is baptized upon his/her faith. The church also accepts into membership believers baptized by a mode other than immersion.

d) Through a re-affirmation of faith by a person who has been out of fellowship with Christ after having been a baptized believer in the past.

Each person requesting membership will be interviewed by the pastor and church leadership team (elders) and will be required to share their testimony of faith with the congregation. Each member will participate in orientation sessions that cover the faith, values, and visions of the church, as well as the policies and history of the denomination. Request for membership is made to the pastor by filling in the request forms provided by the church.

Section 3: Responsibilities of Church Members

a) To pray for one another (Jas. 5:16)

b) To participate in regular worship (Heb. 10:25)

c) To be loyal in fellowship and ministry (Acts 2:42)

d) To give financial support/tithing (2 Cor. 8:5; 9:7)

e) To live a Christ-like life (Eph. 5:18)

f) To participate in witness and service (1 Cor. 12)

g) To uphold the Scriptures (2 Tim. 2:15)

h) To help build the unity and integrity of the church (John 17:21)

i) To support the leadership of the church (Hebrews 13:17)

Section 4: Responsibilities of the Church to the Members

a) To teach them (Eph. 4:11-16)

b) To encourage them (Heb. 10:23-25)

c) To give guidance and leadership (Acts 20:28-35)

d) To admonish and correct them (Matt. 18:15-20)

e) To provide fellowship (Acts 2:42)

f) To help in times of need (Acts 6:1-1 1)

g) To provide service opportunities (Acts 13:1-3)

h) To provide regular worship experiences (Heb. 10:24)

i) To protect them from biblical unfaithfulness (1 Peter 4:1-3)

j) To protect the unity and integrity of the church (John 17:21)

Section 5: Change of Membership

One of the distinctives of the New Testament Church is that membership is by voluntary commitment. Even though individual members are encouraged to commit themselves to a long-term relationship to the church, membership can be terminated or changed in the following ways:

a) By transfer to another church by request from the member.

b) By individual request to have membership discontinued.

c) By congregational action should the member be willfully subscribing to a faith or lifestyle which is in contradiction to that held by the congregation based on biblical teachings.

ARTICLE II—CHURCH GOVERNANCE AND LEADERSHIP

The basic governance structure and leadership involvement of the church is based on spiritual gifting, spiritual maturity, and proven leadership qualities. The church assumes that all believers should be involved in church ministries, and those with spiritual leadership gifts should be involved in church leadership. The governance structure reflects the blended action of discerned leadership elders and congregational affirmation. The leadership selection is a spiritual discernment process rather than a democratic election process.

Section 1: Leadership Team/Elders

The church shall be led by a spiritual leadership team/elders that have first been suggested by the members of the church, then discerned and approved by the leadership team/elders and finally affirmed by the membership. The leadership team/elders shall include the pastor, moderator, secretary and at least three other ministry leaders, with one being responsible for finances.

Section 2: Ministry Committees

The leadership team/elders shall recommend to the congregation for affirmation such committees as needed to oversee its ministry and to accomplish the church's objectives and vision. These committees first report to the leadership team/elders and then to the congregation. The by-laws shall spell out the election procedures and terms to be served.

Section 3: Church Membership Meetings

A minimum of two membership/congregational meetings shall take place annually. The first shall be the church annual meeting, which shall take place within two months of the calendar year-end, to approve the church budget, review ministry reports and approve recommendations. The second meeting shall be in fall, for the purpose of sharing the vision of the church, celebrating God's blessing and dealing with recommendations.

Section 4: Church Membership Responsibilities

The church membership approves pastoral staff appointments, church elder placements, and property or building acquisition. The membership also evaluates and affirms the continuance of both elders and pastoral positions every three years.

ARTICLE III: LEADERSHIP JOB DESCRIPTIONS

The by-laws of the church shall spell out ministry job descriptions for all of the approved leadership roles and define the purposes of each church committee. The by-laws shall describe how the church is to function in its day-to-day activity. The by-laws can be amended as needed by the church leadership team/elders. The by-laws also spell out election procedures and the length of term in office.

ARTICLE IV—DONATIONS AND TITHING

The church understands the spirit of the New Testament giving to be regular, intentional, joyous, and according to ability. The programs of the church and its denomination are dependent on personal tithing, donations and special offerings. The church trusts God to supply its financial needs through the faithfulness and good stewardship of His people. Donations are receipted at the end of the year for tax-exemption purposes.

ARTICLE V—MINISTRY PARTICIPATION

Participation in the ministries of the church shall be open to anyone in the community who is prepared to follow the stated purpose of the church. The church's programs are designed to provide a ministry to the members as well as to community people, and so it welcomes anyone to attend and to participate in its ministries.

NOTES——

[1] Rick Warren, *The Purpose-Driven Church* (Grand Rapids, Michigan: Zondervan Publishing House, 1995), p. 109.

[2] John Haggai, *Lead On* (Waco, Texas: Word Books, 1986), p. 3.

[3] C. Peter Wagner, *Leading Your Church to Growth* (Ventura, California: Regal Books, 1984). *The Bigger Picture Philosophy* is adapted from Wagner's Celebration Congregation and Cell concepts. pp. 206-208.

[4] Wagner, pp. 181-185.

[5] The sample constitution is taken from the British Columbia Board of Church Extension Policy Guidelines and does not represent an actual church document.

NINE

Church Membership

The gifts that appear in 1 Corinthians 12 are clearly reflective of the entire membership, not just of a chosen few: 'All these (gifts) are the work of one and the same Spirit, and he gives them to each one just as he determines' (verse 11). There is something very noble about a community that values and encourages its members (including children) to share their gifts. In fact, what the church says when it values the gifts of individual members, is that it values its members as individuals. In our age of depersonalization, this is a precious gift indeed.

David Giesbrecht, *Mennonite Brethren Herald.*

The church is unique and different from all other institutions in that it was established by Jesus Christ. He said, "I will build My church." It is God's choice way of presenting himself and his ministry of redemption to our neighbourhoods. The church is an institution so closely knit in fellowship with interdependent and indispensable duties to perform, that it is best described as a body. In this fellowship body, distinctions of race, colour, nationality, and social status disappear under the headship of Jesus Christ. The functions of this body are group functions that call for a fellowship of members who devote themselves to the apostles' teachings, fellowship, breaking of bread, and prayer. The biblical nature and purpose of the church is such that it requires the presence of and the action of recognizable local church groups with members who are aware of each other.

This chapter provides some biblical and practical reasons for church membership. It also provides some practical steps and an application to facilitate the entry process of a church. By joining a church, a believer is clearly making a statement of wanting to belong and participate in all of the aspects of a church. By not joining the church and withholding membership, a person is also making a statement. It is first a statement to oneself that church participation is conditional; a statement to the pastor that there is not full acceptance; a statement to the other members of not fully agreeing with the church; a statement to those outside the church who may ask if the church claims to have the answers to life's questions, why its attenders are not even becoming members.

A. Organized Church Membership

PRACTICAL AND BIBLICAL REASONS FOR CHURCH MEMBERSHIP

Most church planters will very quickly discover that there are always some attenders and new converts that have an initial resistance to church membership. With their new-found freedom in Christ, some feel that local membership is unnecessary since they now belong to the so-called invisible or universal body of Christ. It is important that the new believers be fitted and knitted into the functional local body of Christ. Christ clearly showed his discontent about mere secret admirers or distant followers. He listed his disciples by name and number. The full dynamics of body membership comes into clear focus in Acts where the believers are described as being added to the church daily. Reasons for membership today:

1. Membership as a Visible Reality

Christ describes his church as a visible, identifiable reality on earth. The New Testament talks about the church by name and place, i.e. Corinth, Ephesia, Galatia, etc. Christ also lists his disciples by name. The Scripture makes a point of making visible and experiential the believers' deep inner experiences and relationships with Christ. Conversion is connected to a public faith encounter. Water baptism visually expresses an inward reality; communion again is a public, visible confession and proclamation, in the same way membership makes for a public, visible expression of belonging to God and to one another. Membership is a statement of being part of God's family.

2. Membership as a Unity Statement

In church membership the believers declare their unity of faith and common understanding of the scriptures. The members exercise an accountability to one another for biblical faithfulness and spiritual integrity. Membership declares an attitude of submission, humility, and acceptance of body life. Membership brings the body together onto the same theological page for united action. It is a rally occasion, where the church values and orientation are agreed upon and accepted by each member. A formal church role provides for the possibility to set biblical standards and spiritual qualifications for membership.

3. Membership as a Recognition of Need

Individual Christianity tends to develop blind spots in understanding and interpretation of scripture due to environment, attitudes, background, training, experiences, and personal desires. A membership body provides wholesome corrective to such individualism. The sum total of spiritual insight and understanding of a united Christian body exceeds that of anyone's individual understanding. We need to be tied to other believers for spiritual balance. In membership the church recognizes its interdependence.

4. Membership as a Growth Facilitator

The very process and act of officially joining a church is an occasion of personal growth. It is a commitment to support the local church. By joining the church, individuals are declaring their loyalty to be functional members of the church. It is a decision to move from being an anonymous Christian to being identified as a committed church member. Membership is to a church what student enrollment is to a college. It is a commitment to growth and involvement which goes beyond attendance. .

5. Membership as a Sheepfold Home

Membership identifies one's willingness and readiness to be shepherded. In this shepherding process the human shepherd/pastor knows who are in the local sheepfold and the sheep know who is their pastoral shepherd to whom they can turn for pastoral care, spiritual guidance, and protection. A mutual understanding of loyalty and support is established through church belonging.

6. Membership as Teamwork

The united cooperative action of believers achieves more results than uncoordinated individual efforts. When the church works together as a body with its varied spiritual gifts, a harmonious working relationship is achieved. The great commission of going, preaching, baptizing, and teaching is best achieved in a devoted cooperative effort. It is doing together what cannot be done alone. Membership brings structure, order, and reason to the disciplines and duties of a church. It identifies the group that is responsible to act decisively when a decision needs to be made.

7. Membership as an Assimilation and Commitment

There is a significant commitment change that happens when a person takes the step from being a church attender to being a church member. Church attendance does not have the same level of ownership and responsibility that church membership expects. The level of assimilation, connection, involvement, and ownership is measurably increased with church membership. It is much easier to walk away from church responsibility or accountability and even regular attendance when people are not ready to commit to being a church member.

8. Membership as the New Testament Model

A church with members best reflects the New Testament Church model. In the book of Acts, repeated reference is made to people accepting the Word or believing the gospel and being added to the church. Not only are convert's names added to the eternal book of life, as sited in Revelation, they also have a practical need to be added to a local church body. Together in membership the church shares its human and financial resources. There is a strong suggestion that the New Testament church had a formal membership and they knew who belonged to their local churches. They were able to name those who defected.

9. Membership for Protection

Formal membership is a protection against infiltration of enemy forces. It helps to expose people seeking influence and authority. The membership entry process helps to screen and identify the people with false motives from those joining the church with spiritually pure motives of seeking to participate in the family of God. The church membership helps set some logical boundaries for exercising church discipline.

10. Membership as a Spiritual Community

It is within the committed body that true community is experienced. Here grace and love are freely extended and forgiveness is experienced. It is in this environment of covenant that individuals begin to experience the care and love of the body. Church membership helps the leaders to identify the local bride of Christ that is eager to experience the fellowship and care of Christ the bridegroom in his relationship with the church, the bride.

11. Membership for Historic Continuity

The church, through its members, has formed a historic church chain from biblical times until the present. Throughout history, God has used the church to preserve and to propagate the gospel of Christ. The church today needs to assure that the present church link in the chain is strong, so that those after us will have the same privilege of being part of the historic church chain. As a fire burns longer and brighter when many sticks are burning together, so the church in a covenant relationship generates more heat, light, and health when knitted together from generation to generation. As Christ gave his life for the establishment of the church, so its members give themselves to be the church in a visible way. Membership has proven to be useful throughout the centuries of church life.[1]

B. Church Membership Realities

PREPARATION AND UNDERSTANDING

It is important for all born-again believers who have no local church home to attach themselves as members of the church in the interest of their spiritual welfare and continuous growth. Membership means personal attachment and a belonging which is mutually appreciated and recognized in the local church. Therefore, a person should be a member wherever he/she resides whether for a short or longer period. Certificates and papers are important only in so far that they provide for a visible and concrete way of making the attachments and detachments between churches. Membership is an effective way of combatting noncommittal, self-centred Christian living and provides for a wholesome integration and development of the Christian. The Christian life cannot be honestly lived in isolation.

1. Membership Orientation Seminar/Membership Preparation Content

Most churches have a process of membership preparation, instruction, or orientation. For the church planter it is very important to describe the meaning of the local church and to explain the expectations and meaning of membership. This is done in the form of a membership orientation seminar.

(Church membership applications to be handed in after the seminar) **Seminar Course Outline** (To be offered twice before chartering)

• Statement of faith of the denomination local church mission,

values, purpose, structure, and leadership
- Understanding personal commitment/salvation
- Personal faith sharing and mission understanding
- Involvement according to one's calling, gift mix/S-H-A-P-E
- Church ordinances—baptism and Lord's supper
- Membership information/application and covenant
- Church finances and tithing
- Denominational history, distinctives and values
- Global involvements in missions and education
- Conference structures and ministries

2. Prerequisites for membership

a) A credible personal commitment to Jesus Christ and water baptism based upon a confession of faith.

b) A commitment to live according to the biblical guidelines of a holy life separated from the spirit of worldliness.

c) A willingness to be accountable to the spiritual leaders of the church with a teachable spirit and an attitude of mutual submission.

d) A commitment to promote the unity of the church and to support the leaders of the church.

e) A commitment to support the church values, ministry direction, and worship style.

3. Membership Responsibilities

As in a family, so in the church, the members have responsibilities which include: praying and caring for one another, regular worship participation, fellowship, financial support, Christ-like living, witnessing, faithfulness to the Word, building church unity, and supporting the leadership of the church. (For a fuller listing of duties see the sample constitution in Chapter Eight on organization.)

4. Church Responsibilities to Members

The church leaders need to assure that the church members are being cared for, which includes: teaching and leading, encouraging and nurturing, admonishing and protecting, looking after needs, providing worship and service opportunities, and spiritually feeding the flock.

5. Membership Reception

There are four ways that members may be received: (a) through baptism by immersion upon a personal faith; (b) through transfer from another church in the denomination; (c) through a letter of recommendation from a Christian church not in the denomination; (d) through the re-affirmation of faith by a person who has been a member but has wandered away from the faith. All the above assume a baptism upon confession of faith.

6. Membership Changes

Even though long-term membership in a church is encouraged, it is possible to move out of church membership in three ways: (a) by transfer to another church; (b) by request to have membership discontinued; (c) by congregational action when the biblical qualifications of church membership are being compromised.

C. Church Membership Organization Steps

The membership organization service usually takes place several months after the grand opening or official launch of the public worship services of a new church. A new church should consider organizing into a membership church when they have 15 baptized members or more.

MEMBERSHIP ORGANIZING STEPS IN A CHURCH PLANT

1. Inform the attenders well in advance that the church will be having a membership-organizing service and that each attender is invited to consider membership.

2. Announce that this new church will expect to have a baptism service for those who have not been baptized upon their faith.

3. All prospective members are expected to attend a church orientation seminar (membership classes or base 101). This three- to

four-hour seminar should be offered several times before the membership Sunday to give people a choice to fit their schedule.

4. Each person expecting to become a member should indicate this by filling out the membership covenant information application form after attending the church orientation seminar. See sample on page 181.

5. The people planning to join the church as members should be given an opportunity to briefly share their faith journey (testimony) as part of the Sunday worship service. These testimonies could be scheduled over a series of Sundays.

6. Those who are transferring in their membership from other churches should make transfer arrangements before the membership Sunday. The transfer members also participate in the church-orientation seminar.

7. The membership service should involve the church-planting director who usually leads the membership chartering and covenanting ceremony in the context of the denomination. The church planter presents each member with a membership certificate/card.

8. The newly-organized church is usually recommended to be accepted as a member church in the denomination at their annual convention.

9. The names and addresses of all new church members should be submitted to the conference headquarters to receive the denominational periodicals.

10. Church members in a new church usually come from three sources, with about one third of the people coming from each source:

    a) Conversion & baptism of new people
    b) Reaffirmation of faith
    c) Membership transfer from Christian churches

11. Most evangelical churches combine baptism with membership. When a person is baptized they are then welcomed as members of the church. Baptism by meaning symbolizes having died to

the old life and having been raised to a new life in the body of Christ. Baptism is the gateway into the local body of believers, where the true meaning of baptism is lived out in a covenant relationship with one another. True discipleship cannot be lived out in isolation from other believers, and baptism signals the person's sincerity in belonging to and following Christ. Church membership facilitates the commitment made in baptism. Hence, the two belong together.

RICK WARREN, *CIRCLES OF COMMITMENT*

Church membership is part of the Congregational circle and involves an intentional commitment to go beyond the Community and Crowd circles. The committed and core ministry circles of people make even more commitments than membership. Rick Warren depicts this moving from the outer circle towards the centre.[2]

Rick Warren

YOUR COMMUNITY
Those living around your church who never attend or only attend occasionally.

YOUR CROWD
Those who attend regularly, but are not members.

YOUR CONGREGATION
Those who are committed to both Christ and membership in your church family.

YOUR COMMITTED
Those members who are serious about growing to spiritual maturity.

YOUR CORE
Those members who are actively serving in ministry in your church, the community, and the world.

D. Church Membership Application

It is important that the entry process into a church is made simple and uniform. The attendance in a new church will be from a wide variety of church backgrounds and experiences. It is therefore important that specific information pamphlets be available on membership qualifications, reception procedures, membership privileges, and responsibilities. The membership application form facilitates and clarifies the entry process into the church.

(Complete this form and return it to your pastor
after the orientation seminar)

MEMBERSHIP REQUEST FORM

Name _____ Date _____

Address _____ Phone _____

Place/Date of Birth _____ Occupation _____

Marital Status: Single___ Married___ Divorced___ Remarried___ Widowed___

Name of Spouse _____

Names/Ages of Children _____

_____

Name the churches you have been associated with in the past (if any) and indicate if as a member or an adherent: _____

_____

Previous church involvement/positions _____

Indicate by which of the following means you are requesting membership:
_____ 1. Baptism upon a personal faith
_____ 2. Transfer from a church within the denomination
_____ 3. Letter of recommendation from another believers' church
_____ 4. Reaffirmation of faith
_____ 5. Other circumstance (explain)_____

Comment on the following:

1. Describe how you became a Christian _____

_____

_____

2. Describe your baptism _____

_____

3. Why do you want to be a member of this church? _____

_____

4. Provide the name and telephone of a person for a reference _____

_____

My Covenant

    I hereby indicate my desire to be a member of this church and commit myself, by God's grace, to the following:

    1. To live in accordance with the values and lifestyle of the Bible.
    2. To faithfully participate in the worship and ministries of the church.
    3. To actively cultivate friendship and fellowship in the congregation.
    4. To embrace and promote the mission, goals and values of the church.
    5. To get involved in tasks in keeping with my spiritual gifts.
    6. To pursue spiritual growth through regular prayer and Bible study.
    7. To support God's Kingdom through regular church donations/tithes.
    8. To protect the unity of the church through affirmative action.
    9. To seek wherever possible to be a positive witness for Christ.
10. To support and affirm the leaders of the church.

With the help of God I will seek to be faithful to this covenant.

Signature _____Date _____

Using the reverse side, describe your spiritual journey, making reference to your background, spiritual commitments, growth, and church involvements.

Information in this application will be guarded respectfully.

E. Membership-Chartering Celebration

The membership-chartering service is a culminating celebration of the first phase of the church planter's labours. In this celebration the charter members covenant together to be a unified, functional body. In preparation for this celebration, all the prospective members declare themselves through the membership application. Church transfers are arranged and a baptism service planned so that all attenders have equal opportunity to become part of the chartering group. This chartering service is usually expected to happen within three to five months of the launching service. The membership chartering is also known as a constituting service.

1. Membership Chartering Celebration—Sample Order of Service

Worship Time
Greetings and Acknowledgements by the Church Planter
Appreciation of all attenders/community people
Recognition of leadership team contribution
Explanation of the church-planting steps
- preparation, launch, chartering, conference acceptance
- expression of faith, baptism, and membership
Acknowledgement of God's guidance and blessing
Introduction of Guests and Greetings (one or two officials)
Public officials: mayor, principal, etc.
Denominational leaders
One of the guests does a greeting/congratulations
Ceremonial Membership Chartering (denominational leader)
Brief review of membership meaning
Introduction of members joining
Reading of a covenant together
Prayer of dedication and blessing (several people)
Presentation of membership welcome card/certificate
Welcome handshake by church planter and denominational leader

Response
    Testimonials (one or two)
    Parent church pastor, etc.
    New member testimonial
Worship/Music Response
Message
    Charge to the Congregation/Membership
    "Faithfulness to the Purposes of Christ's Church"
Refreshments

2. Charter Members Covenant (Sample)

Introduction

This is the day that the Lord has made; let us be glad and rejoice in it. We believe it to be the Lord's will that believers be united together for the purpose of representing the cause of Jesus Christ here on earth. Today we are officially recognizing that God has raised up a witnessing body in the community, of which we are glad. We believe that God has laid the foundations of this church and that it is by God's grace and according to His plan that this church is being organized.

Charge to the Forming Congregation

Today we are here to acknowledge the will of God for this church. We believe that God has brought together this congregation for the purpose of being the body of Christ in this community. We believe it to be biblical for believers to unite together as churches in mutual and continued love, in support of one another and of the Gospel. If this congregation is of the same mind and is in favour of being the church of Christ as a united body, and is in favour of expressing this unity as the community church within the fellowship of the sponsoring denomination, we ask you to answer "Yes."

Response From the Forming Congregation

We, the members of this new congregation do hereby covenant together to organize as the community church. We have each received the Lord Jesus Christ as our Saviour and sincerely desire to serve him as our Lord. We have also been baptized as a testimony of our faith in Jesus Christ. We are in agreement with the denomination Statement of Faith, and will endeavour by God's help to lead a Christian life consistent with the principles outlined in the church's biblical covenant.

Affirmation by the Denomination
We as a denomination welcome you with joy into our communion and fellowship. We pledge to you our help and prayers. We want to walk with you in Christian fellowship and love. May the unity of Christ and the gifts of the Spirit and the love of God the Father truly cause you to be the body of Christ in every way.

Prayer of Dedication and Commitment

Listing of the Charter Members

3. *Charter Members' Covenant*

(Church) _____

(Address) _____

which organized on the special date of _____

We the members do hereby officially organize as a new congregation of obedient believers and followers of Jesus Christ, the Head of the church. This church is being organized with the understanding that the Bible, God's Word, is the church's rule of faith and practice. We accept the denominational Statement of Faith and commit ourselves to faithful partnership in the ministry and mission of the sponsoring conference.

As members we covenant together to be a faithful Body of Christ in worship, education, fellowship, growth and evangelism.

(signatures) _____

_____

_____

_____

_____

_____

_____

_____

_____

_____

_____

F. New Member Assimilation Factors

KNITTING AND FITTING PEOPLE INTO THE BODY

Bringing people to Christ and into meaningful membership, fellowship and ministry of the church involves a two-track process. The first focuses on salvation, and the second on body participation. The glue that helps people become knitted and fitted into the church varies from person to person. The assimilation and integration process involves:

1. Genuine Commitment

The spirit of Christ that comes to a person through conversion is the basic integrator into Christ's Body. It is hard to assimilate someone who is not fully committed.

2. Christian Friendship

Church friends are indispensable to meaningful church integration. A bond of fellowship built through a trust relationship will have a binding effect.

3. Theological Growth

When newcomers to the church are experiencing growth and theological agreement they will assimilate without reserve.

4. Shared Experiences

Group experiences such as camping trips, picnics, sports events, etc. are great contributors to the incorporation process. These less formal events tend to be less threatening and more attractive to the new attender.

5. Information Flow

For new people to feel a part of the action they need to be well informed on the activity track of the church. Being included on the inside information track signals inclusiveness.

6. Goal Involvement

Newcomers need to be included in helping to achieve major church goals. As in hockey, there is a need for a new team member to get an assist, or in fact score a team-winning goal. So in the church, people need to be contributors to the goal process to feel that they belong and are appreciated.

7. Peer Relationship

Being accepted in a church peer group where one experiences significant commonality of interest, talent and experience, enhances the assimilation process. A peer group relationship is inviting.

8. Common Ground

People with similar cultural backgrounds often find it easier to connect with a church of similar ethnic background and experience.

9. Leadership Personality

Church leaders are an important doorway for new people. These people often first connect with the pastor, then with a group, and finally with the entire church.

10. Celebration Spirit

People like to be part of something that generates enthusiasm. A positive, celebrating church climate will draw people. Fellowship around banquet tables or picnics is important for personalized ministry and relationship building.

11. Harmonious Environment

A new church needs to have a growth-conducive environment. It needs to have a harmonious, non-confrontational, and affirming, warm climate for people to connect meaningfully. You cannot expect a young plant to grow in a garden that is full of rocks and weeds, or if the climate is too wet/dry or cold. Conflict drives people away from the church.

12. Practical Communication

Churchy slogans and complicated theological terminology will not be suitable for the new listener's diet. Both the message and the music need to be simple and practical in order for it to become food for a hungry heart. Wherever Christ is lifted up, people want to be present.

13. Care Group

Regular participation in a care group results in significant bonding with the church. It is here that one experiences significance, belonging and pastoral care.

14. Pastoral Acceptance and Affirmation

People feel integrated when they experience warmth, affirmation, and acceptance from the pastor. In many ways the pastor is the gatekeeper to congregational integration.

NOTES——

[1] *The Organized Church Membership* was adapted from an article written by the writer for Mennonite Brethren Herald.

[2] The *Rick Warren Concentric Circles* diagram was taken from a Saddleback seminar workshop handout.

TEN

Daughter Parenting

Every church contains the seed for other churches. The local church was meant to reproduce itself over and over again. As a healthy plant forms seeds that when planted bring forth other plants, so healthy churches form seeds that produce other churches. There is a price to be paid for planting of that seed. But there is a far greater price to pay if the seed is not planted.

Keith Bailey.

It is widely claimed that church planting is the most effective and biblical way of fulfilling the great commission of making disciples of all nations. Bringing people to Christ and into fellowship in the Body of Christ effectively fulfills the call of going out to preach, to baptize and to teach converts to observe all that Christ taught. Church planting is best done by local churches. This chapter provides a framework for parenting a daughter church. It seeks to break down some of the barriers of resistance and to provide a doable process for a mother church to follow.

A. Developing A Church Parenting Framework

Church planting needs to be seen as the normal experience of every church, just as marriage and the beginning of new families is the normal expectation of young people entering adulthood. Church planting is part of the normal cycle of a church.

1. Determine The Church-Planting Goal

The church-planting goal is to establish self-governing, self-supporting and reproducing congregations, all of which requires concerted focus and effort. The goal is threefold, with the third being the most difficult to achieve.

a) Self-governing

The new church will put into place a biblical pattern of leadership consisting of a spiritually-qualified team of elders who will lead the church into a program of ministry where each one has a ministry involvement according to his/her giftedness. The organizational structures need toreflect flexibility, changeability and practicality.

b) Self-supporting

The new church will develop their ministries according to the size and affordability of the church. Any start-up subsidies should be short-term with a clearly spelled out subsidy phase-out schedule. Stewardship and tithing need to be modelled by the leaders and practised by the people.

c) Self-reproducing

The new church from its very beginning needs to have an understanding to be a witnessing and evangelizing congregation, where each of the members seeks to reproduce themselves by leading others to Christ and where the church itself has a long-range plan of reproducing itself in another church plant. This outreach mind set must be clearly reflected in the church's philosophy of ministry and training focus.

2. Accept Basic Church Motivation for Planting Daughter Churches

It is important for the mother church to enter a church birthing process with enthusiasm and good will. An emerging daughter church wants to be seen as a legitimately wanted child. Launching a church for the right reason is most important.

a) Mission
The vision for growth needs to be developed and cultivated over a period of time. If the church is shown how effective new churches are in reaching new people, a more positive disposition toward church parenting is generated. Planting churches is central to God's global mission design.

b) Privilege
It is a privilege to be a link in the chain of sharing the church of Christ with others around the world. A church needs to see the joys and privileges attached to being directly involved in helping to provide a new church for a group of people who may not otherwise be reached with the gospel.

c) Obedience
The church belongs to Christ. It is never "our church" and so there is nothing to protect or guard. Christians need to reflect a giving and sacrificing spirit at the local church level for the purpose of sharing Christ's church with all groups of people. Church planting by parenting is an expression of obedience to Christ.

d) Diversity
Church planting provides for more church options or choices within a diversified society. New churches can more easily provide the needed ministry styles and worship philosophies that people want and need. The new and younger generation can be attracted more easily to a church model that is current, new, and less traditional. New churches are less encumbered with traditions and expectations.

e) Evangelism
New churches are more effective in bringing people to Christ

and into fellowship in the Body of Christ. People not accustomed to attending church are also more ready to make their re-entry into church life in a new church.

f) Revitalization

A mother church usually experiences revitalization through leadership rotation and recruitment for a church plant. Leaders need new challenges and a daughter church facilitates new leadership involvement. (For a full treatment of church motivations for church planting see the chapter on Crucial Beginnings.)

3. Breaking the Resistance Barrier of the Mother Church

It takes much courage and faith to start a daughter church. Most churches are afraid to launch a new church through a carefully-planned process. Consequently, new church starts too often happen by reaction, division, or at best by permission. Some of the main reasons for the hesitation to daughter church planting occur when the central mission of the church is not kept in focus. Reasons for resisting:

a) Unfamiliar

Church planting is new and unfamiliar. Churches are not used to planning for something that seems as radical as church planting. They are not used to thinking of church planting as a normal function of a faithful church.

b) Unaffordable

The idea of planting a new church brings fear and uncertainty. Church people fear failure, they fear the expenses of a new church, and they fear losing some of their best and most energetic leaders.

c) Disruption

There is a genuine concern that church planting will be disruptive to the church. It will break the unity of family, friends and fellowship.

d) Unnecessary

Church planting can easily be rationalized away as being unnecessary because the church is not yet overcrowded, or the church is too small for such a large undertaking, or because it is considered an optional idea.

e) Lack of Vision

For the most part, churches resist church planting for lack of vision. They have difficulty thinking beyond the needs of their own church.

f) Power Brokers

There could be a group of people who fundamentally resist any advances by the leadership for change. They insist on a unanimous vote to be passed and then usually vote against it. It is important for the church planter to hear the concerns of the opposers and to personally share the vision with them and then to ask for their support for this biblical vision.

B. Preparing The Mother Church For A Birth

Church planting needs to be seen as a normal function and expectation of a church, just as marriage and the beginning of new families is the normal expectation of children entering adulthood. Just as parents do not want their children to stay home all their lives, so the church should be determined to send out missionaries and church planters as a sign of health and faithfulness.

1. Church Continuity

The church needs to be willing to give people for the cause of multiplication. Every church contains "seed" people for new churches. Churches should never see themselves at the end of the line or in a "dead-end-street" situation. Churches need to see themselves as a link in a chain of churches. As someone else has given energy and vision to the planting of the mother church, so the mother church needs to work hard at creating another church link that will serve another group of people with the gospel for generations to come. The church needs to accept the fact that the church does not belong to them. It is the Lord's church and His will and work must prevail in the church. The church must see itself as existing for the purpose of spreading the gospel beyond itself in anticipation of Christ's return. Project ownership may come in bite-size pieces as the project is shared with heartfelt enthusiasm based on the biblical premise that people without Christ are lost.

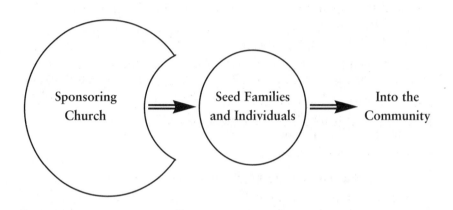

2. Leadership Preparation

The church needs to develop leaders who have a sacrificial and self-giving spirit. A church with a church growth mind set will by definition seek as many ways as possible to extend its influence in the community and give of itself accordingly. Church planting requires a church growth leadership. The church must be willing to make changes in order to prepare itself for church planting. One cannot plant a church and stay the same. Leadership changes, budget changes, organizational changes, and people changes are all part of church planting. The mother church in consultation with the denomination needs to partici-pate in the development of the daughter church's values and overall philosophy of ministry if church planting is to happen. The New Testament pattern of disciple-making begins with wit-nessing, and ends in church planting. Church planting needs to be part of the total ministry of the church.

3. Church Preparation

In church planting, as in any major outreach project, much dialogue and information flow is necessary within the congregation. Messages, workshops, weekend seminars on the subject, all help to make the idea welcome and acceptable. Special guest resource people coming in to share their vision and experience are usually required to help supplement and support the vision leaders in the church. An outreach climate needs to be created. The local church needs to be prepared spiritually for church planting. It needs to develop a genuine concern and compassion for those outside of the church. An emphasis on faith and a dependency on the Holy Spirit along with serious prayer and a concern to labour for harvest fruit, need to be cultivated before a church project is launched.

4. Recovery and Parenting

The mother church needs to know that it will need a recovery time after birthing a daughter church. It needs to recover emotionally from the stresses of changing relationships and friendships. The church will need financial recovery time, and leadership retraining time. Most mother churches recover their attendance and resources within six months to a year. The mother church needs to keep encouraging and mentoring the daughter church. She needs to determine if any other assistance is needed. Sharing with the daughter church some of the group-specific ministries such as youth group and ladies' groups etc. could be helpful. It is easy to forget about the daughter church when the church is in the recovery mode.

5. Daughter Attitude

A new church can easily forget about the sacrifices that the mother church has made. The daughter church often fails to honour the mother and may have unreasonable expectations. The mother church's gifts of money, leaders, people, and the endless amount of planning time, must not be forgotten. It is also important that the daughter church realize that the mother needs some recovery and space to develop. Like a newly-married couple, so a daughter church needs to make its own decisions within a proper context of accountability.

C. Deciding The Level And Type Of Parenting Involvement

There are various ways to participate in a daughter church plant. The mother church will need to decide at which level she is able to get involved. All levels are important.

1. The Pioneer Parenting Plant

At this level the mother church is taking full responsibility for the planting of a daughter church. She will develop the plan, provide the leadership and provide the finances. Usually in such a situation, one of the associate pastors is assigned to be the church-planting pastor and begins to gather the core group. Coaching may be provided by the denomination. It is expected that most of the attenders will be coming from the community through advertising and relationships.

2. The Church Within A Church

In this model the mother church provides the majority of the people. It happens in the same location with a group of church people who want a different church model and maybe at an alternate time. This is somewhat akin to adding another church service.

3. The Church Division Model

In this model the church decides to divide and "hive off" a major part of the congregation. This is a friendly split. In some instances the mother church even builds a new facility for the "hiving off" group. The new daughter church is somewhat like a branch office of a business. Both mother and daughter have similar values and purposes.

4. The Satellite Model

In this model, as was already discussed in the Crucial Beginnings chapter, the mother establishes a satellite location with a separate worship team but with a common preaching pastor. The sermon is either wired in from the mother's location on video, or the pastor commutes to the satellite church for the sermon. The administration of these two churches is the same. This model usually fits a larger mother church.

5. The Partnering Parenting Model

In this situation a mother church partners with one or more other churches to establish a daughter church. This model is often suitable for a group of smaller churches who have limited resources. In this model the churches pool their resources and appoint a church planter who leads the charge. This model is usually supervised by the denomination; otherwise it may have too many bosses.

6. The Replanting Model

This is a situation where a mother church has been declining and is encumbered with difficulties. The contribution by the mother church here is that it liquidates its assets and disbands its membership for the purposes of a complete restart. The restart involves appointing a new pastor, choosing a new church name and designing a new ministry plan. This resembles the death and rebirth of a vision.

7. The Unplanned Parenthood

In this situation God allows two churches to survive and grow out of a church split. When two equally valid visions are being pursued, they need to be expressed in separate groups. Wherever a church split happens, much pain and hurt needs to be resolved.

D. Removing Church Planting Misconceptions

Churches that have not experienced the beginnings of a new church often tend to develop stereotypes and impressions that are conditioned by fears and misunderstanding. Ten of the most common misconceptions on church planting are:

1. Church planting is very expensive and unaffordable for the average-sized congregation.

Church planting needs to be likened to a marriage. It is a venture where people are brought together in relationships of fellowship and worship. This should not be confused with the building of buildings. Church planting is a people program rather than a construction project. Church planting does not need to start with an elaborate facility or a major budget. It usually begins in rented facilities and a moderate budget.

2. Church planting requires a large group of committed people.

Where two or three families are gathered together, there the Lord's purposes can be fulfilled. A new church does not need a fully-orbed program. Six to ten committed families can start a new church. A new church project is not primarily for the purpose of accommodating existing believers but rather to find and bring new people to Christ and His Body. A mother church with an attendance of 150 or 200 or more can well start a daughter church.

3. A Church planting agenda is a reasonable consideration when a church is filled to capacity.

Church planting is first a response to the vision and mandate of Christ. Crowded facilities should not be the major reason for church planting. The decision by a local church to plant a new church should be based on its desire and urge to be faithful to the great commission. Church planting is needed because new communities need to be reached for Christ. If a church wants to conduct a program of evangelism with long-range and ongoing fruitfulness, then let it start a new church.

4. Enlarging an existing church building is an alternative to church planting.

The experience of continuous growth of a local church is commendable, and church enlargement is the natural result. Church expansion is healthy and necessary. This, however, does not provide another community with the privilege of having a local church. Church planting has as its goal to place a gospel preaching centre and a Christian ministry into every neighbourhood. New churches are needed for reaching more people for Christ in more areas.

5. Church planting is for mission organizations and for experienced professionals.

History shows that church planting can be very successful through committed lay people. The book of Acts depicts numerous examples of spontaneous believers' church planting. Wherever committed believers can be found and new converts are identified, there a church might be considered.

6. Church planting must be done only when all questions are answered and all risks are removed.

Faith and risk are to be expected when a new church is started. The only guarantees that a church planter has are a confidence in the gospel and a trust that Christ will draw people to himself and to his body. A new church may well start small like a mustard seed. It begins with a conviction, that God's will is being accomplished. Church planting is always a venture of faith.

There will always be some unanswered questions and some opposition, but this should not deter the church plant.

7. Church planting on a trial basis or for an experimental period can help churches make the right church-planting decisions.

The Body of Christ in worship and fellowship is never an experiment. Churches need to be started upon the conviction that God has written up the church-planting order. New churches are like new families, where strong bonds of relationships are formed. These cannot easily be terminated by a mother church vote after a given trial period. If termination of a ministry is required, it is best done by those affected in the decision.

8. Church planting is an optional consideration for an established church.

The establishment of new churches should be a regular and normal expectation of a healthy church. A local church contains the seeds to reproduce itself over and over again. If a church does not transplant itself it tends to become root-bound. As Christians should be concerned about passing the faith along to others, so churches should be concerned about not being the end link in a chain. Every church should consider daughtering a church.

9. Church planting will destroy church unity and will take away too many good people.

There are sacrifices involved in launching a church-planting project. Church planting is a biblical exercise of giving rather than getting or having. In such selfless giving the church receives a new rallying point, and thus becomes united around a new challenge. Such an exercise of goodwill and obedience to the commission usually renders the mother church more attractive and sets in motion a new impetus for growth. The good people leaving to help plant a church will be replaced by other good people.

10. Participation in a new church planting-project will be detrimental to our children and family.

This parental fear is usually more the concern of the parent than the concern of the children. In many instances, children are more ready for new experiences than are the adults. However, in a new church venture within the same city, friendships can still be maintained and young peoples' meetings or ladies' fellowship participation can be continued with the mother church until the new church has developed its own programs.

11. The parent church loss and recovery process will be insurmountable.

It is true that the mother church will need to go through a recovery process. The birth process takes a lot of emotional energy and time. The recovery time may take from six to twelve months. Leadership training will be needed to replace leaders. Attendance recovery will require new relationship-building and advertising. As new people come ,and new people take on more responsibilities, the financial recovery happens. The mother church usually experiences a revitalization and refocusing through the process of daughtering a church.

E. Action Steps For Planting Daughter Churches

A church that gets involved in planting a daughter church can expect to experience health, vitality and growth. Parenting churches is the biblical model of doing evangelism. This church planting process requires the following specific action steps on the part of the mother church.

1. Catch the Vision

a) Accept the biblical challenge and responsibility of reaching out to a new community.

b) Recognize that community evangelism is most effective and permanent through a church-planting program within the new community.

c) Believe that God wants to build and extend His church within every community and that He is depending on local churches to plant new churches.

d) Build confidence in God's promises to build his church.

e) Give church time to process the church-planting idea.

2. Make the Decision

a) Articulate a clear vision of starting a daughter church.

b) Make a firm decision to start a new congregation within a specific time frame.

c) Build a prayer team of intercessors.

d) Cultivate a climate of faith and expectation within the Body of Christ for a new church.

e) Prepare the church for the tasks and responsibilities of parenting.

3. Assign the Task

a) Get the support of the church influencers.

b) Appoint or assign a church committee or task force within the local congregation to be responsible for church planting.

c) Bless and dedicate this group to the ministry of church-planting evangelism.

d) Mandate and authorize them to actually start the new church.

4. Select the Area

a) Establish the basic criteria to be applied in locating a daughter-planting area.

b) Survey and research several potential communities within reasonable reach of the sponsoring church.

c) Select the most responsive and promising target area for the new church planting project.

5. Develop the Plan

a) Write up the new church's central purpose and give the reason for its proposed formation.

b) Establish the spiritual design and basic program philosophy.

c) Describe the program blueprint and growth expectation.

d) Determine the type of church to be planted.

6. Communicate the Church-Planting Steps— Logan Terminology

a) The Conception Stage of Making the Basic Decisions

b) Prenatal Stage of Preparing for the First Service

c) Birth Stage of Conducting the Launch Service

d) The Growing Stage of Developing Church Ministries
(For details on steps and stages see chapter on Strategic Implementation.)

7. Gather the Core

a) Start with a group that is prepared to bring in the harvest.

b) Rally the support group for prayer, faith and partnership in the interest of the proposed church.

c) Finalize the start-up program plans and arrange for suitable facilities and worship materials.

d) Take care of the count-down preparations and the community worship invitation blitz.

8. Launch the Worship

a) Start with a well-advertised, public celebration worship service and add other programs on a planned time line.

b) Include public, denominational, and church guests in the inaugural dedication service.

c) Charge the new church and its leaders to follow the biblical disciple-making mandate.

9. Establish the Church

a) Involve the congregation in leadership and prepare them for membership chartering.

b) Adopt a preliminary church constitution to stabilize and facilitate church policy, and to affiliate them with the parent body.

c) Lead the church into making plans for the acquisition of facilities.

(For a more complete description of church-planting steps see the Implementation Chapter)

F. Commissioning Send-off Ceremony

THE PARENT CHURCH BLESSING

This is the celebration service of the mother church, where they dedicate the group of members that will be leaving the church to become the core group of the daughter church. It is similar to the "hands-on" ceremony in Acts 13:3 where the church laid hands on Paul and Barnabas and sent them out. It is a kind of ceremonial commissioning and farewell to the leaving group. This service focuses on the church's desire and commitment to help fulfill the great commission.

SAMPLE COMMISSIONING CEREMONY

Parent Church:

Today we dedicate ourselves anew to the purpose for which God has called us. As we enter this church plant, we want to be sensitive to God's guidance. We acknowledge that we are stewards of all that we have, and commit ourselves to give willingly of our time, our talent, our strength, and our material resources, to the accomplishment of God's purpose in this new church plant.

Daughter Church Team:

We thank God for the many blessings we have received here in this church. We believe that God is calling us to a new task: to establish a place of witness through a new church plant. We trust Him to provide strength, wisdom, and love for this work.

Parent Church:

We believe that God is calling you to this new place of service, and we want to commission you to this responsible ministry. As you go, we pray that you may go in the power of the Spirit. May His comforting and guiding Presence ever be with you, and may you bear much fruit. Our prayer for you as you go is expressed in the words of Paul as he prayed for the Christians in Thessalonica: "And may the Lord make you increase and abound in love to one another and to all men as we do to you" (1 Thess. 3:12). As a symbol of the light that you will be, we give to you this lighted candle. (Continued Ceremony)

Daughter Church Team:

We believe that God has given to us this faith-stretching opportunity. We accept this responsibility with faith in God and in his promise to provide all that we will need in order to serve Him faithfully. To you, our brothers and sisters, we pledge our mutual concern and affection. May our fellowship always be close and warm, and may we always remember the blessings we have enjoyed together.

Commissioning Prayer:

All those that have committed themselves to be part of the new church, please gather in front of the stage for a special dedication prayer.

G. Frequently Asked Questions On Parenting A Church

1. Rationale

Why are we talking about planting a church? Is it because our church is full? Are there some people not happy in this church? Are there not enough churches already?

The biblical and most valid reason for parenting is evangelism and disciple-making of all people groups.

2. Impact

Will a church-planting project affect our church adversely? Will we become divided and lose too many people?

Church planting usually unites the church around its new rallying point and makes them ready to invest people into the mission endeavours.

3. Cost

Can we afford it? How much will this church-planting idea cost us? We have a hard time meeting our budget now.

The start-up costs are as follows: advertising, keyboard, offering bags, communion trays, sound system, auditorium rentals, salary, and church ministry materials.

4. Organization

What does a new church need by way of structure? Who will take responsibility for such a project?

A five- or six-person church-planting launch team is adequate for making the church-planting preparations.

5. Control

Where is the church-planting decision made? Who authorizes the program? How much freedom does the start-up group have?

The mother congregation or body needs to approve the church planting design or proposal, which outlines the development steps. All other decisions should be made by the church planters.

6. Process

What is to be done first? Is there a development order?

The master plan or development flow chart as approved by the congregation should be followed as closely as possible. The steps may vary.

7. Location

Where should a new church be started?

The survey data should give some fairly good clues in terms of place. The leading of the Spirit is the final guide.

8. Style

What kind of church should this be? Should it be different?

New attenders are not usually looking for or attracted to maverick churches. Variation is more an interest for those not planning to attend the new church. Most new churches have a contemporary focus.

9. Target

For whom is this proposed church? Is there a special target group to be reached?

The new church will be attended by the residents of the determined area and by interested church members living within or near the area.

10. Facilities

What kind of church facility will be required? Will we need to build?

Most new churches are prepared to spend the first five years or so in rented facilities. This gives them time to build up their attendance and to buy a parcel of land.

11. Leadership

What kind of pastor do we need for church planting?

It is desirable to appoint a church-planting pastor as the first step in the process. A person is needed who is creative and somewhat adventurous, courageous, self-initiating, and full of faith and vision. In some situations a bi-vocational planter is an option.

12. Time

How long does it take to plant a church?

It may take about a year to make the necessary preparations by a parent church before the actual church is launched. Once the decision is made, the launch process can take six to eight months.

Notes——

[1] Paul Becker & Mark Williams, *The Dynamic Daughter Church Planting Handbook* (Dynamic Church Planting International, 1999).

[2] Robert E. Logan & Steven L. Ogne, *Churches Planting Churches* (Alta Loma, California: CRM New Church Development, 1995).

Eleven

Cultural Diversity

The reason that ethnic churches are being planted today is because there have been increases in the immigration patterns to Canada, and there are not enough churches for the new immigrants. These new immigrants bring different cultures, languages, and nationalities to Canada. As a result of this diverse immigration, new and different types of churches need to be planted that allow for this cultural diversity.

> Jim Graham, Southern Baptist Multi-cultural
> Church-Planting Director in British Columbia.

The inter-cultural church-planting chapter assumes that the dominant culture group which usually hosts or sponsors an ethnic church plant is Caucasian. The material presented here is written from a Canadian western perspective and experience. The writer has been involved in planting churches among some twelve different language groups in Canada, including some churches in Quebec. It is a privilege for the Caucasian churches who are well-established and form the dominant culture to become involved in cross-cultural church planting.

A. Cross-Cultural Church Planting

A new church needs to be started wherever a group of people can be identified who are culturally and linguistically too distant from the dominant culture group to be able to relate meaningfully. If language is enough of a barrier to provide a communications breakdown, you need a separate church. Ethnic church planting is categorized in church-growth terms as being an E-3 process of evangelism.[1]

> E-0 Bringing people to a commitment to Christ (new birth) who are already church members.
>
> E-1 Near-neighbour evangelism of non-Christians whose language and customs are those of the Christian who is witnessing.
>
> E-2 Evangelism across a relatively small ethnic, cultural, or linguistic barrier.
>
> E-3 Evangelism across a relatively large ethnic, cultural, or language barrier.

1. Reasons for Church Planting Among International People

Church Planting among ethnic people is an important consideration because Canada is in fact an ethnic mosaic with a diverse population that is about 40% British, 27% French and 33% ethnic other than British or French. When 60% or more of Canada is other than English, church planting among ethnic people must receive a much higher profile. There are three major immigrant groups that could be affected by language-specific church planting.

a) Displaced Refugees

Canada is becoming an international haven for thousands of people fleeing/emigrating from oppressed, war-torn countries. These people see in Canada a place of new hope, peace, and security. A church established for these people could become the main vehicle for returning them to dignity and purpose.

b) Entrepreneurial Immigrants

Canada has become for many overseas business people the country of promise and prosperity. A growing percentage of immigrants coming to Canada each year are coming in search of new opportunities.

c) Foreign Students

Students are coming to Canada from all over the world to get their college and university education. According to the Canadian Bureau for International Education, there are slightly over 30,000 international students in any given year, or 4.9% of the university population (1988). There are now well over half-a-million graduates from Canadian universities who have returned to their homeland to occupy strategic jobs in foreign countries. By involving these students in ethnic churches, one could provide for them a familiar social setting in which the Christian faith and values can be shared. These students can then be sent back home as natural missionaries and church planters.

2. Determine the Nesting Pattern

In many ways church planting resembles the process of building and feathering of a bird nest. Each bird species has its own "at-home feeling" and nesting requirements suitable to its "bird culture." The range is diverse as seen from these examples:

Barn swallow—has a mud nest under the barn eaves

Meadowlark—prefers an open, unprotected ground-level pasture nest

Robin—needs a back yard family environment nesting place

Crow—needs a nest of sticks high in a poplar tree away from people

Duck—needs a ground-level camouflaged marshland nest

Woodpecker—needs a hollowed-out tree stump to feel at home

Oriole—needs a swinging hair and string nest, etc.

The idea that birds of a feather flock together is helpful in the church-planting scenario. Church planting will vary from culture to culture, from region to region, and from mother to daughter churches. Each ethnic group has a "cultural nesting pattern" which provides the group with an "at-home feeling." The church planter needs to discover and discern this reality and build on it.

B. Cultural Sensitivities For The Church Planter

1. Sense of Self, Space and Communication

Different cultures have a varying sense of space when they communicate. While some communicate standing face to face, others do so at a distance. Some communicate indirectly and will not easily say "no," lest they offend. Some speak abruptly and directly, using eye contact while others do not. There are cultures that ignore written communication and respond only to face-to-face dialogue. For some, verbal communication is more binding than a written agreement. Personal communication carries high value in developing cultures.

2. Dress, Appearance and Food

It is important to dress appropriately to the culture. Some have a formal dress code and others are informal. Most cultures have a unique food dish and drink. Some cultures have meals with their worship or business transactions. It is also important to respect food restrictions, such as meat and vegetarian practices.

3. Time Awareness

Time is valued differently in different people groups. Some value punctuality while others come at their convenience.

4. Respect for Age

Some cultures respect age and look up to their elders as authoritative leaders. In western cultures the youth are idealized and in Asian cultures, age is honoured.

5. Family Loyalties and Privacy

Most cultures have close family relations and sometimes family takes precedence over work. If a family member is sick a person may without notice not show up at work. Some cultures value privacy and modesty, while others are more free and open.

6. Families, Children, and Women

In some cultures children do not speak much and remain in the background, while other cultures have their children with them at all times and would be offended to be invited to a parents-only event. Children are closely supervised in some cultures, while in others they mostly do as they please, even in group or church settings. In some cultures the women are treated equal to the men, but in other cultures women have few rights and remain servants. A head covering for the women is required in some cultures.

7. Work, Business, and Finances

Some cultures do not have work training and scheduled work days. Others have a strict workplace discipline and routine. For some, finances are a very private subject, while for others it is an open matter. While some cultures make decisions as a group or as tribal elders, others leave the decision-making to the male family head.[2]

Purpose Vision and Mission

A strong sense of purpose, vision, and mission help bring together a culturally-diverse team because it provides the necessary elements of cohesion and direction.

Terence Brake, *Managing Globally*

C. Understanding Basic Cultural Patterns

Cultures are said to be like icebergs. Above the surface are the characteristics that can be seen, heard, touched, smelled and tasted. Below the service are the attitudes and beliefs that shape decision making, relationships, and conflicts. It is the below-the-surface aspects that cause the greatest challenge in planting churches cross-culturally. It is helpful to categorize cultures in three broad categories with each having their values, beliefs, and cultural patterns. Terrance Blake groups cultures into three categories.[3]

1. Autonomy Culture

This culture values individuality and independence. Decisions are usually made by individuals based on their best judgment. For the most part this describes the western world.

2. Consensus Culture

This culture group values harmony, homogeneity, and conformity. Individual decisions tend to be made to align with the values and practices of the group. These consensus-type cultures are found in many parts of Asia.

3. Status Cultures

The values of this culture are honour and respect, both for individuals and the group. In this culture, an individual culture is closely connected to that of the family, extended family or clan. Loyalty and respect for leaders, group survival, and pride are high priorities. Status-type cultures are found in southern Europe, South America, Africa and the Middle East.

4. Barriers to Cultural Communication

Cross-cultural communication tends to break down under the following conditions:

a) A belief that everybody is the same
b) A presumption that one has nothing to learn from others
c) An attitude that your way is the best.
d) The opinion that those who are culturally different from your culture need to be developed.

Sarah Lanier describes the culture types in terms of hot versus cold climate cultures. The hot climate culture is more indirect in communication, more group-oriented and formal, while the cold climate culture is more direct, individualistic and informal.[4]

D. Lessons For The Caucasian Church Planter

1. Get an understanding of the family, social, and relational structures, and learn how they function as a group.

2. Build meaningful relationships by eating their foods and by showing interest in their ways of doing things.

3. Be willing to invest much time and exercise, much patience and understanding of non-western ideas of time and space.

4. Study the cultural leadership styles and the decision-making process.

5. Be transparent, and ready to be taught and corrected regarding cultural expectations.

6. Avoid becoming the "white cultural hero" who has all the answers and the resources. Guard against paternalistic relationships.

7. Establish clearly-written church-planting goals, guidelines, and expectations.

8. Set clear operational parameters and accountability points.

9. Distinguish between what is cultural and what is biblical regarding the nature and function of the church.

10. Establish clear financial guidelines by which the income and expenses are clearly accounted for and used.

11. Teach the biblical understanding of stewardship, including instructions of tithing and gifts.

12. Recognize that many of the culture groups have two focuses: the new-country home and the home at their country of origin. They will spend much travel time and money on both of these interests.

13. Be prepared to spend much time and money in the development toward an indigenous church.

14. Seek out anointed and qualified ethnic church-planting leader-

ship who understand the values and goals of the denomination.

15. Expect the culture-specific church to have a high level of socialization, meals, and connections.

16. Do extensive research in order to identify the cultural peoplepockets that are often hidden and not easily recognized, as a significant unreached people group.

17. Have a definite time line of indigenisation and financial independence.

18. Leadership internships are a good way to train indigenous leaders.

19. Work diligently at building church unity because some culture groups have tendencies to split churches based on lay leaders desiring to be pastors.[5]

E. The Impact Of Immigration On Churches

1. Population Shifts

Most cities experience the development of culture-specific communities. This means that increasingly more immigrants move into the same neighborhood, giving it a cultural dominant character or ethnic concentration. The result is that the original Caucasian people move out, a phenomenon know as "white flight."

The extent to which a community has changed can be observed by the number of ethnic restaurants, business centres, or ethnic religious centres being built. When these cultural conditions are present in a community, the Caucasian churches are facing the problem of "ethnikitis." This is a church condition where the church attendance is on a decline but the white church is continued as a commuter church because most of the Caucasians have moved out of the area. Such a church faces serious challenges and opportunities.[6]

2. Options for Churches in Cross-Cultural Communities

First the church needs to adopt a positive attitude toward the new Canadians, and show hospitality and love. The first commandment of loving your neighbour needs to become a reality. This will result in becoming comfortable with cultural diversity. The church opportunities could be to:

a) Start a Multicultural Church

The type of church plant has a vision for becoming a church for all nations. It is an intentional model of involving different cultural groups in the dominant-culture English church. The different cultures are included in the worship, the small groups and in the leadership. In this model there is little culture-specific activity. All groups are merging in the Caucasian church.[7] In the multicultural church, an attempt is made to be colour-blind even though white remains dominant.

b) Start a Multi-Congregation Church

In this model the church building is used by many different cultures for their worship. The church is administered by a representative board from the various culture-specific congregations. An attempt is made to have a monthly celebration where all the culture groups come together for a united celebration. This is a church model that recognized the need for cultures to have a worship in their own language.

c) Start a Missional Multi-Ethnic Church

This is a model that seeks to have intentional mission activity for the inner-city hurting people. This effort of social evangelism to many ethnic people from the city core resulted in a multi-ethnic church body. In this model, an attempt is made for the rich and poor to come to God equally. The large Tenth Avenue Alliance Church in Vancouver is seeking to be this kind of church, says pastor Ken Shigematsu.[8]

d) Start a Blended Cultural Church

This model could be described variously. It lives in two culture worlds, the multi-ethnic and the Caucasian. This model is frequently practised in larger congregations. It is a multicultural congregation wherein all the cultural groups worship together in one large English worship service, with simultaneous translation of the sermon for the various language groups. Each cultural group also has an assigned pastor who provides culture-specific activity of fellowship, meals, and small worship meetings. This church operates as one large church with one church board. On the Canadian west coast the Willingdon Church in Burnaby would fit this model with its some 12 different language groups functioning within an English church worship environment.

e) Start or Facilitate a Homogenous Daughter Church

In this situation, the dominant-culture Caucasian church helps a specific cultural group start a worship service using their facilities. The homogenous church is particularly needed for first-generation immigrants of refugee groups. The mother church in this situation usually gives some oversight and church rent concessions. The primary arrangement in this model is the usage of the church. Many English churches, to their credit, are housing and sponsoring homogenous culture-specific groups in their churches. In some situations, this model is like a church within a church plant. One of the advantages for the culture-specific church is that sharing a church building also makes it possible for a gradual attendance transition to the English church of the second-generation new Canadians.

f) Start an International Centre

In the book *Canada New Harvest*, by Brian Seim, Phyllis Orley describes an interesting ministry model of people of all colours, that functions as a community centre.[9] This centre operates as an outreach of the church and gets involved in the various human needs present in the urban centres. The centre appears to have similarities to ministries sponsored by the Salvation Army or Yonge Street Mission. This Oasis Community Center seems to be multi-ethnic or international by virtue of its urban location.

g) Start a Cell Church

Many of the immigrants coming to Canada have experienced cell churches in their home country and so are familiar with the model. It is a model that claims biblical soundness, in that it has no buildings, is flexible, relevant, informal, outreach-minded, accountable, and people-empowering. It is a model that fits into any culture, and adapts itself to the language and values of the participant. Neighbour, one of today's primary proponents of the cell movement says, "A big reason the cell church is effective is that it keeps people in their "oikos" or household, so they are still part of their family or friendship or cultural groups, instead of pulling them out into a forum that is not familiar."[10]

There are many ways to show Christian love to our multicultural neighbours. Canadians have a great opportunity to be host to the nations of the world. What a challenge to share the good news and then have them return to their homelands as witnessing Christians. Every church should evaluate its situation and look for more ways to love and serve our international neighbours.

3. Church-Planting Paradigms

Church planting in multicultural environments differs with the various language groups. The chart identifies four distant cultural church-planting paradigms which help predict the level of progress to be expected in a church plant.[11]

The church planting experience becomes increasingly more challenging when a person moves from the dominant host Caucasian culture church plant of the first circle to the fourth refugee profile circle.

CULTURAL PARADIGM CHALLENGES

DIVERSE CHURCH PLANTING PROFILES

I. Dominant Culture Planting

Dominant Host Culture Profile
- Stable families
- Middle class lifestyle
- Home owners
- Professions, jobs

1-2 years subsidy

II. Integrating Culture Planting

Integrating Immigrant Profile
- Business owners
- University students
- Home land investors travel integrate

2-3 years subsidy

III. Non-Integrating Culture Planting

Immigrant Non-Integrating Profile
- Keep dress code
- Keep the culture
- Keep religious practice
- Christianity on surface

4-6 years subsidy

IV. Refugee Culture Planting

Refugee Immigrant Profile
- Social upheaval
- Fearful & disadvantaged
- Minimum wage
- Welfare • Displaced

6-10 years subsidy

NOTES——

[1] C. Peter Wagner, *Church Growth—State of the Art* (Wheaton, Illinois: Tyndale House Publishers, 1986), p. 289.

[2] Jim Graham, Church Planting leader for the Southern Baptists in B.C. Some of this material was adapted from an article provided by Jim Graham in 1997.

[3] Terence Brake, *Managing Globally* (London, England: Darling Kindersley, 2002), p. 21.

[4] Sarah A. Lanier, *Foreign to Familiar* (Hagerstown, Maryland: McDougal Publishing, 2000).

[5] Some seed thoughts of this section were provided by Jake Balzer and Nick Dyck, who were both church-planting directors for the B.C. Mennonite Brethren denomination.

[6] Vern Middleton, a former missionary and seminary professor at Acts, describes the concept of Ethnikitis in an article, *Ethnikitis May be Fatal*, in the Antioch Blueprints manual, 2001.

[7] This model was presented by Pastor Ken Peters at the IMC Symposium at the Acts Seminary, Langley, B.C., June, 2002.

[8] Ken Shigematsu in a paper on *Becoming a Multi-ethnic Church*, at Acts Seminary, B.C.

[9] Brian Seim, *Canada New Harvest* (Canada: Evangelical Fellowship of Canada, 1999), p. 137.

[10] Seim quoting Neighbour, p. 171.

[11] This paradigm analysis was created and presented by the author of this book to the B.C.M.B. Church Extension Board retreat at Stillwood Camp, B.C. in September 2001.

- TWELVE

Apostolic Leadership

A church will never rise above its leadership. If the leadership of the church isn't committed to church planting, the entire membership will not be committed. If the leadership doesn't pray for daughter churches, the membership will not pray for daughter churches. The leadership must set the example for the congregation.

Aubrey Malphurs, *Planting Growing Churches*.

The apostolic leadership chapter brings together the various leadership qualities and functions needed for a successful church plant. A major part of this chapter is about understanding the leadership role and functions of a church planter. The other priority has to do with the spiritual profile and character necessary for a successful church plant. It is clear to the writer that a church plant rises and falls on the strength of the church planter. The spiritual life of the church planter is all-important, since the plant is in partnership with Christ who is building His church. This co-labouring with Christ brings many joys and also many challenges, because it involves people who need to hear the gospel. It is for this reason that the planter needs to exercise self-care and growth. A special part of this chapter is the ministry focus of the planter's wife, written by Elfrieda Nikkel, the spouse of the writer.

A. Leadership Conceptualizations

EXPECTATIONS—INFLUENCES—CAUTIONS

Leadership styles change from church to church and from generation to generation. Leadership in a small group obviously needs to be different from that of a large group. Leadership and tasks are related. The bigger the task to be done, the stronger and more pronounced the leadership roles need to be. Leadership is related also to spiritual gifts and special calling. Someone with a vision and call from God will be energized and enabled to complete their God-given tasks like Noah, Gideon, or Moses. The leadership that is required for church planting is very broad and yet very focused.

1. The Parishioners' Expectations

Some see the pastor/church planter as a white-collar scholar; others see him as a blue-collar servant. Some respect him as the Very Right Reverend and others call on him for tasks that suggest janitorial or "coverall" tasks. Some expect him to serve as kind of a church security guard and others want him to function in the community as a public relations officer. Some want him to be a perfect managerial leader and others want him to be a humble servant leader. Amidst all these conflicting images, the church planter needs to know that he has been called of God as an ambassador and steward of the Gospel.

2. The Professional Influences

Much discretion is required for ministry leadership in our highly-specialized society. The various disciplines of learning and corporate business are having a creeping influence on the pastor's leadership style. The pastor, along with the leadership, needs to use as much as is relevant and reject what cannot be used for church leadership. The contributions are many:

- Electronics has brought sound systems
- Business has brought goals and procedures
- Education has brought evaluations and progress
- Science has brought measurements and graphs
- Sociology has reinforced small groups
- Psychology has suggested personal counselling
- Media has pushed for stage performance
- Politics has brought about church constitutions
- Athletics has introduced success and competition

3. Church Planter Expectations

- Establishing a dynamic-balanced worship service
- Setting up the pathway from attendance to full commitment
- Developing team leadership and governance structure
- Organizing the church membership and ministries
- Setting up the financial system and structure
- Maintaining a priority on evangelism
- Keeping the church plant well advertised
- Connecting with the sponsoring church conference

Leadership

Leadership is a God-given capacity and responsibility to influence God's people to fulfill God's purposes. Leaders inspire, unite and motivate God's people over an extended period of time.[1]

Terry Walling, *Focusing Leaders*

B. Building Personal Church Planter Confidences

1. Clarify the Ministry Objectives of the Church planter

The effectiveness of a church planter is clearly related to the clarity of his work parameters. How the church planter will schedule his time will again be related, to how he sees the scope of his assignment. The church planter's objectives are:

a) To do the work of the great commission
  - Moving into a designated new area
  - Relating to the people in witness
  - Preaching the gospel of Christ
  - Baptizing the converts
  - Teaching them to observe Christ's commands

b) To help people make three basic commitments
  - The commitment to Christ for salvation
  - The commitment to the Body of Christ for growth
  - The commitment to the work of Christ in obedience
  - The commitment to the global mission

c) To establish and organize a believer's church
  - Adding converts to the membership
  - Facilitating fellowship events
  - Providing opportunity for service
  - Affiliating the church with the denominations

d) To establish a permanent meeting and office place
  - To give permanence to the ministry
  - To facilitate program development
  - To provide a corporate church home

In order to implement the church planter's assignment, a careful timetable of activities will need to be developed. The planter will need to decide daily between doing that which appears urgent and that which is in fact important. The church planter needs to keep a disciplined routine of mornings spent in preparation and study, and the afternoons given to community outreach and relationships. It is not possible to successfully plant a church and not have regularly scheduled time away from the office doing visitation and making contacts. The church planters need to see themselves as the pastor to the "one," outside of the "ninety and nine" in the fold.

2. Establish Church Planter Priorities

a) Pray for the Harvest
- For the leadership
- For the people
- For direction/wisdom
- For salvation of people

b) Preach the Word with Power
- God speaks through the Word
- God makes his appeal through human witness
- Spend time to prepare heart and head
- When they hear you they hear God

c) Promote the Church Plant in the Community
- Survey the community regarding needs
- Advertise the various ministries
- Telephone invitations to participate in worship
- Attend public community events

d) Present Christ—Share your Faith (up to 40% of time)
- Meet the leaders of the city
- Meet business people
- Make courtesy drop-in visits for new attenders
- Visit institutions: hospitals, prisons, etc.
- Do follow-up visits of various contacts
- Prayer walks

e) Present the Vision to your Team—Follow the V.H.S. Model[2]
  - i) Vision-casting by the pastor—for direction, inspiration, and team ownership
  - ii) Huddle with the leaders—for ministry, prayer, and feedback
  - iii) Skill development—for ministry improvement, strategizing, and expansion

3. Plan And Follow a Daily Schedule (sample)

6:45	Shower and Shine
7:00	Bible/Prayer
7:30	Breakfast/Meetings (Wednesday & Friday)
8:00	Travel to Work
8:30	Office—Day Planning
9:00	Study—Preparations
11:00	Phone Calls/Administration
11:30	Letter Writing, E-mails, etc.
12:00	Luncheons/Leisure
1:30	Community Visits/Appointments
3:30	Office
4:00	Family
5:30	Supper
7:00	Meetings (Tuesday and Thursday)
9:00	Family
10:00	Debriefing, Devotions/Spouse
10:45	Retire

4. Practice the Personal Godly Behaviours Required

Church planters are a specialty group, a kind of type unto themselves. They are a leadership group that have a special task, have special gifts, have special needs and consequently need special resources. Their specialty task is to carry the gospel out and to enlarge the Kingdom of God. Church planters officially and formally do that which all Christians are called to do more informally and unofficially. Some of the significant behaviours for leadership would be:

a) Spiritually Conditioned
Spiritual maturity is an indispensable part of church-planting leadership. A new church leader needs to be noted for faith and hope, joy and peace, prayer and power, courage and confidence, vision and optimism.

b) God-Directed
The actions of church planters must flow out of a personal

relationship with Christ, the church founder. They lead because they have been led; they can shepherd because they are being shepherded; and they can give direction because their life is directed.

c) Self- Disciplined

Church planting requires leadership that is self-accepting and growth-focused. The church planters must discipline themselves to balance people time with preparation time, family time with personal time, community time with congregation time.

d) People-Oriented

Church planters must build bridges to people through wholesome, warm and cordial relationships. They need to major in common courtesies, people interest, and spiritual needs satisfaction. They must accept and understand the feelings and fears of people as they relate to their backgrounds and experiences.

e) Servant-Postured

Church planters need to come with a good service track record. They must present an articulate, simple, and credible gospel message. Their words and work must reinforce each other.

f) Church-Committed

Church planters need to have a high view of the church. They are committed to bringing people to Christ and into the fellowship and ministry of the local church.

g) Ministry Philosophy

Each church planter needs to develop a definite and workable philosophy of ministry to avoid being tossed to and fro by program crises or ministry bandwagon fads.

h) Community-Related

The church planters' major focus needs to be on the community. They must move among the masses, participate in projects, penetrate barriers, and share the gospel of Christ freely. Contact with new people in their context of life must be their constant objective.

C. Committing To The Ministry Job Description

MINISTRY OUTLINE

Being called to develop and pastor a congregation is an awesome calling. It is an appointment to serve the Body of Christ which Christ Himself makes. He provides the church leaders as God's people pray. To serve as a church planter/ pastor must be seen as being God-appointed, and is therefore a position of great honour. The scriptures refer to ministry assignments as being divinely-given.

"You did not choose me, but I chose you and appointed you..." (John 15:16).
"To complete the task the Lord Jesus has given me" (Acts: 20:24).
"Complete the work you have received in the Lord" (Col. 4:17).
"I have become its servant by the commission God has given me" (Col. 1:25).
"I thank Christ Jesus our Lord, who has given me strength that he considered me faithful appointing me to his service" (1 Tim. 1:12).

THE CHURCH PLANTER'S MINISTRY OUTLINE—JOB DESCRIPTION [3]

1. Concerning the Spiritual Soul Ministry

- Preaching the Word of God
- Pray for the people regularly
- Provide spiritual shepherding and mentoring

2. Concerning Church Leadership

- Develop and lead a team of leaders
- Equip others for ministry
- Develop and share the church vision/values
- Make leadership changes where needed

3. Concerning Pastoral Care

- Love, encourage, and visit the people
- Develop a covenant community of Kingdom people
- Help people to be biblical disciples

4. Concerning Church Integrity

- Guard the church from heresy
- Keep the unity of the faith
- Apply discipline to the willfully erring

5. Concerning the Church Ordinances

- Baptize believers upon their confession of faith
- Conduct the communion service for believers in Christ
- Add the baptized believers to the church membership

6. Concerning the Great Commission

- Do the work of evangelism
- Lead the church in mission ventures
- Plan for regular community outreach
- Be involved in the events of the local community

7. Concerning Church Administration

- Keep accurate church records
- Keep phone calls, e-mails, reports, correspondence up to date
- Lead in the preparation of worship services

8. Concerning Life Modelling

- Watch over yourself spiritually
- Model regular financial tithing
- Observe the elder qualifications

9. Concerning Family Ministries

- Conduct child dedications
- Perform family marriages
- Assist in family funerals

10. Concerning Community Involvements

- Participate in the ministerial
- Attend public community events
- Participate in one volunteer agency

11. Concerning Denominational/Conference Networks

- Participate in denominational meetings
- Support the mission and education ministries
- Be loyal to your overseers

D. Church Planter's Ministry Success Principles

Church planters need to be committed to a practical set of guidelines that serve as protection rails to keep them from losing valuable time in unproductive activity. Their time must be used to the greatest possible advantage.

1. Spiritual Growth Principle

Ministry effectiveness is directly related to the leader's faithfulness to Christ. Time must be taken daily to nurture one's faith and to practice the spiritual disciplines.

2. Work and Family Principle

The church planter's family is part of the ministry and not in competition to it. The church planter's date book needs to include family and spouse appointments and a block of time for vacation and days off. Church planters must put in a regular day's work. They themselves, their family, and their church must know when their day begins and when it ends. The key is to get an early start time and to respect the day as a work-day for the Lord.

3. Outreach and Involvement Principle

The church planters must move out into the community and mix with the people. They cannot stay within the safety of the church, home or office walls. Up to 40% of the week should be outreach-directed. The church planters should seek to be involved in one or more community-based caring organizations and so demonstrate their credibility and integrity.

4. Evangelism and Lost Sheep Principle

The church planters need to be practising evangelists. It is not enough to believe in witness; they must do it and model it to others on a daily basis as a witnessing lifestyle. They need to talk about Jesus and His gift to all people. Church planters need to develop eyes for those outside the fold. They must learn to see the needy and the responsive people in the community. Their hearts' compassion and concern must be for those that are straying as sheep without a shepherd.

5. Acceptance and Adaptation Principle

The Greek-Jew principle of Paul, which involves being flexible and adaptable, is very important. Church planters must adjust themselves to the context. The church planters need to express full acceptance of all community people groups. They cannot harbour prejudices, give preferential treatment or express shock to people's problems.

6. Harmony and Control Principle

Church planters must strive for a harmonious working environment. They need to be at peace with their fellow men and women. It is important that they cultivate a relational, non-confronting way with people. Conflict kills the church. Church planters are not miracle machines that can go on endlessly. They are subject to burnout and fatigue and so need to put controls on their life and practice self-care. Church planters need to have a positive, upbeat spirit, and should not easily be given to discouragement. Seeing the positive side of things as well as having a sense of humour and a joyful spirit, is most helpful for the church planter.

7. Time Investment Principle

Church planters need to invest their prime time in potential leaders. As Christ had his priority twelve, so the church planter needs to give quality time to the developing leaders. Church planters must be careful not to get locked into a situation where their time is being monopolized by a few people with unsolvable problems. Such needy people must be kept to scheduled appointments. Church planters need to have a knack for getting things done on time. They cannot be procrastinators. There may not be anybody around to pick up the pieces that are dropped.

8. Institutional Principle

It is important that the church planters establish a good ministry relationship with the existing institutions in the church planting area, such as hospitals, jails, schools, major employers, newspapers, etc.

E. Ministry Focus For The Church Planter's Wife

God has given to the wife of a church planter an important ministry alongside her husband. In order to face the demands and pressures in this ministry she must have a strong commitment to the Lord as well as a strong sense of God's call on her life.

1. Committed to Being a Woman of God

A priority for the church planter's wife is to nurture her relationship with God and to strive to be all that He wants her to be.

a) Woman of the Word
  - Committed to the Genesis model of being a "suitable helper" for her husband
  - Living her life according to the principles of Scripture
  - Receiving encouragement and direction through the Word

b) Woman of Prayer
  - For her husband and her family
  - For her own personal needs
  - For the ministries and people in the church plant
  - For the salvation of people
  - For open doors to share the gospel

c) Woman of Faith
  - Believing that God called them to this particular church plant situation
  - Believing that God will see them through the ups and downs of their ministry

- Believing that God will meet all their personal needs as a family
- Believing that people contacted will accept Christ
- Believing that God will build His church through their ministry

d) Woman of Outreach
   - Seeing the opportunities to reach out to people
   - Sharing the gospel intentionally
   - Building bridges to the uncommitted within the church and in the community

2. Committed to Personal Growth

The role of a church planter's wife is often very demanding. There must be a readiness to take risks, to serve endlessly but at the same time to remain positive in this ministry.

a) Servant Heart
   - Seeing all her tasks, mundane or overwhelming, as assignments from the Lord
   - Filling the gaps where needed
   - Serving regardless of human recognition
   - Looking to God for his approval
   - Being content with her situation and responsibilities

b) Positive Attitude
   - Helps her cope with the stresses of the ministry
   - Affects the attitude her children will have toward the ministry
   - Encourages her husband
   - Blesses the congregation

c) Flexible Mind set
   - Accepting of changes that are a constant in her life
   - Taking demands and schedule revisions in her stride
   - Enjoying the creative approach to ministry

d) Risk Taking
   - Being open to learn and try new experiences

- Moving outside her comfort zone
- Experiencing church in a non-traditional way
- Exposing her children to the demands of church planting
- Willing to have her husband involved in a ministry that requires a greater commitment and involvement on her part as a wife

e) Balance Time Priorities
- Between church and community involvement
- Between time for family and time for church ministries
- Between time spent with husband and time with children
- Between time in team ministry with husband and time in personal ministry
- Between time with Christians and time with the unchurched
- Between time for household tasks and time for relationship building

f) Personal Self-Care
- Setting appropriate boundaries
- Cultivating a mentoring relationship with a mature Christian woman
- Self-resourcing through seminars, reading, workshops, etc.
- Taking time for herself: rest, recreation
- Developing friendships that are life-giving

3. Committed to Ministry Involvement

A church planter's wife has a special opportunity to work alongside her husband. However, it is also important for her serve in areas that are uniquely suited to the gifts that God has given to her.

a) Team Player
  i) Working in team with her husband in the church—Bible Studies, visitation, church programs, relationship building, etc.
  ii) Parenting as a team—helping her husband be a good father by keeping him updated on family issues, making plans for family times, consulting with him, etc.

  iii) Participating in community events together—building relationships

  iv) Having regular planning sessions to build togetherness, keep informed and set goals

b) Encouragement Role

  i) To her husband—being a listener, friend, sounding board for ideas, encouraging him to take his days off, relaxing together over a cup of tea at the end of a busy day

  ii) To her family—at school, in their faith life, activities and achievements

  iii) To the congregation—sending cards, e-mails, telephone calls, coffee, hospitality

  iv) To newcomers—follow-up, hospitality

c) Gift Involvement

  i) Participating in her areas of giftedness—Bible Studies, programs, visitation, hospitality, coffee contacts, etc.

  ii) Using opportunities to serve beyond the church—children's school, community activities, coffee with neighbours

g) Leadership

  i) Giving leadership during start-up period of the church plant until others take responsibility—children's programs, hospitality food/fellowship occasions, women's ministries, etc.

  ii) Delegating as people get involved and their giftedness is discerned

  iv) Coaching, training, and mentoring in areas of her strength

e) Care Giving

  i) Making relationship-building a priority

  ii) Caring for hurting people in the church

  iii) Being a ready listener and an encourager

  iv) Following up with cards, e-mails, phone calls and visits

f) Hospitality

  i) Meeting/welcoming people in the formal church setting

  ii) Inviting people into her home for coffee, meals or lodging

4. Committed to a Sense of Call

The church planter's wife who sees her many responsibilities as tasks that God has called her to do, will experience peace and joy in her ministry.

a) Calling as a Christian
- Living out her personal commitment to the Lord
- Using her God-given gifts
- Growing in Christ-likeness
- Being an impact person in her world—recreational, church, neighbourhood, etc. Sharing the gospel

b) Calling as a Wife
- Helping her husband reach his God-given potential
- Partnering with him in the church planting ministry

c) Calling as a Mother
- Parenting the children entrusted to them as a couple
- Building a positive attitude within the children toward God and the ministry
- Helping children experience and grow in a personal relationship with Christ

d) Calling as a Homebuilder
- Making home a place of joy, peace and rest for her husband and children
- Touching the lives of Christians and the unchurched through home hospitality

The above section was contributed by Elfrieda Nikkel wife of the author.[4]

F. Developing Church Planter-Specific Ministry Statements

PURPOSE—MISSION—VISION—VALUES—MINISTRY—GIFTS

1. Developing and Understanding One's Personal Statements

a) Develop your Biblical Purpose Statement (God's design for me)

The Bible is clear about the reason for one's existence. The basic purpose is the same for all believers, but it needs to be expressed and worded personally. The biblical purpose does not change from person to person. It answers the questions of what the Bible calls them to be and do.

b) Develop your Personal Mission Statement (my response to God's design)

The personal mission statement spells out how we want life to reflect and implement God's design. It is a statement of what people want to do in their life, given how He has created them and given the opportunities and needs around them.

c) Develop your Personal Vision Statement (my future—God willing)

The vision statement is a faith statement of what a person believes God wants to accomplish by prayer, faith and action in their lives. It describes life from the end result, given the promises of God for them.

VISION—getting a telescopic glance of what God wants to accomplish
  - *vision maps out the next leg of one's spiritual journey*
  - *vision is the etching of God's will upon one's heart*
  - *vision is an urgent declaration about a future reality*
  - *vision declares what God wants done at this point in history*

---

d) Develop your Personal Value Statement (what is important in my life)

The value statement declares what is important to a person's faith journey. This statement identifies the non-negotiable values that they will be faithful to on a day-to-day basis.

e) Develop your Ministry Statement (my ministry priority)

The ministry statement is a commitment and dedication statement that summarizes the strategic priorities that individuals will pursue for an effective ministry.

2. Steps in Identifying God's Design for an Individual

a) Commit Yourself to the Biblical Purpose
   Glorify God in whatever you do
   State the reason for your existence

b) Dedicate Yourself to the Present Will of God
   Give priority to seeking God's Kingdom
   Follow God's moral will
   Make the most of every opportunity
   Pursue the way of service and sacrifice
   Obey the biblical mandates of making disciples and loving your neighbour

c) Make Observations From Your Past
   What has God blessed in your past?
   What opportunities of service have come your way?
   Are there some re-occurring themes or issues?
   Are there some weaknesses that need addressing?
   What are the things you value?

d) Identify People of Influence in Your Life
   What are these influencers affirming about you?
   What do they say about your strengths?
   What cautions do they give?
   What do they see as your personal mission?[5]

3. Develop Your Understanding of Spiritual Gifts

Your mission and calling will be in keeping with your own being. It is God that has created us unto good works. The acrostic: S-H-A-P-E is often used to gain an understanding of your gift mix. Assessing yourself on the basis of your "shape" helps to determine your gift mix.

S—Spirituality
   Your spiritual gift hunches?
   What spiritual ministry invigorates you?
H—Heart
   - what do you feel passionate about?
   - what does your heart say about your calling?
A—Ability
   - what can I do well and enjoy doing?
   - what am I suited for in the Kingdom of God?
P—Personality
   - what is my character suited for?
   - what are my natural tendencies and traits for mission?
E—Experience
   - what do my experiences affirm?
   - what do I know I can do well?[6]

A person's mission statement usually flows out of how one understands one's spiritual gifts and mission in relation to family, work associates, the church, the Bible and the world. It should be noted that Christian involvements are not only based on spiritual gifts but also on the needs or special circumstances as exemplified by the good Samaritan. It should also be noted that spiritual gifts in a person are often better determined by others rather than by the persons assessing themselves. Where spiritual gifts are self-assessed they often become an excuse for not doing what one does not like or enjoy.

4. Differentiate Between Strong and Weak Spiritual Leadership

Though the characteristics selected are especially true of Western-type leadership, the comparison between natural and spiritual leaders is worthy of careful consideration.

THE NATURAL LEADER	THE SPIRITUAL LEADER
1. Self-confident	1. Confident in God
2. Knows people	2. Also knows God
3. Makes his/her own decisions	3. Seeks to find God's will
4. Ambitious	4. Self-effacing
5. Originate his/her own methods	5. Finds/follows God's method
6. Enjoys commanding others	6. Delights to obey God
7. Motivated by personal considerations	7. Motivated by love for God
8. Independent	8. God-dependent

Weaknesses/Cautions

There is a fine line between a leadership strength and leadership weakness. When a leadership strength is pushed too far it becomes a weakness. There is a fine line between a person's strengths and weaknesses. Paul refers to this concept in a warning to the Corinthians by saying, "so if you think you are standing firm, be careful that you do not fall" (1 Cor. 10:12). Note the contrasting combinations of positive and negative characteristics.

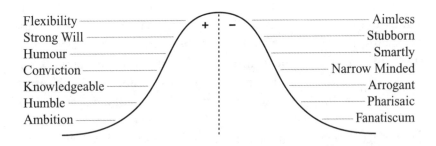

Flexibility	Aimless
Strong Will	Stubborn
Humour	Smartly
Conviction	Narrow Minded
Knowledgeable	Arrogant
Humble	Pharisaic
Ambition	Fanatiscum

5. Understanding the Value of Coaching in Church Planting

The coaching systems that are effectively used follow a definite strategy. Robert Logan and Steven Ogne have given the coaching movement significant shape and direction.[6] What most church-planting supervisors have been doing intuitively for years has now been packaged into a useful coaching system as follows:

The Coaching Process

1. Listen empathetically
2. Care personally
3. Celebrate wins
4. Develop strategy
5. Develop skills
6. Disciple the whole person
7. Challenge specifically

The Coaching Relationship

The church-planting coaches in their sessions seek to cover the church planter's ministry and personal life, as well as the relational and accountability areas. Their effectiveness depends on the right balance of the five possible authority approaches being used.

1. Positional authority
2. Spiritual authority
3. Relational authority
4. Experiential authority
5. Skill and expertise authority[7]

G. Lessons From The Church Growth Environment

1. They Talk About Leadership Types

Catalyst—the pioneer, creative enterprising leader
Organizer—specializing in making things orderly and workable
Operator—is adept at keeping things going and making things nice
Renewalist—is able to redevelop and rebuild a situation[8]

The church planter is identified as a catalytic leader whose energies are directed toward the community.

2. They Talk About Leadership Classes

Class I—Leaders who work primarily within the church body, working with believers

Class II—Leaders who work primarily outside of the church structure in an effort to bring people to Christ and into the body.

Class III—Leaders who are full-time paid pastors in the church

Class IV—Leaders serving in denominational leadership roles[9]

The church planter is classified as a class-two leader whose primary concern is community outreach.

3. They Talk About Pioneers and Homesteaders

Pioneers are the founding members or old-timers who fought the early formation battles and have become a tightly-knit group, as the originals.

Homesteaders are the second group who have moved in and become involved after the church was established, and do not identify with the past.[10]

The church planter is often caught between these two leadership groups who tend to have conflicting visions.

4. They Talk About Shepherds and Ranchers

Shepherd leaders keep close contact with all the people and minister to their individual needs.

Rancher leaders delegate and oversee the work of ministry, but do not necessarily have close contact with individual attenders.

The church planter needs to start off as a shepherd leader and as the congregation grows he needs to switch to the rancher model.[11]

5. They Talk About Enablers and Equippers

Enablers function as a relational facilitator among equals, who are content to see what the agenda of the group might be.

Equippers have a defined goal and seek to prepare and motivate the group to fulfill some given goals.[12]

The church planters need to see themselves as a combination of the enabler and the equipper. They have an agenda to move forward in a relational way and to create a sense of ownership within the group.

6. They Talk About Modality and Sodality

Modality leaders are congregational and pastoral in focus
Sodality leaders are frontier and expansion in focus.[13]

The church planter needs to have a sodalic, apostolic spirit and a venturing faith.

7. They Talk About Church Culture and Mission Culture

Church culture leaders assume that outreach can happen from the church
Mission culture leaders assume that outreach needs to be done away from the church.[14]

The church planter needs to realize that the church exists in a non-church culture which requires outreach in the community with a missional mind set.

8. They Talk About Growth Eyes and Visitor Eyes

Church Growth Eyes—Describes a vision of the harvest that looks for growth opportunities and ways to maximize growth principles
Visitor Eyes—Describes the church from the perspective of what the visitor experiences or sees with a view to improving areas of weakness.

Church planters need to have church growth eyes and visitor eyes. They need to be aware of the feeling of new people, and so provide a ministry with sensitivity.

9. They Talk about Leadership Style and Church Size

Spiritual leadership is the primary factor in church planting.

Except for the blessing and actions of God, everything rises and falls on the ability of the church planter to give leadership. The style of leadership is related to the size of the church, the vision of the group and the theology of the church on leadership. The role of the pastor changes with the size of the church.

Church Leadership and Church Character and Size

0 to 50—**Family-Centred Church**—with association based on belonging to one another

50 to 150—**Pastor-Centred Church**—association based on knowing one another

150 to 350—**Program-Centred Church**—association based on involvement/committees

350 Plus—**Staff-Centred Corporation**—association based on celebrations and quality

In the large churches the pastors symbolize unity, quality and church stability.[15] Carl George uses animal terms to describe church size and leadership relationships. His terms are: mouse size—home group, cat size—small church, lap dog size—medium church, yard dog size—large church, horse size—super church, elephant size—mega church and metropolis of mice—meta church.

The mission of the church succinctly and simplistically stated, is to proclaim the gospel of Jesus Christ in the power of the Holy Spirit among all the social groupings of mankind and to gather those who hear into churches. Planting churches is right at the heart of the Apostolate of the church of the New Testament. Planting churches is the essence of the apostolic gift.

Baptist General Convention,
Bold Missions Multiplying Churches

H. Church Planter Stresses And Self-Care

FACING THE STRUGGLES AND STRESSES OF MINISTRY

1. Spiritual Stresses in Church Planting

a) Stress of Open Doors
Paul talks about having no rest in his spirit or peace of mind about the opposition he faced, despite many open doors. Opportunity doors with road blocks create much stress (2 Cor. 2:12-13, 1 Cor. 16:9).

b) Stress of an Earthen Vessel
There are always limitations to the ministry because of human weakness. The answer is God's sufficiency (2 Cor. 4:7-10; 7:3-6).

c) Stress of Daily Caring
There is the constant pressure that comes from carrying the concern and responsibility for the Church (2 Cor. 11:27-29; Col. 2:1-2).

d) Stress from Desertion and Hypocrisy
Discouragement can be very disheartening, when people turn away or against the planter after endless time has been spent on their behalf (Gal. 1:6;2:13).

e) Stress of Sleepless Nights
Paul talks about praying night and day for the church's spiritual welfare and encourages Timothy to endure hardship in the face of difficulties (1 Thess. 3:10; 2 Tim. 4:5).

f) Stress of Evangelism Warfare
The work of evangelism is hard work, and requires much endurance. It is a fight against the powers of darkness (Eph. 6:12;11 Tim. 4:5).

2. Professional Stresses in Church Planting

a) Stress of the Caring Profession
Caring for people, keeping confidences and resisting manipulation makes for a stressful work week.

b) Stress of Emotional Ministry
Carrying the emotional concerns of the poor, the despairing, hurting, sick and dying creates much stress.

c) Stress of Congregational Insensitivity
Working overtime to keep unity, harmony, and satisfaction within the body without appreciation, is discouraging.

d) Stress of Evening and Weekend Work
Being on call constantly and working evenings and weekends creates constant stress for the family.

e) Stress of Social Vulnerability
Working and living, often with only few friends but many critics and advisors, is especially stressful for the pastor's family.

f) Stress of Spiritual Fitness
There is often the expectation from the church that the church planter always needs to be strong and spiritually fit.

g) Stress of Denominational Expectation
Answering questions on progress, and giving conference reports, can be burdensome.

h) Stress of Isolation and Separation
A church planter can feel very alone and often deserted by conference leaders, and misunderstood by peers.[16]

3. Warning Signs of Ministry Burn-out

a) Energy Depletion—lack of priority and enthusiasm
b) Negative Feelings—short tolerance level
c) Stagnation—lack of accomplishment or progress, resistance to change
d) Self-Interest—preoccupation with self and little concern for others
e) Self-Esteem—negative disposition, indifference, hopelessness, poor self-image
f) Lack of Planning—work maintenance, spinning wheels, poor motivation

g) Irritable Behaviour—impulsive decisions, cynical attitude

h) Social Withdrawal—locked into defeatist relationships

i) Immobilization—due to physical, emotional and mental exhaustion

j) Physical Signals—overeating, headaches, sleeplessness, depression, fatigue

k) Spiritual Apathy—minimum output, spiritual defeat, poor choices

l) Blurred Vision—rejecting new information, distortion of perception

4. Spiritual Self-care to Avoid Ministry Burn-out

a) Practice Basic Self-Disciplines
Adequate rest, good diet, exercise, recreation

b) Self-Assessment
Do a realistic self-evaluation of abilities and gifts, know work limits and energy levels, set realistic goals, consult with a mentor or coach

c) Revitalization
Nurture your spiritual self through regular prayer, Bible reading, reflection, journalling, and personal retreats, etc.

d) Peer Support
Build a support system of peers for friendship, fellowship, trust relationship, recreation, etc.

e) Home Reinforcement
Strengthen your home life and marriage by having regular days off, spousal dates, regular holidays, and time with your children, etc.

f) Personal Growth
Cultivate a personal growth edge through reading, continuing education, outdoor activity and community involvement, etc.

g) Lighten Up
By having more fun times, laughter, walking and camping. Enjoy life!

h) Health Care

Adopt a lifestyle that protects against stress-related health conditions—heart problems, low immune system, ulcers, muscle tensions and nervous conditions, etc.

I. Church Planter Profile Assessment System—PAS

DR. CHARLES RIDLEY ASSESSMENT TOOL

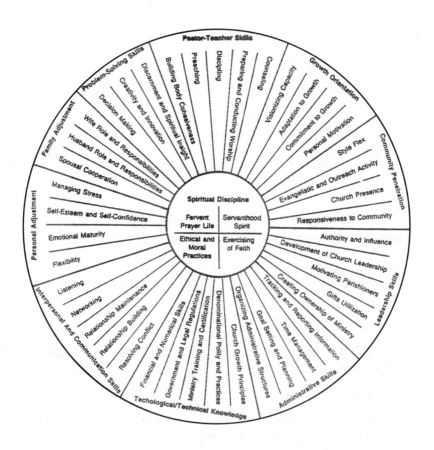

The result of a survey of church planters in Canada and the United States has produced the Church Planter Performance Profile. The characteristics of the profile wheel can serve as a grid for ministry evaluation. The church planter will need to keep the wheel in balance. While all the forty-six specific performance dimensions are important, five have been identified as critical; they are the spiritual discipline core, growth orientation, community outreach, leadership skills, and family adjustment.

The profile was developed using a state-of-the art industrial organizational technique called "job analysis." Thirteen denominations, including the Mennonite Brethren, formed a consortium led by the Fuller Institute of Evangelism and Church Growth, which sponsored a research project resulting in the identification of the skills, abilities and qualities that are essential for effective church planting.[17]

ESSENTIAL CHARACTERISTICS MEASURED IN THE
PAS ASSESSMENT INTERVIEW

1. Visioning Capacity

A person who can project a God-given vision of the future. Such a person can see the finished project before it is started.

2. Intrinsically Motivated

A self-starter with a willingness to build from nothing. Having a high energy, vitality, and motivational level.

3. Creates Ownership of Ministry

Helping people to "buy in" and feel responsible for the growth and success of the church.

4. Relate to the Unchurched

Ability to communicate with the unchurched and break through the barriers they tend to erect.

5. Spousal Cooperation

Having mutual understanding of each other's roles in the home.

Enjoying hospitality and willing to pay the price for the many demands and uncertainties in church planting.

6. Effectively Builds Relationships

Making others feel secure and comfortable in their presence and showing compassion to expressed needs and concerns of individuals, making them feel worthwhile and wanted.

7. Responsive to Community People and Needs

Ability to understand, identify and assess community needs and target people.

8. Committed to Church Growth

Appreciating steady and consistent growth without preoccupation with quick success factors. Not satisfied with maintenance ministries.

9. Utilizing Giftedness of Others

Releasing, equipping, and matching giftedness of people with ministry tasks that need to be done.

10. Flexible and Adaptable

Coping effectively with constant and abrupt changes and learning how to shift priorities and emphasis during various stages of church growth.

11. Builds Group Cohesiveness

Developing a nucleus group who catch your vision of ministry and run with it.

12. Resilience

Ability to rebound from setbacks, disappointments, failures, and criticism.

13. Exercise Faith

Possessing a conviction regarding the call to church planting as well as believing that God will provide and answer prayer for both the church planter family and the ministry.

14. Sense of God's Call to Church Planting

Having a growing, continued interest and desire to plant churches with a God-driven conviction and a sense of call. (Number fourteen was not part of the original PAS.)

Rating

The rating of these fourteen characteristics is on a scale of 1 to 5, with 5 being the ideal. If the candidate scores lower than 3.5 on more than 3 of the first 5, or below 2.5 on any one of the first 5, the likelihood of a person succeeding as a church planter is slim.

> Leadership is the discipline of deliberately exerting special influence within a group to move it toward goals of beneficial permanence that fulfill the group's real need."
>
> John Haggai, *Lead On*

J. Causes For Church Planter Resignations

1. Lack of a Divine Calling

Church planters must know that they are called by God to a church-planting assignment. Only the conviction of God's will and vision provides adequate motivation for long-range church planting.

2. Stepping-Stone Assignment

If the church planters are using church planting as a ministry start-up step to gain experience for another assignment, they will not last.

3. Spousal Partnership

Church planters cannot go it alone. If their spouses are not supportive and co-operative to this ministry, the church planting assignment will be short-lived.

4. Maintenance Philosophy

One cannot plant a church by remote control out of an office. Unless there is a strong commitment on the part of the church planters to do community evangelism, they will have a short term.

5. Negative Disposition

Church planters who take a pessimistic or confrontational approach toward the congregation and conference leadership will soon be without a congregation. A positive spirit is essential for an ongoing ministry of attraction.

6. Flamboyant Approach

Church planting requires a steady and stable involvement. When the church planters depend only on their winsome personality and novel ideas for church growth, they will soon run to the end of their resources.

7. Role Confusion

A person who is perceived as being "high browed" or is seen as being more interested in books and lectures than people and needs, will not make it in the long run. Church planting is a people-ministry task rather than a professional teaching position.

8. Spiritual Burnout

Church planter resignations are inevitable when they lose sight of the power and resources of God. Spiritual drought and personal fruitlessness will quickly lead to the termination of their assignment.

9. Over-Confidence

When leaders overwork their strengths, these qualities turn into weakness and failure. When strong leadership turns into aggression, ambition becomes fanaticism, and confidence becomes arrogance; a church planter will soon lose the confidence of the group.

10. Independence

Church planters need to be willing to share the ministry with others. There is a danger for church planters to claim ownership of the work and make decisions independent of the group, thereby creating alienation. Unless there is a willingness to adjust ministry goals to incorporate the visions of the church, the church planters will soon find themselves alone, irrelevant and unwanted.

11. Lack of Vision

Church planters need to be able to visualize the development steps and see the end product from the beginning. Church planters that minister from week to week or from crisis to crisis without planning ahead and anticipating future decisions or needs, will not see growth.

12. Spiritual Compromise

When a church planter violates the moral and ethical values of the Bible through ministry indiscretions, moral failure, or dishonest business practises, he or she has then compromised the integrity and qualifications that the Bible requires for church leadership.

13. Spiritual Gift Mix

The church planter needs to have an apostolic spirit and the spiritual gift mix needed to see the formation of a church. If the planter does not have the personality and gifting for church planting leadership, the assignment will be short-lived or unproductive.

14. Claiming Ownership

The church belongs to Christ. However, after the church planters have put so much time and effort into establishing the church, it begins to feel like it belongs to them. When the church planters take church decisions into their own hands and so demonstrate an attitude of church ownership, the congregation soon feels as though they do not matter and do not count. Such disconnection between the planter and the congregation often results in alienation and resignation or termination.

NOTES——

1 Terry Walling, *Focusing Leaders* (Carol Stream, Illinois: Church Smart Resources, 1997), p. 4, Module Two.

2 Carl George, *Prepare Your Church for the Future* (Tarrytown, New York: Fleming H. Revell, 1991), p. 136.

3 *The Church Planter's Ministry Outline* was first presented in Lithuania at a leaders' Seminar in 2000.

4 The section, *Ministry Focus for the Church Planter's Wife* was written by Elfrieda Nikkel, the author's wife. She has participated in many church plants and works as a professional family counsellor.

5 Some of this material has been adapted from the Terry Walling *Focusing Leaders* manual.

6 Rick Warren, *The Purpose-Driven Church* (Grand Rapids, Michigan: Zondervan Publishing House, 1995), p. 370.

7 Steve Ogne, *Boot Camp Manual* (Cedar Springs, Washington, 1996), pp. 1-9.

8 Carl George, Lecture Handout, Fuller Institute.

9 C. Peter Wagner, Class Notes, *How to Plant a Church*, Fuller Theological Seminary.

10 C. Peter Wagner, *Leading Your Church to Growth* (Ventura, California: Regal Books, 1984), p. 209.

11 Wagner, p. 173.

12 Wagner, pp.75-79.

13 Wagner, p. 146.

14 Kennon L. Callahan, *Effective Church Leadership* (San Francisco: Harper & Row, 1990), p. 34.

15 George, pp. 44-50.

16 Adapted from The Albon Institute, *Clergy Stress and Burn-out* Seminar by Ray Oswald, Winnipeg, 1983.

17 Charles Ridley, Church Planters Consortium and Consultation, Fuller Institute, 1985.

- THIRTEEN

Personal Witness

Christians have the job and potential for becoming spiritual meaning-makers. Of all the people on the face of the earth, the followers of Jesus are in a position to make most sense of life. They have access to the Creator's plan. They are in a position to unscramble TV channels. Christians have the capacity to bring a clear picture of what God intended when He set the world in motion. We can sort out the jumble and chart a life with coherent design.

Don Posterski, *Reinventing Evangelism.*

There are three basic outreach tracks to making disciples. There is the witness that individuals do to the best of their ability, and then there is that which the Christians do together through the church, and then there is the corporate witness that all the churches do together in the community. In this personal faith-sharing chapter, an attempt is made to cover the personal witness practice and understanding. This chapter is essential to church planting, since evangelism is church planting and church planting is evangelism.

A. Introductory Outreach Insights For Church Planters

HELPING PEOPLE INTO THE KINGDOM

1. Variation

Golf Bag witnessing is an appropriate witness analogy. Just as one needs different clubs for the different positioning of the golf balls on the golf course in relationship to the flag pole, so one needs to use different spiritual strokes depending on where people are in relationship to the cross of Christ. Different clubs or approaches are needed to help people cross the faith line.

2. Readiness

God is already at work in people's lives, and it is for the Christian to identify the people that are ready, and to help them understand how they can become Christians.

3. Friendship

Friendship leads to understanding, relationship and commitment. The building of relationships usually precedes the sharing of the gospel and brings people into a commitment to Christ. Often church involvement leads to a personal acceptance of Christ.

4. Actions

People today are word-weary and respond much more readily to deeds of love and acts of kindness than they do to theological truth as a starting point of faith sharing.

5. Dialogue

Witnessing within our pluralistic society needs to flow from a non-judgmental, accepting and caring position. Dialogue needs to flow conversationally and respectfully, somewhat like a ping-pong rally with no quick spikes.

6. Prayer

Christians need to learn that prayer must precede witness. Prayer cultivates and prepares the heart for the seeds of the gospel.

7. Mentoring

Faith sharing is most effective in a step-by-step faith mentoring and spiritual direction-giving; which leads people to the cross of Christ for forgiveness and new birth, in an environment of trust and caring.

8. Process

Conversion is most often experienced within a process or a series of steps. It is not uncommon for people to need up to seven or more different exposures to the gospel before they are ready to make a commitment.

9. Progression

Conversion can also be described as a chain of events that lead to the ultimate "chain link" of faith in Christ. Some of the lead-up chain events may include infant baptism, church participation, doing good deeds, years of searching, and finally accepting Christ as their Saviour and Lord. Helping people take the final faith step is the challenge.

10. Initiative

The most effective witness will take place in non-Christian places and likely not in the church. It will require the Christians to take the initiative in reaching out to the unchurched.

11. Timing

Timing is important in people's openness to the gospel. They may express openness in spring, but by the time fall comes, they are on to something else. Taking the harvest when it is ripe is essential.

12. Response

Bringing closure to the witness conversation is important. Giving a definite opportunity to respond is necessary. It is important for the witness to clarify what kind of a faith response Christ is looking for.

13. Jesus

Talking about Jesus is the key. General dialogue about a loving

God does not provide enough content to the gospel. Jesus is the way, the truth and the life. He is the door. He died in our place. Salvation has to do with accepting what Jesus did for us. This goes beyond general God talk. The issue is one's response to Jesus, who offers Himself as Saviour and Lord.

14. Journey

There are many pathways to Christ, but only one way to God, which is through Christ. There is only one mediator between God and mankind, which is Christ Jesus.

15. Messenger

The adage that the medium is the message has much truth to it. The witness embodies the message. The integrity and sincerity of the witness will lend credence to the gospel. The lives of Christians validate the gospel.

16. Patience

For effective evangelism, one needs to be thinking of a process of time involving friendship, relationship and witness. In the past, evangelism was more often thought of as an event, rather than a journey leading toward an understanding and entry into a commitment.

17. Involvement

Active church involvement before a commitment is made often moves people towards salvation. As seekers connect with Christians in ministry, they see their need for making their own commitment. Involvements could be in the area of hospitality, music, maintenance, etc. In times past the emphasis was that people needed to make a commitment first before any church involvements would be possible. Involvement evangelism is proving to be an effective approach to outreach.

B. Double-Diamond Disciple Making

The individual outreach aspects in the role of bringing people into the Kingdom can be described as the Double-Diamond process.

The writer has developed this diamond analogy as a witness-training tool. It traces the believer's faith activity in two spheres, starting with the church body and then out to the Community diamond.[1]

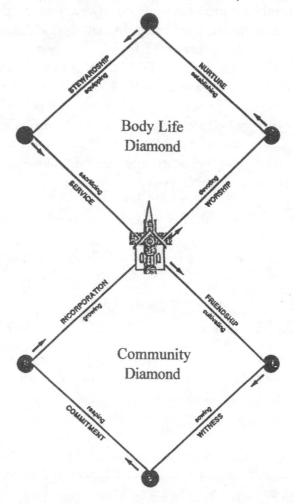

The Double-Diamond disciple-making plan calls for the involvement of the believer in two different spheres. The Body Life diamond represents the believer's activity pattern within the Body of Christ. A growing disciple will cover each of the four bases of the Body diamond. Believers need to be careful that they are not left on first base of the discipling plan. Each believer needs to move slowly along the bases of faith into nurture, stewardship, and service.

Serious disciples of Christ will make sure they do not only run the Body diamond over and over, but will assure that a balanced portion of the faith life is run on the Community diamond.

The community involvement diamond describes a definite pattern or plan of outreach. The strategy of making disciples or of winning people to Christ begins with friendship. Once the friendship base has been reached, the discipler begins to move toward the second and third bases of witness and commitment, and then onward to body incorporation. The Community diamond is helpful in that it gives the believer a definite pattern of witness involvement. Often Christians get left on the friendship base, without a definite second and third base of witness and commitment in mind. Satan will do everything possible to keep a person from progressing past the first Community base. In fact, he would prefer for the Christian to remain on the Body diamond only. For the church to be effective in continuous disciple-making, it will need to take both the Body life and the Community diamonds more seriously and to keep them in balance.

C. Charting The Faith-Sharing Journey

INDISPENSABLE TO CHURCH PLANTING

Witnessing is the natural overflowing of the new life that has come to the believing person through the Holy Spirit. In a world of unbelief, faith sharing has become more of a duty driven by guilt, rather than being a privilege to represent Christ as His good news ambassador. We are to be witnesses for and unto Christ (Acts 1:8). In a world of growing religious diversity, it is more critical than ever that the Christians articulate their convictions and experiences of new life in Christ in a meaningful and non-judgmental way.

1. Establishing the Personal Witnessing Goals

a. To help people understand God's view on issues of life and death.

b. To help people believe and accept Christ as the basis of their salvation.

c. To help people commit themselves to the body or family of Christ for fellowship, nurture and worship.

d. To help people assume responsibility for the work and mission of Christ in this world.[2]

2. Balancing the Witnessing Expression

Each community needs to experience three levels of witness.

a) The Individual Witness

The faithful and sincere expression of word and deed, friendship and relationship, are most effective and attractive to a hurting, broken world.

b) The Church Witness

Seeing the vibrant and joyful Body of Christ united in fellowship and worship is in itself a powerful witness to the watching world. The Body of Christ has a magnetic attraction as it lifts up Christ the Saviour.

c) Agencies Witness/Church at Large

The many mission and para-church agencies have had a vital role in sharing Christ. With their single focus they are effective evangelists. This broader witness also includes the united action of all the churches together. The local church gathers up the fruit generated through cooperative church and agency witness.

3. Developing a Life of Integrated Witness

There are five witness aspects that work together for impact in the life of a Christian.

a) Inner Witness

This is the inward witness of holiness and devotion to Christ as Saviour reflecting the life between you and God (the witness that God sees).

b) Body Witness

This witness involves the cooperation in the Body of Christ expressing unity, love and participation with other believers (faith witness among Christians).

c) Deed Witness

This witness of faith and works includes community involvement, social concerns and deeds done in the community (Christian's reputation outside of the church).

d) Word Witness

This witness is the verbalized faith of explaining and sharing the meaning and importance of Christ for people (conversational witness to the unchurched).

e) Peace Witness

This witness is a character witness. The community of faith is about showing the alternatives of love and peace within a society of alienation and violence (general kingdom value witness).

D. Believer Preparation For Effective Witnessing

1. Experiencing Kingdom Empowerment

a) The presence of Christ gives confidence
b) The power of Holy Spirit brings fruitfulness
c) The Word of God gives authority
d) The Body of Christ provides support
e) One's personal experience of salvation gives integrity
f) By faith, fears and barriers are overcome
g) From a servant heart comes opportunity
h) A bold vision provides direction
j) A disciplined life gives credibility and inner strength
k) A praying posture provides power and conviction
l) Spiritual gifts provide balance and believer participation

2. Learning and Sharing the Simple Message of Hope

a) God's Intent—Eternal Life for All!
  • God loves and desires all to be saved (John. 3:16)
  • Heaven is a free gift (Rom. 6:23)

b) Human Problem—Separation from God
  • People have sinned and walked out on God (Rom. 3:23)
  • Sin must be punished (John 3:36)

• People cannot save themselves (Eph. 2:8-9)

c) God's Solution—Christ as a Ransom
  • Christ died in our place (Rom. 5:6-10)
  • Opened the doorway to God
  • Offers free salvation (John 14:6)

d) Individual Response—Personal Acceptance
  • Believe on Jesus Christ (John 1:12)
  • Trust Christ alone for salvation (1 John. 5:11-13)
  • Repent and confess your sins (Acts 16:31)
  • Ask Christ to take over your life

e) Changed Life—Together With Christ
  • New creation (2 Cor. 5: 17)
  • Following Jesus
  • Serving one another
  • Worship the living God
  • Walking in the Spirit

3. Preparing Your Own Testimony (My Faith Story Outline)

a) My life before I accepted Christ
  • How I lived and thought (if converted as an adult)
  • How the Bible describes life without Christ (if converted as a child)

b) How I came to realize that I had a spiritual problem
  • How God sought me and spoke to me
  • How I became restless—convicted—attracted to Christ

c) How I received Christ
  • The role of others in my salvation
  • How I made my confession of faith—acceptance of Christ

d) How things have changed after my conversion
  • New understanding of life and its purpose
  • New activity involving God's family

e) How I try to share my new discoveries with others

- The power of Christ in us as a witness
- God's forgiveness, grace, and mercy

E. Developing Eyes For Witnessing Opportunities

1. Identifying the Witnessing Worlds and Friendship Webs

Contact and concentrate on two or three in each world for spiritual influence
a) Family World
b) Neighbourhood World
c) Employment World
d) Recreational World
e) Peer Group World
f) Situational Need World—Good Samaritan type
g) Providential Unplanned World—one-time meetings

2. Recognizing the Distance Factors Between People When Witnessing

Accept and appreciate the differences between people
a) World view spectrum of distance from Christianity to secularism
b) Tradition distance from church to non-church
c) Educational and economic/social distance factors
d) Cultural mosaic distances and differences
e) Generational distances/peer group differences
f) Geographic and locations distances
g) Language and color distances[3]

3. Learning to Recognize People Responsive and Interested in the Gospel

A sensitive and loving faith expression is required for:
a) People in social or political upheaval, persecution, and turmoil
b) People in disadvantage—poverty and suppression
c) People in dissatisfaction—loneliness and disappointment
d) People in crisis or need—illness and family failure
e) People in transition—job, family, and health
f) People with Christian connections—family and friends [4]

F. Leading Someone To Faith In Christ

THE NEW BEGINNING

1. Pre-commitment Phase

After having established a common-ground relationship, move toward telling your faith story of how Christ has made you a new person by faith.

2. Commitment Phase

Begin by inviting the person to become a follower of Jesus. Help the person accept the gift of spiritual life to start the Christian life. The seeker needs to realize that God is the One Who provides forgiveness through Jesus

Sample commitment conversation:

a) Draw near to God and He will draw near to you (Jas. 4:7-10). "As we speak to God in a prayer, picture yourself in God's presence."

b) Search me, Oh God, and see my heart (Ps. 139:23-24). "Ask the Lord to point out the things in your life that you need to confess. Ask the Lordto forgive you and to lead you in the way of righteousness."

c) "But as many as received Him, to them gave He power to become the sons of God, even to those that believe in His name" (John 1:12). "In a sentence or two, receive Christ by inviting him to be your personal Saviour. Ask Him to forgive your sins and give you the gift of eternal life through your faith in Christ" (Eph. 2:8-9).

d) Express your thanks to Christ for dying on the cross for you (Rom. 5:8). Ask him to fill your life with the Holy Spirit so that you can overcome the temptations of the enemy. The Father gives the Holy Spirit to those who ask.

Sample Prayer of Commitment

Dear Father in Heaven I know that I am a sinner and need Your forgiveness. I believe that Christ died in my place, paying the penalty for my sin. I am willing to repent and turn from my sin with Your help. I now invite Jesus Christ to come into my heart and life as my personal Saviour. I ask you to fill me with Your Holy Spirit and to take control of my life. I am willing, with Your help, to follow and obey Christ as the Lord of my life. Thank you for giving me salvation as a gift. Thank you for accepting me as your child into your family. Amen.

---

3. Celebration Phase

Welcome the person into the family of God on Christ's behalf. Give the new convert immediate assurance that he/she now is a child of God. Assure the new believer that the following has taken place as a new follower of Christ:

Their sins are forgiven (Col. 1:14)
They have become children of God (John 1:12)
They have been made an heir to all of God's blessings (Rom. 8:16-17)
They now have everlasting life (John 3:16)
They are a new creation (2 Cor. 5:17)

Part of the celebration is the sharing of their conversion with someone else.

4. Becoming a Follower

The Application of Faith: To follow Christ involves sharing His values, adhering to His teachings, and obeying His commands. The Christian life has now begun involving the various aspects of being a disciple or follower of Jesus.

5. Understanding Conversion

The conversion process is a partnership involving God and the human witness. The diagram below shows the progressive response patterns of the person receiving the message. Note the three interactive aspects of salvation in the diagram adapted from the Engel scale.[5]

UNDERSTANDING THE SALVATION PROCESS

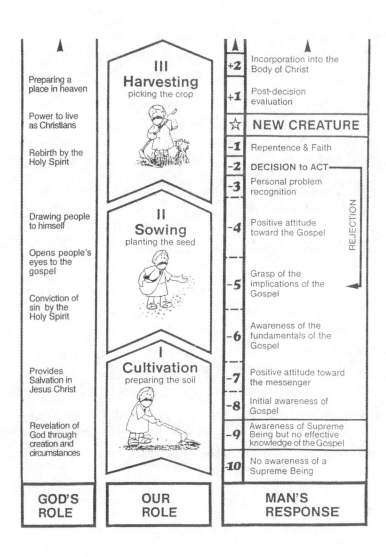

| GOD'S ROLE | OUR ROLE | MAN'S RESPONSE |

G. Understanding The Market-Place Person In Witness

1. The Needs of the Market-Place Secular Person

a) Credible Christianity

The market-place secular person needs to see a credible expression of faith. There is a need for a real-life demonstration of what a believer is like.

b) Friendship

The market-place secular person needs to have a caring Christian friend who understands and expresses a loving concern regardless of circumstances.

c) Conversation

The market-place secular person has a need for dialogue to answer questions on subjects of the Christian faith. A non-judgmental and non threatening conversation is required.

d) Acceptance

The market-place secular person needs to be accepted and appreciated at the level of faith and commitment that the person is presently holding.

e) Guidance

The market-place secular person needs to be led to experience his/her full spiritual potential through a loving witnessing, friendship; he/she needs to be helped into the Kingdom by a friend through the new birth.

f) Instruction

The market-place secular person needs to see that people are being deceived by Satan with various misconceptions. People need to understand that salvation cannot be earned or merited by good works or achieved through the association with religious groups or the involvement of sacred exercises.

2. The Feelings of the Market-Place Secular Person when Among Christians

Some market-place people fear being exposed due to their limited knowledge of Christianity. They may have a sensitivity about some past religious experiences and so they fear being judged when among Christians. Their past efforts and participation in religious life may have resulted in disappointment and disillusionment. Secular people tend to feel uncomfortable in Christian crowds and fear being seen with Christians by their friends. They try to avoid being among Christian pros, who sing nicely, pray fluently, and read confidently. A growing number of Canadians feel that the church is irrelevant to their situation, and consequently are not giving it much attention. Many secular people do not feel any need for a personal faith in God.

3. Faith Levels Identified by the Market-Place Person

People often first experience the four levels of faith below, which can serve as a staircase to a personal salvation faith. Witnessing is dialogue about salvation faith.

   a) Historic Faith is the belief that Christ was born as the Son of God and that there is a Creator God Who is revealed in the Bible.

   b) Physical Faith is the dependence and involvement of God for the physical dimensions of life such as food, clothing and physical health. Here the involvement of God is in the temporal affairs of this life.

   c) Emergency Faith is the turning to God in times of trouble and stress while the rest of life is lived mostly without God. It is a faith of last resort to help cross an emergency crisis.

   d) Institutional Faith involves a level of relationship and participation with the church. It is often an outward conforming to the behavioural expectations of the body. This may include baptism, membership, weddings, funerals, and occasional attendance.

   e) Salvation Faith is a personal faith that reaches to God in Christ for eternal life, where forgiveness of sin and peace with God is given as a gift from God. This faith accepts and focuses on what God has done through the death of His Son instead of what people do to win salvation. It is a response to accept salvation to become a follower of Christ.

> ... radical conversion can never be the achievement of any human persuasion, however eloquent. It can only be the work of God. True conversion, therefore, which is the proper end toward which the communication of the gospel looks, can only be a work of God, a kind of miracle--not natural, but supernatural.
>
> Lesslie Newbigin, *Foolishness to the Greeks*

H. The Winning Combination In Witnessing

WORKING THE SPIRITUAL HARVEST

1. Declare your obedience to the witness assignment of Christ
2. Identify your friendship worlds and select three or four people for regular witness
3. Pray regularly for them and for their salvation
4. Exchange visits, courtesies, and friendship
5. Build relationships through coffee times and meals
6. Attend social and recreational events together
7. Open the subject of faith, dialogue with discussion
8. Invite a third party to explain the faith picture
9. Invite the person to join you at a special church celebration event
10. Encourage participation in neighbourhood Bible discussion group
11. Lead toward a definite decision to accept the offer as given by Christ
12. Stay in touch with them and start the discipling process

> More people become part of God's kingdom because of love than by rational persuasion. We don't argue people into the church; we love them into it.
>
> Herb Miller, *Magnetic Church*

I. Overcoming Personal Witnessing Fears And Neglects

REASONS FOR INEFFECTIVENESS IN, OR LACK OF WITNESSING

1. Some think they need a special gift or calling
2. They don't realize that Christ expects all Christians to witness
3. They don't know how to do it—no guidance or model
4. Some think church attendance is their witness and service to God
5. They are overcome by their spiritual fears and personal limitations
6. They are intimidated by the unbelieving majority
7. They are too busy and have no time for witness relationships
8. They are preoccupied and isolated in their Christian worlds
9. They are spiritually weak and too undernourished to do the work of spiritual combat
10. They are intellectually too sophisticated and proud to share the simple gospel of Jesus
11. They are ashamed to identify themselves as simple faith-sharing people of God
12. They have stereotyped witnessing as door knocking, confrontational embarrassments, and bad press experiences
13. They are not living the life about which they are witnessing

NOTES——

[1] The *Double-Diamond* expresses the writer's philosophy of evangelism. It first appeared as an article in the *Evangelism Canada Digest*, Vol.5, No.2, 1988.

[2] These evangelism goals were first printed by the writer in a church pamphlet entitled, *Church Evangelism in the Local Church*.

[3] Donald McGavran, *Understanding Church Growth* (Grand Rapids, Michigan: Eerdmans Publishing, 1970), p. 192.

[4] McGavran, p. 256.

[5] The *Understanding the Salvation Process* diagram is the product of several agencies and people. It first appeared as the Engel scale at the Lausanne Conference in 1973, and was later adapted by the Christian Business Men's Association, and has been further revised by the writer.

Fourteen

Church Outreach

New churches need to be planted because younger and smaller new churches tend to be more energetic, creative, and evangelistically efficient than are older and larger churches. Churches seem to have their greatest evangelistic potential during the first thirty years of life. While older churches can be redeveloped, new churches generally baptize more new converts per 100 members than will older churches.

Murray Moerman,
Church Planting: The Key to Growth.

The outreach ministries of any church need to be intentional or they will gradually drop out. Church evangelism is difficult because it invades the kingdom of darkness. It is an exercise of entering enemy territory to claim and free individuals who have been victimized by Satan. This is what the great commission is all about. With church outreach the first part of the great commission is achieved, and the second part is done through spiritual nurture.

It is important that the church outreach ministry be a

central part of the church's purpose and ministry philosophy. Furthermore, it is essential that the outreach responsibility be lodged with a designated group for planning, implementation and evaluation. It is to be expected that when the church does outreach events as a corporate body, the quality of the message presentation will be more formal and polished than what the people are able to do through individual witness. The church outreach events are needed so that the members of the church can bring their unchurched friends to hear a formal presentation of the gospel as a continued step in the relationship they have built with their friends.

This section is about assisting the church planter in developing a year-round philosophy and pattern of church outreach. The church planter must keep in mind that church planting is evangelism, and evangelism is church planting. Effective church outreach combines the various individual efforts of church people along with the official outreach ministries of the church for the common purpose of bringing new people to Christ and into the fellowship and ministry of the local church.

A. Establishing New Church Outreach Goals

1. To help each church family bring its own children and family to Christ and into responsible church membership.

2. To assure that the gospel of Jesus Christ is regularly presented in the church's public worship services, whether in sermon, song, testimony, video, or drama.

3. To provide instruction that will help each worshipper develop a strong life of personal witness.

4. To help each local church agency or committee carry out its particular part of the great commission.

5. To take responsibility for sharing the gospel with the people living within a reasonable driving distance of the church.

6. To develop a church leadership team that will model a vision and a plan for bringing the lost to Christ and his church.

7. To extend the church's outreach ministry beyond the church by taking responsibility for planting a new church in the next three years.

8. To develop a balanced and growing mission budget for local, provincial, national, and international mission programs.

B. Program Principles For Church Outreach

1. Relevance

The programs have to meet the everyday needs of the people. The programs should be formulated on the basis of a person's felt needs, and so find entrance to their real needs. The ministries must be practical.

2. Inspiration

The ministries should provide for an uplifting experience. They should inspire faith and hope, and bring encouragement to the participant. The ministries should have a celebrating dimension.

3. Relationship

Loving and caring for people is basic to church planting. Friendship and trust relationship is essential to winning people's confidence and getting their response.

4. Adaptation

The new church must adjust its music, message and ministry to fit the understanding and needs of the people present. The Christians need to learn how the unchurched think, and then anticipate their response.

5. Hospitality

For new people to feel comfortable and welcome in the church, they must experience warmth and hospitality. A regular pattern of welcoming should be implemented.

6. Sensitivity

New attenders usually come with many fears and anxieties. The church must provide acceptance and understanding of the new worshipper's situation.

7. Visibility

New churches will grow in proportion to the church's community contact and people-visibility. The church must make its presence known in the community.

8. Publicity

Community people are more ready to become involved in new programs if the ministries are clearly described and introduced through well-done public advertising. Special event advertising is usually effective.

9. Proclamation

It is important that the gospel be simply and clearly presented, with ample opportunity for discussion and response. All the programs must contribute to the understanding of the gospel.

10. Family Focus

Church-planting programs need to show a priority for reaching community families and adult singles. For church planting to succeed, it needs the commitment to the family. Children's ministries are often the reason adults will stay with the church.

11. Peer Experience

Growth and fellowship are the result of peer programming. Personal identification between people who have commonalities is important for response and progress. Small group fellowships are proving to be very productive in disciple-making within peer groups.

12. Variation

Church programs need to vary in content and in style from weekday to Sunday, and from seasons to special days. The programs need to move toward a culmination and conclusion, so that another entry and beginning point can be created for new people to get involved.

13. Growth

New church programs need to grow and progress both in quality and in quantity. The climate needs to be such that a growth environment is present. New ministries need to be added with ample lead time and leadership preparation.

14. Centred

The church programs need to be centred around a worship core. Worship needs to be the anchor around which all other ministries are established. Worship has become prime time for reaching new families.[1]

C. Community-Centred Outreach

MINISTRY TARGETS FOR CHURCH PLANTING

It is important that the church planter identify the potential target people in the community and then develop programs to meet their needs. The church planter needs to recognize his responsibilities of setting up appropriate communication channels, and programming systems that assure that the message is in fact reaching into each part of the community. A serious church planter will plan for ways to reach the four levels of people represented in the church and the community.

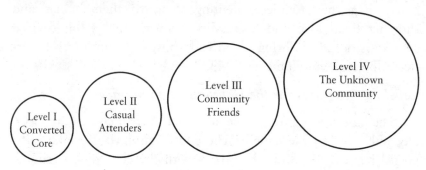

Level I: Programs for the Church Core

The group that the church planter is most aware of is his committed church core. The programs generated for this group must be for the purpose of strengthening the committed core through worship, fellowship, teaching, baptizing, and the breaking of bread. This core group is also the body which makes things happen for the other three community levels. The church planter must disciple his core in the direction of becoming program producers rather than being mere recipients.

Level III: Programs for Community Friends

Every church has a sizable group of people in the community, known by the members, who do not worship anywhere. Most of these are friends of the committed core or the attender group. The church planter along with the committed core must set their minds to reaching these identifiable people with the gospel, by taking the initiative of going out to them. The kind of programs these church friends may respond to by special invitation are community Bible studies, special events, banquets and picnics.

Level II: Programs for Casual Attenders

The casual attenders are an easy-to-win group since they have already volunteered their presence at the church. The committed core should not be satisfied to have a segment of the church people in attendance only. Every effort should be made to lead these people into salvation, commitment, and then into baptism and full membership. In terms of program this may mean individual families befriending the attendees, inviting them to their homes and showing them love and hospitality. Informal fellowship-centred activity is needed to bring the attender target group into full participation and church membership.

Level IV: Programs for the Unknown Community

The largest group of people around an urban church are virtually unknown to the church. The entire initiative of making the gospel heard and known here rests with the church. The church planter along with the core will need to penetrate into this unknown community and so begin to tackle the most difficult job of winning the unknown community. The program plan in this instance might include blanket mailings, door-to-door visitation, newspaper articles and advertising, and one-to-one friendship building.[2]

D. Outreach Master Planning

PHILOSOPHY OF CHURCH GROWTH

The different days and the different seasons offer a variety of program possibilities. Community people are more likely to respond to the special-day celebration programs than to the more regular and routine ones. The church planter needs to take advantage of all the ministry outreach options.

1. Sunday Programs—The Church Gathered

As the church planter plans the programs for Sunday, the first day of the week, he/she must plan for the total church involvement. On this, the Lord's Day, the church can be expected to give priority to the program of the church over other interests. Sunday is the day that the church reaffirms its interdependence as the different parts of the body unitedly express their togetherness. It is on this day that the church brings together its full complement of resources and talents in celebration of its salvation. The church planters must teach these new worshipping converts to hold to a high and responsible view of the Lord's Day of worship. They must also assure that the Sunday celebrations are joyous occasions. The Sunday worship is the heart of the church, around which all its other activities are focused.

Formal Church Outreach

When the church is gathered together as a body, you can expect that the gospel presentations will be verbalized more formally, more precisely, and more systematically. The fruit of the informal evangelism of the congregation is often reaped through the more formal efforts of the church. The formal work of evangelism by the church corporately needs to be expressed regularly through its ministries. The individual attenders depend on the outreach events of the church for a place to bring their friends to hear the gospel clearly presented.

2. Week-day Programs—
The Church Scattered

The church planter must look at the week-day activities with considerable flexibility. Since the church is scattered during the week, a variety of individual and small group community-centred outreach activities should be planned or encouraged to run simultaneously in different places according to time available, personal interest, and spiritual need. Programs that require the presence of the entire church should be shifted to Sunday, leaving the full week for ministries of personal choice and preference. Each church member should be encouraged to participate in at least one church-related activity during the course of the week and strive to be involved in one activity in a community organization. The week-day activities need to have mission and witness as a focus. The church planter should be encouraged to exercise generous flexibility concerning the week-day programs.

Informal Personal Outreach

Each Christian seeks to witness as they are able during the week. This witness is usually casual and spontaneous. In this informal, away-from-the-church witness, the believers apply their spiritual gifts for the sake of influencing and winning people for Christ at their

workplace and in their neighbourhood. This process of "being salt and light" frequently involves deeds of mercy and actions of love. In this informal process the good news is shared in many ways.

3. Semester Programs

Short-term programs offer particular opportunities and challenges. Certain programs lend themselves best to operating in blocks of several months with breaks in between, similar to seminary and college semesters. Such programming provides for short-term commitments of both the program leaders and the participants. It also allows newcomers to become involved, and others to exit at the semester break. It is also easier to get new participants involved in programs of six to ten weeks than on a year-long basis. Lecture series, Bible studies, visitation programs, and even Sunday School seem to thrive best in semester arrangements. Summer, Christmas, and Easter times make for convenient program breaks. New enthusiasm and participation is fostered through such block programming.

4. Seasonal Programs

A church planter cannot afford to miss out on seasonal program opportunities. With each season change the church should make seasonal program adjustments in its community-centred programs. At various times of the year the church needs to put together a concentrated specialized program feature or thrust, to help the congregation in its celebration. Each season might be planned in such a way that it climaxes in a weekend of celebration or in a banquet setting. It is very important for a new church to banquet and celebrate together often. Each season may also have its particular focus on a certain age group or family group. Summertime could be children's focus time, where attention is placed on recreation and camping. The fall season lends itself to family programs in banquets, conferences, or competitions. The winter season could focus on couples in retreats, crusades, and study groups; while the spring season could feature special youth events in festivals, excursions and coffee houses. Such variety can bring new life and spice to the church planter's career.

5. Special Day Programs

Every church planter knows that the church's special days also bring special opportunities. Christmas, Easter, Mother's Day, and Thanksgiving must be dressed with special program care. It is on days like these that the community is open to the church's ministry. The church planter must maximize these special-day occasions with additional community visibility and advertising.

6. Crowd Events—Fishing Pool Situations

Beyond the seasonal and special-day emphasis, the church planter needs to plan for some major attention-getting events to bring in the crowds. From the perspective of the community people, they may only see this as an evening out at a concert, a carnival, or a picnic. For the church it's an outreach, with people deciding to come to church again.

7. Worship Evangelism

The main worship service of the church is becoming an effective evangelism time. Many churches are making a special effort to develop the worship time to be a "seeker-sensitive" or "seeker-targeted" service. When visiting seekers feel the warmth and welcome of Christians they are attracted to the gospel. The pastor also makes a special effort to speak with relevance and invitation.

8. Meal Outreach

Today, as in biblical times, eating together as a group creates an environment for special spiritual reflection. Breakfasts, lunches, banquets, picnics, or coffee time with friends we care about can be prime times for personal faith sharing. The monthly breakfasts or lunches for outreach have proven to be very effective.

9. Entertainment Outreach

Hospitality outreach in a group setting through an evening of entertainment is well modelled by Campus Crusade. It is an informal evening of fun activities such as games, swimming, boating, or doing some athletics, combined with a meal or a backyard barbecue. The evening concludes with an assigned couple sharing their story of how they came to faith in Christ and the difference this has made.

10. Home Group Evangelism

The small neighborhood home group is an effective relational way to do evangelism. It combines fellowship, friendship, and sharing. The small group is a very important part of the church-planting process. It is in the group that new people find a sense of belonging and appreciation. These factors combined create a fertile heart for the gospel.

11. Outreach Visitation

Community or neighborhood visitation is very important to the church-planting process. Contacts made during the course of the week need to be followed up by a home courtesy or contact visit. If the church has a regular visitation ministry, it should follow a structured pattern. In a group of five to eight people forming visitation teams, the evening could begin with a half hour of instruction and encouragement. They would then go out on assigned visits, in teams of two or three, for an hour, and then return to the church, or an arranged home, for coffee, debriefing, sharing and rejoicing.

12. Contact Ministry

An important part of the new church's life and presence is its regular contact with the various parts of the community. Regularly scheduled contacts during the day or evening need to be maintained. The church planter needs to visit institutions such as the hospitals, jails, colleges, and businesses. Sometimes the contact is also with business clubs, care organizations, etc. Church planting is not an office job, it is a field assignment.

Contacts include:

Farm system advertising
Telemarketing invitations
Contact month—high profile month once a year

Brochures and newspaper visibility
Door step visits—area blitz

13. Visitor Hospitality

The church needs to have an intentional hospitality process whereby it makes visitors feel welcome. Guests have their minds made up about coming back based on the church's hospitality. There are at least four phases to the hospitality track:

a) Arrival hospitality
- People are welcomed before they enter the church, either at the parking lot or outside the church door.
- Warm greetings in the foyer, just inside the church doors, with expressions of appreciation for coming, and name introductions.
- Sanctuary ushers provide bulletins and seating.

b) Sanctuary hospitality
- Pastor's comments of appreciation to guests present.
- Offering disclaimer, that guests are not obligated to give.
- Protecting anonymity by not singling out guests or having them stand.

c) Departure hospitality
- Roving guest book by a church hostess.
- Foyer coffee and greeting of guests.
- Exit door greeters saying "good-bye, best wishes, come again."

d) Follow-up hospitality
- Pastor's appreciation letter to recognize the visit with a "welcome back."
- Lay person telephone call to guests, thanking them for the visit and asking if they have any questions or needs.

14. Master Outreach Planning Calendar

Maximizing special days and seasonal opportunities for church outreach.[3]

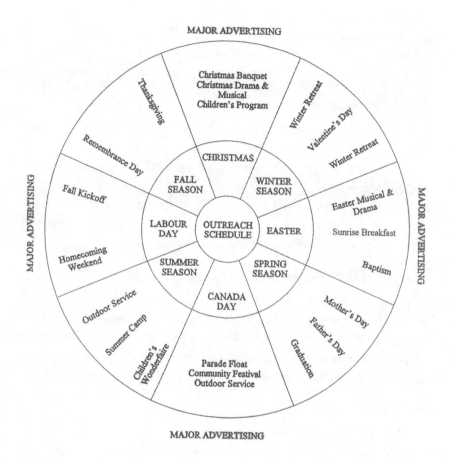

E. Church Entry Points

<small>ATTRACTING PEOPLE BY BEING ATTRACTIVE</small>

1. Church Responsibility

The road to and into the church for new people is often cluttered with many road blocks. For most non-worshippers it will require a specifically arranged occasion for them to find their way into a church fellowship. Church people will need to take more responsibility in providing special attractions or program doors through which the community people can enter and experience the love and warmth of Christ's Body. The church cannot rely on its routine activity for attracting first-time attenders. It must create special program highlights or attraction points to which church people can invite their employment partners or neighbourhood friends.

2. Church Attitude

The church must change its mind about the people outside of the church. Most of the non-worshipping secularized people are not rabid atheists or arrogant opposers of the faith. And most are also not deliberate church "runaways" or theological "backsliders" who need to be hit with a hard sermon. It is probably fair to describe the average non-worshipper as one who has dropped out by a natural process or simply followed the secular crowd.

3. Church Preoccupation

Maybe it is fair to suggest that many non-worshippers are in their position somewhat by church default. Perhaps the church people have not demonstrated the kind of sincerity and vitality to provide much attraction or drawing power. In many instances they have possibly closed the church doors to people by their own preoccupation.

4. Church Responsibility

The responsibility of believers is to create a welcoming open door for newcomers. They must develop an ongoing openness and excitement for new people. Newcomers are attracted by love and genuine hospitality. For the church to be the church in its fullness, it must be known for its effectiveness in reaching and drawing people to Christ and then fitting and knitting them into the body.

5. Church Entry Points

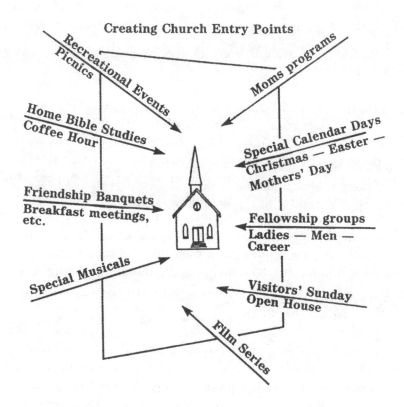

Creating Church Entry Points

Recreational Picnics
National Events
Home Bible Studies
Coffee Hour
Friendship Banquets
Breakfast meetings, etc.
Special Musicals
Moms programs
Special Calendar Days
Christmas — Easter — Mothers' Day
Fellowship groups
Ladies — Men — Career
Visitors' Sunday
Open House
Film Series

F. Life-Changing Home Groups

SMALL GROUP EVANGELISM

Home groups usually have four basic components: loving, learning, ministering, and serving. Time spent on each of these will vary according to the needs and priorities of each group

1. Core Values for Life-Changing Home Groups[4]

a) Building Relationships
Loving and caring for one another in an environment of trust, respect, and friendship.
b) Loving Unchurched People

Caring and befriending the people that matter to God but may not have yet responded to Christ.

c) Caring Ministry
Sharing and caring for one another's concerns and difficulties through encouragement and prayer.

d) Truth Discovery
Exploring the Bible together for spiritual growth and new commitments.

e) Mission Initiatives
Taking responsibility for task involvement as a group, for team-building and mission or service involvement.

f) Accountability
Where the group members are accountable to one another and the group leaders are accountable to the church elders/pastor.

g) Life Relevance
The group experiences need to be relevant to the life of the participants.

h) Grace Giving
The group provides a positive environment where weakness and failures do not need to be hidden for fear of rejection, but where brokenness can be shared, forgiven and rebuilt.

i) Expansion
Each group has a goal to multiply itself and to keep inviting new people into the experience of life-changing home groups.

2. Key Principles for Launching Community Home Groups

a) Composition Principle
The goal for each home group is to have an attendance mix of some church people and some neighbourhood people. The size may vary from two couples to six couples.

b) Friendship Principle
The home group assumes that the participants will know at

least one other person in the group. The group is based on the premise of one neighbour meeting another neighbour for the purpose of study, sharing, and friendship.

c) Location Principle

The neighbourhood home group needs to meet where the non-churched person is most comfortable, which is likely in their own home. The unchurched are often reluctant to go to a Christian's place for any kind of religious activity.

d) Biblical Principle

Since the home group is also a Bible study, it is advisable to use the Bible as the text. A New Testament should be supplied by the leader since the community people often do not have one readily available. The Living Bible or another contemporary paperback makes for a good group study Bible. The Bible is at its best in the presence of learners and seekers. It is also advisable to stay with a given passage rather than jumping to various verses in the Bible.

e) Sensitivity Principle

A wide range of maturity levels could be present in the group. Therefore it is important not to expose the knowledgeable and less knowledgeable in the group. New people should not be asked to read lengthy passages or be placed into an uncomfortable prayer circle. Page numbers rather than book, chapter, and verse should be used. The leaders must understand the fears of new people in a Christian circle.

f) Seasonal Principle

The studies should have a specific time frame. The attenders should know that the group will terminate after eight or twelve weeks. At the end of a series it can divide, reorganize, relocate, or discontinue. Having a fall term and a winter term has proven to be a workable arrangement for many home groups.

g) Growth Principle

Both the seasoned Christians in the group and the non-practising or potential believers will experience growth in such a mixed setting. The studies should lead the seeking person step by step toward a personal commitment in a non-threatening way.

h) Organization Principle

There should be a minimum of three parties in the neighbour-hood home group: the hosting person, who should preferably not be a regular church attender; the study leader, who is committed to Christ and the church; and two or more neighbours, one a friend of the host, and the other a friend of the leader.

i) Result Principle

Expect growth from each participant. Depend on the power of God's Word. Research shows that one in four home groups see con-versions happening. Keep a non-judgmental attitude to all contri-butions, whether theologically right or wrong. The Spirit will bring the needed corrections.

j) Ministry Principle

As needs are shared by the group members, take time to pray for the needs that are shared.

k) Participation Principle

The reading of the study text should be assigned to a person ahead of time. The reading of verses in circle by different people usually means people will be looking ahead to practice their verse, thus missing most of the Scripture reading. People may participate at their level of readiness and comfort.

3. Home Group Format (90 minutes)

a) Group Building and Welcoming
- Welcome, socializing and refreshments
- Chat with each participant upon arrival
- Make personal statements of affirmation and apprecia-tion to each attender
- Describe the open and non-threatening nature of the group
- Exchange participants' experiences of the week

b) Group Bible Study and Interaction
- Hand out study Bibles
- Pray a short prayer of guidance and blessing
- Read or have the text read by an assigned person (not

everyone likes reading)
- Do a paragraph-by-paragraph study of the text
- Look for daily applications
- Have each person share what has been their insight of the evening
- Ask for any needs to be prayed for
- Have one or two people volunteer to lead in a ministry prayer

c) Group Fellowship and Refreshments
- Another round of coffee/refreshments are offered
- Adjournment[6]

G. Summary Inventory On Outreach Strategies

There are many ways to do evangelism with varying degrees of effectiveness.

1. Arm's Length Evangelism Strategies—Impersonal

a) Display Evangelism
Instant non-personal visuals—posters, billboards, T-shirts, bumper stickers, etc.

b) Literature Evangelism
Making reading materials available—gospel tracts, book racks, Why Magazine, Gideon Bibles, etc.

c) Electronic Outreach
Using variety of electronic media—television, videos, music, CDs, radio, lecture tapes, etc.

d) Internet Outreach
Using the Internet for faith sharing—e-mails, web sites, sermons posted, Power to Change campaign, etc.

2. Personal Evangelism Strategies—Individual

a) Entertainment Outreach
Using fun times for witness—rock concerts, athletic events,

entertainment parties, recreational activity, etc.

b) Friendship Evangelism
Outreach based on relationships—neighbours, work colleagues, recreational partners, friendships, etc.

c)Visitation Evangelism
Taking the initiative to go to people—personal contacts, courtesy calls, crisis calls, business calls, contact follow-up, etc.

d) Prayer Evangelism
Praying people into the Kingdom

e) Encouragement Evangelism
Exercising the gift of encouragement and support—telephone calls, e-mails, cards, letters, visits, gifts, food, flowers, care packages, etc.

f) Lifestyle Evangelism
Winning respect by your life—good deeds, responding to crisis, philanthropy, etc.

g) Door-to-door Evangelism
Visitation teams going door to door with a structured presentation, etc.

3. Mission Agency/Parachurch Strategies—Sodality Group Efforts

a) Holistic Strategies
Looking after social concerns—food banks, victim shelters, recovery groups, clothing, recycling, etc.

b) Crusade Evangelism
Organized crowd events for outreach—week-ends, week-long crusades, preaching, music, altar calls, etc.

c) Confrontation Witness
Assumes people need to be challenged—door-to-door, street witness, surveys, four spiritual laws, etc.

d) Power Evangelism
People responding to signs and wonders—healing meetings,

power worship services, etc.

e) Classroom Evangelism
Training to share your faith—witness seminars, lay retreats, school of evangelism, college courses, etc.

f) Church Planting Evangelism
Starting a new congregation—reaching a new area, new people groups, new formats, etc.

g) Saturation Evangelism
Saturating the community with the message—Bible distribution, Luke, *Power to Change*; *I Found It* Campaign, Jesus video, etc.

4. Church Outreach Strategies—Modality Events

a) Meal Evangelism
Eating together with a witness purpose—banquets, prayer breakfasts, business luncheons, coffee times, etc.

b) Retreat Evangelism
Getting away for relaxation and reflection—day camps, family camps, week-end retreats, camp outings, etc.

c) Small Group Alpha
Combine fellowship and learning—care groups, seniors' groups, youth groups, hobby groups, Alpha, etc.

d) Worship Evangelism
High-energy, uplifting worship—attractive worship, good music, contemporary communication, etc.

e) Crowd Events
Fishing pool evangelism crowd events—special attractions, concerts, rallies, carnivals, picnics, etc.

f) Side Door Evangelism
Ministries that address a special need—child care, parenting classes, resume writing, retraining, etc.

g) Annual Special Days
Capitalizing on public celebration days—Christmas, Easter,

Thanksgiving, Valentine's, Mother's/Father's Day, etc.

h) Sunday School 101
Teaching the basics of Christianity—pastor's classes, discovery class, church orientation, etc.

i) Life Cycle Evangelism
Witnessing when individuals or families are in transition—birth of child, weddings, funerals, illnesses, baptism, etc.

j) Involvement Evangelism
Church participation before a commitment is made—ushers, band members, child care workers, maintenance, etc.

k) Children Evangelism
Programs for children are planned—clubs, camps, parties, etc.

NOTES——

[1] The *Program Principles for Church Outreach* were developed by the writer for church planters in Manitoba, Alberta.

[2] Rick Warren lists five target church circles from outside to inside, to be: community, crowd, congregation, committed, and core. p. 205.

[3] *The Master Outreach Planning Calendar* was developed by the writer as a church planter in northern Manitoba.

[4] Carl George in *Prepare Your Church for the Future* describes the church entry points as front door entry and side door entry, p. 75.

[5] Bill Donahue, *Leading Life-Changing Small Groups* (Grand Rapids, Michigan: Zondervan, 1996) pp. 88-89.

[6] The house group format and the key principles for launching home groups were developed and implemented by the writer for the Neighbourhood Life Groups, in The Pas, Manitoba.

Fifteen

Church Finances

...the needs of others, feelings of gratitude, the privilege of sharing, the needs of the church for operation money, the place of giving as an act of worship, the biblical teachings that undergird stewardship, and the guidelines supplied by the church, are important factors when an individual or household decides how much to give.

Nordan C. Murphy, *National Council of Churches.*

One of the major challenges of church planting is to establish the church onto a secure financial base. New churches do not always have the needed people who have experience in financial matters. So many times the skills in these important financial positions need to be taught and developed. Added to the lack of experience among financial church volunteers in a church plant, there is also the challenge of teaching biblical stewardship. New Christians need to learn how to give according to the biblical patterns. This chapter lays out some of the biblical expectations and motivations for giving. It also provides some guidelines on how to set up a financial system in a new church. For a veteran church treasurer some of these guidelines may appear somewhat elementary, but for a new church planter who has never been on a church finance committee, they are foundational insights.

A. Developing The Biblical Giving Base

BIBLICAL LESSONS ON GIVING FOR CHURCH PLANTERS

1. Why the Subject of Money is Important

The Bible devotes some 2000 verses to money, giving, and possessions, while prayers and faith both have only some 500 references each. Jesus talked about money in eleven out of thirty-eight parables and in one out of ten verses in the gospels. It is an important subject because money and possessions can keep people from God. Money can become one's master, priority, and symbol of position and power. The Bible describes the love of money as being the root of all evil which often becomes an addiction or an obsession, which then results in conflict and self-destruction. Selfishness and hoarding are in conflict with Christian growth. How people view and use their money is a sign of what they treasure in their hearts. In our materialistic and selfish culture it is important to present the biblical meaning and purpose of money, wealth and generous giving.

Money can also be a great blessing. Generous giving has resulted in major mission exploits over the years. Many Christians of wealth have been a great example and a blessing in the Kingdom of God through their generosity.

2. There are Different Kinds of Givers

    a) Token givers—smallest bills in wallet, change, loonies
    b) Project givers—special projects that have enough appeal
    c) Secret givers—nobody knows if they give or how little
    d) Impulsive givers—they give after an emotional appeal or according to feeling

e) Rare givers—negative spirit, selfish attitude, dislike sermons on giving

f) Potential tithers—learning to give, sacrificial attitude

g) Regular tithers/givers—giving with joy and regularity, 10% and more

3. Why Christians Should Tithe

a) Tithing is biblical

The Old Testament practice went far beyond a 10% tithe. It started with a 10% giving to the temple and included 20–30% for the care of the widows. Beyond the financial giving, grain gleaning for the poor and the birds was expected. Giving also included providing sacrifices from their livestock for their festivals. The New Testament practice was built on Old Testament giving principles. In the New Testament giving takes on the idea of appreciation in response to salvation. It is not by law, but by an inner spirit of generosity and gratitude. New Testament giving was assumed to go beyond the requirement of the law of the Old Testament.

b) Tithing provides spiritual growth

Tithing blesses the giver because it is more blessed to give than to receive; it increases a person's faith, and fosters contentment. Giving to the Lord and at the same time helping others is very satisfying.

c) Tithing is a blessing to others

The practice of tithing encourages others. It expresses that unselfishness is the answer to the prayers of many people in need. It makes others thankful.

d) Tithing makes missions and evangelism possible

Tithing and special mission offerings keep missions going. Finances are needed to send out missionaries and operate mission programs. The great commission can be implemented as people give their tithe.

e) Tithing makes the local church possible

The New Testament idea of having all things together and in common, as in Acts 2, is today done by sharing finances. The church is about doing together what cannot be done alone. The needed church rent, equipment, and salaries are met through giving. Church needs are met by giving as an expression of united action.

f) Tithing honours God

Tithing is an expression of thanksgiving. It reveals the treasure in a person's heart. Tithing is a demonstration of obedience to God's will. God loves a cheerful giver.

g) Tithing recognizes Christian stewardship

Everything a person has and is belongs to God. He has bought the believer at a great price. As a result, Christians are stewards of all that they have. They now have the responsibility of managing what belongs to God.

h) Tithing expresses Kingdom citizenship loyalty

By tithing and giving, a person participates in God's Kingdom. It is a tangible expression of laying up treasures in Heaven.

4. The Bible Teaches Much About Tithing and Giving

a) Giving the tithe is for everyone (Deut. 16:17; 2 Cor. 9:7).

Everybody is to give, according to God's blessing, and this includes one-income families. Each one is to give as they also worship, pray, and sing.

b) Giving the tithe is to be a joyful experience—
not grudging (2 Cor. 9:7; 2 Cor. 9:2).

God loves a cheerful giver. Generous people are joyful people, while greedy, selfish people are difficult people. Giving with enthusiasm and eager willingness encourages others. It is more blessed to give than to receive.

c) Giving the tithe is part of the Sunday worship
(1 Cor. 16: 1-2; Cor. 8:9).

On the first day of the week they brought their offering.

d) Giving the tithe is to be according to income and ability
(Deut. 16:17; 2 Cor. 8:2 ; Acts 11 :29; 2 Cor. 8:3).

Giving is acceptable according to what one has and what one

earns. New Testament giving was according to their ability and even beyond. Many gave from a context of extreme poverty and persecution.

e) Giving the tithe is to be outstanding and a model of excelling to excel and to model (2 Cor. 8:7).

Having a generous reputation is a great personal attribute. Just as one excels in knowledge, speech, and faith; so giving is to be with distinction and honour.

f) Giving the tithe is to be from a clear conscience (Matt. 5:23-24).

The giving is to come from a clean heart. First comes the act of forging, then the offering. The Bible always warns against hypocrisy and a double standard. One cannot serve two masters: God and money.

g) Giving the tithe is to be with heart and mind (2 Cor. 9:7; Matt. 5:21).

Giving is to be voluntary but it is an intentional and regular practice. It is to be a decision of the heart and according to the treasure of one's heart.

h) Giving the tithe is storing up treasures in Heaven (Matt. 6:20).

Heavenly treasures are safe against rust, thieves, and loss. Giving is building heavenly investments.

i) Giving the tithe is to be with right motives (Matt. 6:1-4).

Giving is not for self-glory. It is not to get rich in return, and is not to be done boastfully or for praise.

j) Giving the tithe is consequential (Mal. 3:8-11).

Withholding tithes means robbing God, but giving opens the floodgates of Heaven to pour out blessings.

5. Personal Steps to Becoming a Biblical Tither

a) Give yourself to God first (2 Cor. 8:5).
   - personal commitment

b) Recognize that all you have belongs to God
- we hold it in trust
c) Depend on God to be the source of your supply
- the Lord's prayer instructs us to pray for our daily bread
d) Accept tithing as God's will
- giving is God's design for every Christian
e) Make a decision to start tithing immediately
- start with three months and see how God supplies joy
f) Calculate the tithe on your income
- do it for the Lord
g) You can do all things through Christ (Phil. 4:13).
- Christ is present in our life and knows our need

6. Common Resistance Factors to Biblical Tithing

Situations that make tithing difficult:
a) When Christians come from a State Church background which has a church tax
b) When Christians come from a dictating, legalistic church background
c) When the cultural background resists openly giving information
d) When a person is rich and feels exploited
e) When a person is poor or on welfare and feels exempt (2 Cor. 8:7).
f) When Christians love money and practice hoarding
g) When the stewardship principle of everything belonging to God is not understood
h) When Christians reject and disobey biblical tithing principles
i) When the church planters see the new church as their own project
j) When the church plant is seen as the financial responsibility of the denomination.
k) When prayer and pseudo-spirituality becomes a substitute for responsible giving
l) When the pastor and elders are not setting an example in tithing

B. New Church Financial Responsibilities

1. Basic Assumptions on Church Finances

a) Every church is responsible to manage its finances well

b) The church today follows the Jerusalem principle of sharing and having all things in common through shared facilities, program, staff, denominational mission, and ministries, etc.

c) All Christians are expected to express their "salvation thankfulness" through regular tithing (10% of income). Coffee break-sized gifts are not an adequate expression of gratitude for God's gift of eternal life at the ultimate price.

d) Biblical giving is to be sacrificial, joyful, by ability, regular, given heartily, and prepared in advance (2 Cor. 8-9).

2. The Church has Financial Responsibilities and Privileges

a) Privileges include: to be registered with the government, to receive tax deductible receipts, to participate in the denominational programs, etc.

b) Responsibilities include: employer responsibilities, income tax deductions, Canada Pension Plan, employment insurance, employer's portion of the deductions, Compensation Board fees, and annual reports.

c) Denominational responsibilities include providing adequate benefits and protection.

3. Understanding the Budget and Subsidy Program

a) The church program expenses must remain within budget.

b) The budget should not exceed the church's giving potential.

c) Local church programs come before extra mission projects.

d) When there is a financial shortfall, the church should immediately be encouraged to give.

e) The financial needs and offering totals received must be made known regularly to the congregation.

f) The denominational subsidy portion is based on agreed monthly amounts given towards the approved church budget.

g) The denominational subsidy partnership program is there to help the church get started and become financially independent. The subsidy is annually determined on a decreased schedule.

h) The elders of the church have the responsibility to pay all bills promptly, assure that the expenses are in the budget, and report to the church periodically.

i) The denomination is not to be seen primarily as a funding source, but rather as a fellowship of churches who submit to each other in doctrine and mission.

C. Developing The New Church Financial System

1. Essential Beginnings for the Church Financial System

- Open a church bank account
- Assign the signing officers other than the pastor
- Adopt a suitable record-keeping system
- Print church offering envelopes
- Set up individual, confidential donor cards
- Print payment requisition forms
- Have an approved annual budget
- Sunday offering report forms in duplicate
- Deposit book
- Master accounting ledger/software
- Weekly offering report form for the pastor's office

2. Offering and Deposits

a) The designated ushers will take the offering and bring it to the church stage as a symbolic expression of thanksgiving

b) Immediately following the service, two members of the finance committee will count the offering, fill out the offering report form and sign for the offering amount, with one offering report form staying with the offering and the other going to the church office. Personal offering information is open to the pastor.

c) The offering is stored in a safe in the church office or taken home in a briefcase by the person making the deposit.

d) The deposits are made early in the week by a designated church officer.

e) The personal donations are recorded on confidential individual donor cards/software.

f) The total of each Sunday's offering should be reported to the pastor's office.

g) Year end receipts are issued to each individual for their donations

SAMPLE OFFERING REPORT FORM FOR PASTOR AND TREASURER

Church Offering Report Form

Date Offering Taken _____

Total Amount in Cheques $ _____

Total Amount in Cash $_____

Total Amount in Coins $_____

Total Amount in Pledges $_____

Total Offering $_____

Offering Counted and Signed by:

1) _____ 2) _____

(One copy stays with the offering—one copy to pastor/office)

Comments or Instructions: _____

_____

3. *Cheque Writing*

a) All expenditures are to be paid with a church cheque blank with double signatures. There should be no cash transactions for church expenditures.

b) All payments of bills are to have a payment request form indicating the budget line to be debited.

c) All payments made need to have a purchase receipt or bill attached to the payment request form.

d) Before payment is made, the appropriate person needs to authorize payment to be made, by a signature on the payment requisition form.

e) Maintain an accurate bank balance by keeping the disbursement journal and the deposit book up to date.

f) The pastor should not be a cheque-signing officer but could sign expenditure requisition forms.

Payment Request Form/Sample

Date: _____

Payment to be Made to:

Name _____

Address _____

Bill is Attached _____ Other _____

Payment Amount $_____

Expenditure Description_____

_____

Church budget Line to be Debited _____

Expenditure submitted by _____

Payment Authorization Signature _____

Payment Cheque Number _____

---

4. *Financial Reporting*

a) Periodic financial reports, usually monthly or quarterly, should be presented to the church elders, tracking the income and expenses.

b) Keep the congregation informed on the status of church finances in summary form on a monthly basis.

c) Prepare complete financial statements for the church's annual meeting.

d) Prepare and approve the church's projected budget.

e) Churches receiving denominational subsidies need to provide periodic financial reports to the Church Extension office.

f) Appropriate reports will need to be made to the government annually to assure that the charitable registration privileges and responsibilities are maintained.

5. *Financial Debt*

a) It is important that the church live within its financial means.

b) The church mortgage payments should not exceed 25–30% of the church's annual income.

c) Whenever possible, a local church should arrange its facility financing through its denomination.

d) The church should have raised from 30–40% of the facility costs before launching a building project.

Church Plant Budget Format

CHURCH _____ YEAR _____

CHURCH PLANTER _____ DATE _____

PROJECTED INCOME	Monthly	Annually
Church Offerings		
Fund-Raising Projects		
Parent Church Help		
Conference Subsidy		
Total Income		

EXPENDITURES

Worship Space Rental
Office Space Rental
Telephone/Internet
Office Supplies
Equipment
Church Maintenance
Other/Utilities
Children/Youth
Church Ministry Refreshments
Program Supplies
Advertising Brochures
Leadership Training/Retreats
Conference/Support
Evangelism/Outreach
Missions/MBMSI etc.
Pastor's Salary
Salary/Benefits (13%)
Ministry Coffee Meetings
Travel Costs
Conference/Seminars
Guest Honorariums

Total Expenses
Total Income
Balance

D. The Church Offering Process

OFFERING UNDERSTANDING

1. The offering process must be treated with respect, for it is a gift to the Lord.

2. The offering is part of the worship that individuals bring to the Lord.

3. The offering gives the pastor an opportunity to encourage generosity.

4. The offering should be blessed, as it is a sacrifice for the Lord.

5. The offering bags should be passed through the pews, so that every person is encouraged to give to the Lord.

6. The offering should be taken with sensitivity toward guests and unchurched people that are present in the service. Their presence is their gift.

7. A box on a table at the back of the auditorium could communicate the message that some cost-sharing of church expenses is appreciated. This process often fails to acknowledge the offering as a part of the worship experience in which a sacrificial gift is given and dedicated to the Lord.

OFFERING ENVELOPE—SAMPLE

1. Should be letter envelope size—large enough for cheque

2. Should be professionally printed

3. Should clearly identify church name and address, donor and date of offering

The offering envelop below was designed by church planter Peter Nikkel at the beginning of the Panarama Church plant in Surrey, B.C. This format has been widely used in other church plants and has set a new standard for offering envelopes that have traditionally been much smaller. The envelope used is a regular-sized lette envelope, larger than the sample shows.

A GIFT TO BUILD
GOD'S KINGDOM

Name or No. _____   Date _____

Address _____   Postal Code _____

Tithes and Offering (General Treasury) $ _____

Other (Specify) $ _____

Total $ _____

*"Every man shall give as he is able, according to the blessing
of the Lord your God which He has given you." - Deut. 16:17*

PANORAMA COMMUNITY CHURCH
Mailing Address: #5 - 13415 76th Avenue, Surrey, BC V3W 2W2

Panorama
Community Church

• SIXTEEN

Church Facilities

Mission congregations should defer building plans until the congregation has developed sufficient strength and stability to shoulder such efforts themselves. The mission congregation should assign a higher priority on ministry to people than to building and budget. It should be content with a temporary place for central worship and use many satellite home activities that tremendously assist a church in growth and effective ministry.

Jack Redford,
A Guide for Establishing New Congregations.

While the acquisition of property and buildings is usually several years down the road from the beginning, it becomes a significant part of the congregation's long-range goal. Already, in preparation, the congregation can celebrate the various steps in the direction of getting its own church home. In some settings the church's anniversary is celebrated in a banquet format with a special offering towards the acquisition of the property. The tradition of banqueting on the church's anniversary for the purpose of reviewing and renewing the vision of the church can be very effective.

A. Facilities Planning Principles

To start with, the church needs to realize that our society has become less efficient and is more demanding of church space. It takes more foyer space for the same number of people than it did in times past because it has become a space of socialization. It takes larger Sunday School classrooms today because they have become activity centres. It takes more cars to bring the same number of people to church, requiring more parking spaces. It takes larger church lots since most cities require a sizable green belt and a high ratio of parking spaces to the number of seats in the auditorium. The church needs to build for the future and should build for at least twice the number that are presently in attendance. It must, however, stay within its financial means.

1. Program Suitability

It is important that the building be constructed upon a careful projection of the church's program needs. The program plan must dictate the design of the building. It should be a facility that combines function with beauty.

2. People Compatibility

The new facility must be compatible with the lifestyles of its members. The church is an extension of the people's homes and needs to reflect their values and understanding.

3. Area Contextualization

The new building must be made to fit the general architectural characteristics and standards of the community. It should enhance the beauty of the community.

4. Government Standards

The church needs to be exemplary in following or exceeding standards established by the building codes and government regulations. In the parking requirements, for example, the church should seek to provide more parking than the law requires.

5. Public Expectations

The church should be ready to go beyond the minimum legal facility expectations. In some situations, the expectations of handicapped's organizations are pushing for standards beyond that which the law requires. Wherever possible, the church should seek to satisfy the handicapped people's needs.

6. Worship Design

The building should communicate a spiritual identity and presence to the people at large. It should be so constructed that it is obviously recognized as a place of worship. It should be a facility that combines architectural beauty with financial modesty.

7. Faith Enhancing

The building needs to be in keeping with the theology of the people. The design and symbols need to reflect the particular emphases of the church's tradition and heritage.

8. Symbolism

There needs to be harmony between the building and its art forms and suggested theology. The designs need to symbolize a centred life in Christ, and a close relationship between the people. The building should symbolize both continuity and community. It is a place of celebration and faith expression. The church itself is a symbol of providing service in the world, while at the same time not being of the world.

9. Anabaptist Considerations

The church building of most Anabaptist churches reflects a congregational approach to worship. The clergy are not seen in an elevated position or as a separated group. The pulpit and platform are usually built to reflect easy access to all people. The centrality of the

Word is signified by a centred pulpit, and the importance of music is shown by the location and space for the musicians or choir. Most churches have a visible baptism font and a communion table to depict the importance of the two ordinances in the believers' church. The building needs to be helpful in integrating and unifying the people.

B. Motivating Factors For A Church Building

PROBLEMS CONNECTED WITH RENTING SPACE FOR WORSHIP

1. Temporary Sunday School classrooms are inconvenient for teachers and do not provide for a good teaching environment.

2. People in the community are more likely to visit and attend a church that has a building.

3. Local church members would have a higher level of commitment to invite people to the service if they had a permanent site.

4. Membership discouragement sometimes results from long-term arrangements in rented facilities and repeated problems with the facility usage and set-up.

5. Facilities are not always available or suitable for the various church programs, and so church ministries become restricted.

6. Worship environment in multi-purpose rooms/halls are not always conducive to worship after Saturday night community parties, etc.

7. Worshippers tend to be preoccupied with set-up and clean-up before and after the service, rather than fellowship with one another and meeting new people.

8. A building would facilitate a sense of oneness. It is one of the ways that a church today has all things in common, as did the church in Jerusalem.

9. Rented facilities for a church gives the impression of transiency and of short-term ministries. A building facilitates permanence.

10. A visible facility also serves as a reminder to the public that there are Christians in the community that take their faith seriously.

11. A public place of worship encourages open attendance and guards against unintentional social, ethnic, or cultural exclusiveness.

12. As a garage mechanic needs a service bay and as a carpenter needs a workbench, so the pastor and his church need a workplace within which the great commission can be carried out.

13. A church sanctuary atmosphere is more conducive to worship with less noise, more reverent atmosphere, and easier control of young children.

14. In rented facilities, mothers with small children often have no place to go when a child is unruly, and so decide to stay home.

15. School use for Sunday School frequently creates ill will between classroom teachers and the Sunday users. School teachers' and students' supplies often get moved around or lost through the activities of the Sunday worshippers.

16. Sunday School teachers often end up spending valuable teaching time in policing their classes and keeping them from touching the attractive school items. This is not a very good long-term environment for spiritual growth.

17. The exorbitant rental cost could be better used to make facility mortgage payments.

C. Church Site Selection Guidelines

The location of the church is considered to be one of the major long-term health factors for a church. It has been said that "the church that locates well, reaps the benefits throughout its lifetime, and the church that locates poorly, lives to regret it or dies because of it." Bert Cavin of the Baptist General Convention, lists location among the top three priorities of a new church. He says, "There are three basic ingredients in beginning a new church or mission. These are: (1) Lordship, (2) Leadership, and (3) Location."

GUIDELINES TO BE CONSIDERED WHEN SELECTING A CHURCH SITE

1. Attraction Power

By the site the congregation determines whether it wants to attract the general public to its services. If the public is to be attracted, then the same criteria for site selection would apply as that of a fast-food restaurant or a gas station. Just as business success is determined to a large extent by location, similarly the church's power to attract casual attenders is determined by location.

2. Visibility

Visibility is one of the most important factors in church site selection. A corner lot is preferred to a middle-of-the-block property. The church building itself is its main advertising all week long. A church that is hard to find is also hard to attend.

3. Accessibility

A church property should be easily found and described. If at all possible, a church should locate at a junction of several major traffic arteries to accommodate quick entry and exits. A church should, if possible, be approachable from at least two different directions.

4. Centrality

A church should seek to locate somewhere in the centre of community life. Locations around shopping centres, colleges, or hospitals make for a good church site. This provides for the possibility of offering programs related to the needs of the institutions around the church. Such a church also has the advantage of having the traffic already naturally flowing in the church direction during the week.

5. Parking

Surplus parking is essential to a growing church. Community people will be more ready to attend a church where they know they will not have to fight for a place to park. The site in consideration should be large enough to accommodate more than enough parking.

6. Public Transit

The church must take seriously the fact that gas prices are forcing more people to use the public transit systems. The new church site should be chosen on a regularly serviced bus route, and so accommodate a large potential group of worshippers.

7. Prime Property

The church should seek to build its sanctuary on prime property. Leftover properties may not be the best investment. The less expensive property may be the most expensive in years ahead, in terms of possible church growth. Undesirable properties or wrong-side-of-the-track areas should not be considered for church sites. Suitable property should take priority over private good deals.

8. Adequacy

The site must be suitable for the proposed church campus. Rectangular or square property is preferred. Triangular or other odd-shaped pieces make for too much waste area. A minimum of three to five acres is necessary for a congregation of 300-500 worshippers. Both the site and the proposed building must be adequate to embody the vision of the church people.

9. Stewardship

Church buildings and land acquisition that is needed to facilitate the programs of the church should not be regarded as second-rate use of money. The Lord's work deserves the best of location and buildings. Money spent for the purposes of facilitating the hearing of the gospel is money well spent.

10. Identity

The choice of church site and building will determine the kind of identity and profile that the church will have in the community. An attractive building and site will attract, and an obscure, poorly-built facility will do the opposite.

It is important to underscore that the church that locates well is likely to do well, and the one that locates poorly will suffer its consequences with no recourse.

SEVENTEEN

Information and Technology

We have entered into this new age of information—or whatever label one prefers, much as our forefathers entered the Industrial Age. They energized the means of production and nothing—socially, economically, politically, was ever the same. Today we are 'informationalizing' everything, because our convergent technological information resources are becoming more and more abundant and more and more versatile.

–Benjamin M Compaine and William H. Read,
Information Resources Policy Handbook.

The church is in the business of communications. It communicates in different directions, upward would be to God, lateral would be to its own people and outward would be to society at large. While the message to be communicated is constant and unchanging, the method of communication needs to be ever-changing to adapt to the broader communications environment. The church has not always had a mind or appetite for much change. In the church planting environment, the likelihood of communication in current forms is much higher than that of an established church. This chapter seeks to explore the various communication and information forms as well as identify the challenges and responsibilities that come with the use of electronic communications in the context of the church and beyond.

A. Identifying And Protecting Information Assets

In the same way that the church has physical assets it cares for and protects, it also has information assets it owns which need protection and care. Examples of information assets are: church membership lists, church policies, budget and financial information, vision and value statements, minutes of meetings, etc. Although all of these are examples of information assets, not everyone is freely permitted to arbitrarily view information whenever they want. Some information can be public, some information should be limited to church members, and some information may need to be restricted to staff or elders.

In order to implement a policy for protecting information assets, it is helpful to classify various sensitivity levels and to designate groups of people who are allowed access to a particular piece of information. The higher up in the organization, the greater the need for information protection. This applies to both physical or digital storage of information.[1]

Shown here is an example model of classifying the sensitivity of a Church's information assets. Also shown are example groups of people permitted to view this information.

1. Elder Information

The elders deal with leadership information, pastors' reports, minutes, salary issues , employment and budget issues, all of which need to be guarded and treated as sensitive information. Therefore, appropriate security and protection of this data is required. Information classified at this level should be restricted to elders and not be freely accessible to staff, church members or the general public.

2. Staffing Information

The church staff deals with program planning, staff meeting minutes, member records, church discipline, offerings, prayer requests and bulletin production, etc. Again, much of this information is not open to everyone and so needs to have information protection and security. Information classified at this level should be restricted to elders and staff. It should not be generally available to church members or the public.

3. Member Information

Issues that concern the members have broader boundaries and have wider areas of concern. They deal with ministry issues, caring for one another, worship and faith sharing. Protected data here would include member-related problems, member-only bulletin information and internal issues. Although this information is not as sensitive as that of the elders and staff classifications, there must be a distinction between information for members and information for the public at large. Information classified at this level should not be conveyed outside the church, i.e., through the Web, advertising, etc.

4. Public Information

The data for public information are the open items that the church seeks to make known about itself. These include program options, services available, the church purpose statement, vision and values. These are the issues that the church puts in its public bulletins, on Web sites, billboards, TV and newspaper advertising. There are no restrictions on reading this information, but care should be taken to protect the modification of the content.

Each of these classification policies requires a mechanism to ensure that information is appropriately accessed. Examples of this are locks on doors, locks on filing cabinets, firewalls, passwords on computers/networks, password-protected files and encrypted remote access. This is the implementation of the policy which protects the information.

It is important to note that information assets can be stored in a physical or digital format. Care needs to be taken to protect these assets regardless of the format.[2]

B. Using Technology For Communication

The church as an institution has used a wide variety of communication methods in its history. It is to the church's credit if it seeks every possible way to get its message communicated. Here are some examples of technology used by churches today:

1. Visual Technology

A variety of presentation software and hardware has become available to assist the church in its communication. For many years the church has used slide projectors for its missionary reports and overhead projectors for music and sermon outlines. More recently, churches have introduced video presentations and Powerpoint presentations with attractive picture background for music slides and sermon material.

2. Audio Systems

In the field of sound systems, most churches have maintained a significant level of expertise. The various shapes of buildings and the acoustic variations make for many sound system challenges. There are new audio services such as live translations, audio for the hearing impaired, audio or video feeds to church nurseries and hallways. These services may use may different technologies to transmit the message, including wireless, satellite, streaming audio, AM/FM radio, etc.

3. Video Transmissions

In a growing number of churches, the worship services are televised into senior citizen homes or into private homes of shut-ins. In other situations, the service is transmitted to a screen at the site of an emerging congregation. In other cases, the service is publically broadcast on television or streamed over the Internet.

4. Lighting Effects

Increasingly more lighting effects are used to focus the attention of the audience and to provide an intended mood or environment. The spotlight has become for many churches a way to focus on the stage presenters.

5. Audio/Video Recording

Churches have for many years made available services and sermons on tape·recordings. Duplication equipment has made it possible to also provide video tapes or CDs for the people on short notice. Possibilities also exist for providing MP3 audio or digital video for download over the Internet.

6. Public Billboard

A growing number of churches are using the message board in front of the church to list the sermon title or other program features. This form of communication is very public and requires regular maintenance and updating.

7. Internet Publicity

In times past, people looking for a church to attend would look through the yellow pages or the church page in the newspaper. Increasingly more people check the Internet for available worship services. Internet search engines and directories have become the main vehicles for providing public information. For many churches, this has not yet become their main source of information flow to the public at large.

8. Church Web site

The church Web site, another usage of the Internet, is gradually replacing or supplementing the general church information brochure. Church Web sites have the potential to provide a wide range of information about the local church, including its history, statement of faith, staff listings and the ministries provided. Many churches are also posting public versions of their church bulletins and the pastor's sermon on the Web site. The church Web site is crucial to building bridges of information to the outside world.

9. Electronic Mail

Electronic mail is an addition to conventional communication systems. There are basically three applications for e-mail: a) It's an addition to the traditional postal service, b) a compliment to the telephone service and c) an optional medium for interaction, planning meetings and holding discussions. It must be remembered that e-mail is unprotected and is much like an open postcard. It is therefore important not to send sensitive information like banking data, credit card numbers, medical records or anything else that could be misused, stolen or become a violation of privacy.

C. Managing Technology For Quality Control

The exploding information age that has become the new reality needs special commitment regarding quality standards and control.

1. Commitment to Technology Management

This is a process that assures that the various information systems are well managed, monitored and maintained. This would include such things as: system updates (patching), virus signature updates, data backups and Web site content updates. Technology management also includes capacity planning and the monitoring of computer hardware and software. Proper systems management will assure that all systems remain operational.

The practical application of this management commitment to the church setting could apply to the church bill board situation. Management has failed when the Easter program announcement on the outside message board or Web site is still there two weeks after Easter or when the message board is blank several weeks running because no one has taken time to letter an up-to-date message. Another example of management failure is when the Web site has not been changed or updated since it was first established .

2. Commitment to Information Availability

This commitment assures uninterrupted access to services and information. It monitors the systems to prevent potential break-downs. This section also concerns itself with service continuity during possible disaster situations through Business Continuity Planning (BCP) where critical operational data is maintained at a remote location. This is so that the availability of service and information is not interrupted in the event of a disaster. Some examples of work disruption are fire, theft, power outage or acts of terrorism.

3. Commitment to Information Security

As in the public sector, so within the church environment there must be adequate data security policies, guidelines and practices to protect and filter inside networks from outside network communications. Firewalls are needed to limit access only from certain places, users or activities. The use of passwords or encryption should be a regular practice.[3]

For example, firewalls would protect a church's infrastructure from external attack and encryption would prevent passwords and data from being stolen during transmission.

4. Commitment to Workplace Excellence

The quality of excellence needs to be applied to the management and maintenance of technological systems, in order to provide the best possible service within a changing society.

The application to church planting would mean avoiding sound system glitches by doing sound checks before every performance to avoid the embarrassment of the sound finally coming through in the middle of the first sentence or finding that the speaker has a dead mic.

Another application of excellence in a church situation applies to the use of stage lighting. An obvious breach of excellence has happened when the spotlights are not adjusted to the speaker's location and the audience tries to follow the speaker in and out of the spotlight.

A further example of reaching for excellence would be making the Web site available to any computer, new or old, and regardless of vendor.

D. Ethical Use Of Technology

Significant ethical and professional issues arise in the field of technology particularly as they apply to the church and its leaders. Leaders need to be models of ethical standards and professional practices. In the face of rapidly changing leadership environments and communication technologies, it is important for Christian leaders to anchor their leadership moorings around a code of leadership conduct.

ETHICS AND LEADERSHIP CONDUCT IN TECHNOLOGY

1. Leaders need to be an example of resisting, on principle, the accessing of illicit material (pornographic, racist, satanic,etc.).

2. Leaders need to avoid any inappropriate chatroom or discussion group activity that would compromise the integrity of their Christian character.

3. Leaders need to maintain a high standard of complying with software copyrights and licenses.

4. Leaders need to be sensitive to the rapid pace of technological change and budget for continuous education of staff as required.

5. Leaders need to give full credits to the authors and the sources when using information off the Internet.

6. Leaders need to pay attention to the ergonomic conditions of the physical working environment.

7. Leaders need to practise promptness and politeness in responding to e-mail communications.

8. Leaders should ignore unsolicited junk e-mail (spam) and never open attachments from unknown senders.

9. Leaders should guard against computer addiction where large amounts of time are spent for trivial gain.

10. Leaders should strive, in a computer-driven environment, to maintain a healthy balance and priority of family relationships and ministry duties.

Effective ministry requires the best involvement of Christian leadership, the best application of technical communication and the empowerment of God's spirit if maximum Kingdom results are to be achieved in church multiplication. Finally, it is Christ who is building His church.

NOTES——

[1] Much of the technical content of this chapter needs to be credited to Bruce Nikkel, the writer's son, who works in the field of computer security in the banking industry in Switzerland.

[2] Matt Bishop, *Computer Security*, (New York: Addison Wesley, 2003) p. 152 . Provides for comprehensive treatment of the various levels of communication security as first developed by the military involving four levels of responsibility and security.

[3] Charles Pfleeger, *Security in Computing* (Preutic Hall International, 1997) Provides a comprehensive treatment on the subject of information security.

Conclusion

With this book I have revealed some of the life-long visions and passions of my heart. It has been my goal to make at least a small contribution to the fulfillment of the great commandment of love, and the great disciple-making mandate of Christ. I have written this as one more way to realize my personal mission statement, "To passionately follow and serve Christ my Saviour and Lord." The writing of this book is true to my ministry slogan "making the most of every opportunity" (Eph.5:16).

This book also expresses my mission statement which reads:

> I dedicate myself to advancing the kingdom of God through the use of my natural talents and spiritual gifts, as the Lord opens the door of opportunity. I commit myself to strategic involvements of leadership discerning, training, and mentoring for the purpose of raising up leaders for the spiritual harvest, who will be effective in making disciples and multiplying churches that will effectively reach emerging generations among

different people groups. I want my life to be a statement of personal integrity, biblical faithfulness, effective evangelism and servanthood leadership.

I am deeply grateful to God for the privilege of many years of evangelism and church-planting ministry. This book is a theological and practical reflection from the involvement of church planting, pastoring, teaching and mentoring. It is my prayer that this book will be one of the many resources that church planters will want to have as an outreach tool in their arsenal of valuables. If this book has served to motivate and encourage more church planting to happen, it will have achieved its intended purpose.

Subject Index